Taking the Long View
70 Years of Fianna Fáil

Taking the Long View
70 Years of Fianna Fáil

edited by

Philip Hannon
Jackie Gallagher

BLACKWATER PRESS

Editor
Deirdre Bowden

Design & Layout
Paula Byrne

ISBN
0 86121 894 9

© 1996 Fianna Fáil.
Contributors retain copyright of their individual chapters.

Produced in Ireland by
Blackwater Press
c/o Folens Publishers
8 Broomhill Business Park
Tallaght, Dublin 24

In memory of the late Brian Lenihan TD 1930–1995.

Contents

Foreword

Fianna Fáil has reached its 70th year as the largest and most enduring political party in the State. After that period of time, it is appropriate that there should be an examination of what has made Fianna Fáil so different and distinct, but not just in nostalgic terms.

This book is not designed to be a definitive history of the party since 1926, more a reflection on the magical mix that makes up Fianna Fáil.

In *Taking the Long View*, Fianna Fáil has invited historians, academics, politicians and individuals from within and without the party to give their assessment of aspects of Fianna Fáil over the last 70 years. These individuals were invited to avail of the recently catalogued archives at party headquarters in Dublin. (Fianna Fáil is unique in Irish political terms in having organised and catalogued historical archives. This situation came about because of the foresight of the late Brian Lenihan and Party General Secretary, Pat Farrell.) The authors have written their assessments as they saw fit. The result is this collection of essays on some of the people, events and achievements associated with Fianna Fáil over the last 70 years.

The editors are very grateful to all the authors who delivered their contributions to us on time despite their own busy schedules. Thanks also goes to the Fianna Fáil Leader Bertie Ahern and the Party National Executive for commissioning the book, to Pat Farrell for his support, and to Paddy Duffy and Martin Mansergh for advice and invaluable assistance. We would like to thank colleagues at Headquarters and at Leinster House, especially Karan Finn, Evelyn Eager and the staff of the Fianna Fáil Press Office. We would also like to acknowledge *The Irish Times*, the Franciscan Fathers in Killiney, Dublin, RTE's Cashman Photograph Collection, Colman Doyle, Maxwell Pictures, the Fianna Fáil Press Office, Fianna Fáil Archives and Photocall for permission to include photographs in this book.

Finally, our thanks to John O'Connor, Anna O'Donovan and Deirdre Bowden at Blackwater Press.

Philip Hannon and Jackie Gallagher
Fianna Fáil, November 1996

Notes on Contributors

Bertie Ahern is the sixth leader of Fianna Fáil. He has been a TD since 1977 and has served in a number of governments, first as Minister for Labour and later as Minister for Finance. He has been leader of Fianna Fáil since November 1994.

Síle de Valera is Fianna Fáil TD for Clare and is Frontbench Spokesperson on Arts, Culture and Heritage. She is a granddaughter of Eamon de Valera.

Frank Dunlop is a public relations consultant and was Fianna Fáil and Government Press Secretary from 1974–79. He worked closely with Jack Lynch over a period of years.

Dr Richard Dunphy is Senior Lecturer in Political Science at the University of Dundee, Scotland. He is the author of *The Making of Fianna Fáil Power in Ireland 1923–1948* (Oxford University Press, 1995), from which the essay included here is an edited extract.

Dr Yvonne Galligan is a lecturer in Politics in the Department of Political Science, Trinity College Dublin and has done extensive research on women in politics.

John Garvey was Deputy Editor of the *Irish Press* when it closed.

John Horgan is Senior Lecturer in Communications at Dublin City University, and is currently engaged on a major biography of Seán Lemass, which is due to appear in 1997.

Dr Declan Kiberd is the author of *Idir Dhá Chultúr* and *Inventing Ireland: The Literature of the Modern Nation*. Until its demise, he was a weekly columnist with the *Irish Press*.

Joe Lee is Professor of Irish History at University College Cork and is an independent member of Seanad Éireann.

Margaret MacCurtain is a Dominican Sister, historian and was the recipient in 1993 of the Éire Society of Boston Gold Medal for her work in women's history.

Dr Breandán Mac Giolla Choille was consultant archivist to the de Valera papers. He is a former Keeper of State Papers and Deputy Keeper of Public Records of Ireland.

Dr Martin Mansergh is Head of Research with Fianna Fáil. He worked closely with Charles Haughey and Albert Reynolds during their terms as leaders of Fianna Fáil and as Taoisigh. He is an editor of *The Spirit of the Nation*.

Eunan O'Halpin is Associate Professor of Government at Dublin City University. He is currently writing two books *The State and its Enemies: Defence, Security and Subversion in Ireland 1922–1996*, and *The Forgotten Bond: Anglo-American Security Co-operation 1914–1945*.

Sari Oikarinen is a Finnish scholar. This book includes an edited extract of her article which appeared in the conference report of the IV Nordic Women Historians' meeting of May 1993. In it she offers an interesting external view on Irish history and Countess Markievicz.

Eamon Ó Cuív is Fianna Fáil Spokesperson on Rural Development and the Islands. He is a grandson of Eamon de Valera.

Nollaig Ó Gadhra lectures at Galway Regional Technical College in Communications, Irish and European Studies. He is widely experienced as a print journalist and broadcaster, and is a member of Comhairle Teilifís na Gaeilge.

Mary O'Shea is a part-time lecturer at UCC. She was National Youth Organiser of Fianna Fáil from 1984 to 1989.

Notes on the Editors

Philip Hannon works as an assistant to the General Secretary at Fianna Fáil Headquarters. A qualified archivist, he has catalogued the Fianna Fáil Archives and previously worked on the de Valera Archives in Killiney, Dublin and at the EU Historical Archives at the European University in Florence.

Jackie Gallagher works as an adviser with Fianna Fáil at Leinster House and was formerly Industry and Employment Correspondent with *The Irish Times*.

1

Celebrating 70 Years and Towards the New Century

by Bertie Ahern

(This essay is a continuation of themes first addressed by Mr Ahern in a speech at Fianna Fáil's 70th Anniversary dinner, Berkeley Court Hotel, Dublin, April 1996.)

Fianna Fáil has good reason on its 70th Anniversary, to be proud of the party's central role in many great national events. The party, during seven decades, has adopted the spirit of the 1916 Proclamation where it says: 'In every generation, the Irish people have asserted their rights to national freedom and sovereignty.'

That spirit was there in 1938 when, after the adoption of a new Constitution, Fianna Fáil negotiated the return of our ports. That spirit was also there in 1973 when we enthusiastically took our equal place as a sovereign nation at the table of the European Economic Community.

The real heroes of Fianna Fáil are the thousands of men and women in every townland, every village, and every urban area, who have been our Fianna Fáil presence in their own communities. While the Leaders may take the laurels, and at times the sharp end of criticism, it is the organisation which is enduring, flexible, vibrant, and always ready to fight the good fight.

It was an important evening for the fledgling democracy in May 1926, when de Valera spoke to the new Fianna Fáil Party in La Scala Theatre, and challenged them with these words:

> The freeing of our country is not an easy task. It is a task that can never be performed except with the enthusiasm and energy that spring from the passionate feeling of the people, and such passionate feeling cannot be aroused if we move away from the realities that affect their daily lives.

Having survived the death sentence of 1916, the struggle for independence and then the cruel carnage of the Civil War, de Valera accepted that the people would not support or condone further violence. The genius of the man was in convincing those opposed to the Treaty that democratic dialogue and debate were the only acceptable and appropriate means of winning a national argument. But they still maintained their republican credentials. And so do we, in Fianna Fáil.

The immense moral courage shown by Fianna Fáil in entering the Dáil after its successful contest with Sinn Féin in 1927 marked a decisive and historic moment for the new party and the new State. And the words spoken by de Valera to that first gallant band on 16 May 1926 are as relevant now, as they were then:

> We must not allow ourselves to be hypnotised by our prejudices and feelings on the one hand or by our opponents' propaganda on the other. To underestimate our strength is even a worse fault than to overestimate it. We must not let our opponents dissuade us from attempting a task that is well within our power by suggesting it is impossible. We must, if we really want to succeed, endeavour to judge the situation just as it is, measure our own strength against it, lay our plans and then act with courage and tenacity.

The great victories of the 1930s saw Fianna Fáil undertake a massive housing programme, enlightened social welfare, health and employment legislation, pragmatic protectionism and a restoration of national morale. Our first Fianna Fáil Cabinet went into pioneer country:

> They hungered as they went the sharp-stoned road
> And only one small lamp above them glowed.

That was the lamp of destiny and the lamp of duty. Like the powerful *Men of Destiny* by Jack B. Yeats, landed fresh on a new quayside, they were about the nation's business.

Fianna Fáil were the youthful champions of the New Deal and the Irish Five Year Plan. With our radical policies we 'subsumed within our expansive electoral embrace' the working people of Ireland, urban and rural, middle class and no class, civil servants and those in service.

'The stormy petrel, the Fiery Cross of Irish politics in the twentieth century' as Ó Faoláin rather colourfully calls Dev, with his assistant, and confidante Seán Lemass, carved out a pro-active political agenda which captured the imagination of the nation, and for many years answered their needs and desires.

The relationship between Dev and Lemass was an equal relationship, where both understood the talents of the other and appreciated them. Dev with his innate political sixth sense, his inspiring and scholarly aloofness, and his spiritual politics, Lemass with his great administrative competence, his practical and innovative nature, his superb personnel and organisational abilities, and his robust independence. They and their Cabinet colleagues believed, in the words of Lemass, that: 'National progress of any kind depends on an upsurge of patriotism directed towards constructive purposes,' and the opening of over 900 new factories and workshops, the development of Bord na Móna, Aer Lingus, the Irish Shipping Fleet, building over 130,000 houses, the land divisions, major programmes of hospital construction, the enlightened welfare, employment and education provisions of social reconstruction, paved the way for the next phase – industrial development, also to be undertaken by Fianna Fáil.

In 1938, after a referendum on the new Constitution and the General Election victory, *The Irish Times* wrote:

> We are glad that he [Mr de Valera] has been returned to power.

We all appreciate the remarkable success of that Constitution in meeting the needs of modern Ireland, in showing itself to be an adaptable instrument for a changing nation. As has been said about the US Constitution, Bunreacht na hÉireann 'is a living organism, and as such is capable of growth, of expansion, and of adaptation to new conditions.'

As de Valera himself said in a radio broadcast in 1938:

> The Constitution is a practical, flexible instrument of Government, embodying principles just in themselves, and long associated with the ideals to which our people are devoted.

During the Second World War, we opted for a friendly neutrality which we now treasure and export as peace-keeping, medical, educational, agricultural and managerial expertise. Even though times were tough, people understood well that serious work was being undertaken in their name. When we remember that Lemass got his best vote ever – two and a half quotas in 1944, having been 'Minister for Shortages' since the outbreak of the Second World War – we can begin to understand the impact that the radical Fianna Fáil programme of Government action had. As has been observed, 'they had indeed created a philosophy and code of practical statecraft.'

After the war, there was a period of stagnation, as governments of all shapes, for a time, failed to come fully to grips with post-war conditions.

Tánaiste at 45 and Taoiseach at 60, Lemass's seven-year stint was action-packed, with 'protectionism giving way to active competitive participation in a free-trading world.'

Now he was free to chase the industrialisation, the inward investment, the exports, the challenges of a new TV culture, the swinging 1960s and the rapid rise of individualism and business. With the First (Economic) Plan devised by Whitaker and championed by Ryan and Lemass, Ireland was well on its way to economic planning and learning how to spread its economic wings. Lemass set Ireland on the road to Europe. He captured the new mood of optimism, with the picture of the rising tide lifting all boats. The unexpected high growth created a political and economic optimism, which Lemass constantly used to refer to the possibilities of tackling similar economic problems North and South, on a one-island basis.

His Oxford Union speech of October 1959 was timely, non-threatening, statesman-like and comprehensive. Opposing him in the debate was the young Patrick Mayhew. Building goodwill measures, removing barriers to fear and suspicion, asking the British Government to act as persuaders for mutual cooperation, justice and esteem – these all remain topical and have now become British Government policy in the Downing Street Declaration, and the Framework Document, at least on paper. Lemass used simple, direct language to make his point.

'It is a fundamental right,' he said, 'of every local minority that their legitimate interests should be respected, and that there should be no economic or social discrimination against them.'

Lemass was determined to ease himself out, once he had the new policies and the new generation of Fianna Fáil political leaders in place. As he drily commented, 'It is time I passed on. I don't want to become a national monument around the place.'

It is hard to beat Senator Joe Lee's epitaph:

> It was neither his manner of gaining power, nor his manner of holding it, that distinguished him uniquely among Irish prime ministers. It was his manner of using it.

The visit of President Kennedy in 1963, the cup of tea with Captain Terence O'Neill at Stormont in 1965 and his promotion of 'the youngest cabinet in Europe' are three pen pictures of a sunny time under an outstanding Fianna Fáil leader, to whom we owe so much, and who continues to inspire all his successors.

When Jack Lynch took the helm in 1966, Fianna Fáil had proceeded with its second Five Year Plan, and three high-powered groups – a Committee on the Constitution and Commissions on Higher Education and the Public Service were working and free Second Level Education had been introduced. The electoral campaign of 1969 took little notice of Northern Ireland or its problems.

Fianna Fáil, the Republican Party, could not be immune or unmoved by the civil disturbance in the North, and the 1970 Árd Fheis was tense and heated as a result. Nevertheless, national politics continued as usual, paralleled by the Northern troubles, and our entry into Europe in 1973 offered us tremendous opportunities, many of which we have realised. Fianna Fáil has always believed firmly in an active European role for this country in developing social, agricultural, and financial linkages which raise our standards and the quality of life here at home. Structural and Cohesion Funds as well as CAP Reform and GATT and access to a market of 400 million have made us party to the greatest economic developments of our time, and have given us opportunities to benefit from our participation in a greater Europe ahead of many other countries.

The 1970s gave us all the unwanted highs – high inflation, high strike days, high wage settlements, high government spending and then as we were swamped by the first and second oil crises, massive borrowing. The new over-confident economic policies first pursued by the National Coalition were unsound. The great electoral advance of 1977 – our greatest ever – was unfortunately accompanied by a continuation of policies for full employment, which gave the country an artificially high growth, not based on sound foundations.

The Haughey era ushered in a political whirlwind of elections and heaves. A Paddy Kavanagh line is very apt:

He could not walk the easy road to destiny.

The Way Forward of 1982 was indeed the correct medicine, but unfortunately we had to wait until 1987 to tackle our structural deficiencies properly. The man who had always shown flair, innovation and style in his ministerial posts found it difficult to get a good run at Government but then he presided over one of the best governments ever from 1987 to early 1992.

The Temple Bar district and the International Financial Services Centre were established. The 1990 EU Presidency was an outstanding success. Then the foundations of our present economic success were laid, and I was proud to play my part in creating our National Agreements, which have given us ten years of industrial peace. The work we did then, and continued under Albert

Reynolds has given us the best growth rates in the EU, low inflation, low interest rates, reduced the debt GDP ratio, achieved a massive transfer of European funding up until 1999 to implement our National Development Plan, record employment and inward investment in spite of a currency crisis and monetary turbulence in the ERM, and at last, a rising tide of prosperity based on sound financial management and strict adherence to the Maastricht criteria. Fianna Fáil was central to that outstanding work, as we also dealt sensitively with major social issues which were issues of lively public debate, at that time and more recently.

Albert Reynolds' risk-taking with John Hume and Gerry Adams, and our helpful American friends brought us a golden peace in the autumn of 1994, and we are proud that it was a Fianna Fáil Taoiseach, who made that historic breakthrough, who pushed and persuaded and persisted, until the IRA accepted the case for adopting an alternative political strategy. Albert Reynolds built on the sound foundation of previous Fianna Fáil leaders. De Valera had often said that partition could not be resolved though violence. Lemass clearly spelled out the language of reconciliation and mutual cooperation which was in everyone's interest, and this was replicated by Jack Lynch. Charles Haughey established the Anglo-Irish framework, and extended the range of language we use with regard to the North.

Albert Reynolds built on that well-developed basis to partner John Major in producing the Downing Street Declaration, the IRA Ceasefire and the Framework Document.

As we face into the next general election, the words of de Valera at the 1933 Árd Fheis are apt:

> We have a tough struggle before us, a long fight to fight. If we are going to win, it will be by cool action, taking thought as to the directions in which we move, calculating what the best chances of success are.

Seventy years of independence have brought many positive advances to this country, and Fianna Fáil has been at the heart of the action. We have a proud tradition of serving the nation. As we prepare to return to government, we must re-dedicate ourselves to that task.

2

The Soldiers Set Out: Reflections on the Formation of Fianna Fáil

by Richard Dunphy

It has sometimes been implied that, organisationally at least, Fianna Fáil took up where the old Sinn Féin left off, albeit with a greater degree of effectiveness. There is certainly some evidence to suggest that, on the surface, this is true. One of the main sources of recruitment for Fianna Fáil had indeed been Sinn Féin; the number of affiliated Sinn Féin cumainn fell from 275 to 173 between March and April 1926 and, at the level of national leadership, there was a considerable overlap between the old and the new (17 of the 37 Sinn Féin Standing Committee members and 21 of the party's 47 TDs joined Fianna Fáil; moreover, they were later joined by some highly-regarded Sinn Féin leaders, such as Oscar Traynor and Seán Moylan, who had at first greeted the new departure with caution). But this should not blind us to significant organisational differences between Fianna Fáil and Sinn Féin. These differences are not simply related to the fact that Fianna Fáil cumainn were a good deal more extensive than Sinn Féin cumainn had been; they consist in the membership composition, political ideology, and structural orientation of the new party.

First, it seems clear that the existing Sinn Féin network was not the most important source of recruitment. Arguably of greater importance was the large pool of disillusioned republicans who had not been politically active at all since the end of the Civil War: many of them may not even have voted in 1923. Indeed, it was not so much the old Sinn Féin model of organisation, as the IRA model, which was adopted. Party organisers toured the country, contacting local IRA commanders, many of whom, due to their (real or legendary) exploits during the War of Independence and Civil War, had established themselves as heroic or charismatic figureheads in their localities. In this way, numerous old IRA companies were transformed into Fianna Fáil cumainn. Also of importance was the network established among republicans imprisoned during the Civil War period. Indeed it is reasonable to assume that it was some time before all those who followed de Valera into Fianna Fáil actually severed their connections with the IRA, and certainly many of them regarded their republican oath of allegiance as still binding with the force of military discipline.

This fact is significant from a number of angles. The highly disciplined nature of Fianna Fáil has frequently attracted comment, both positive and negative. Boland has recalled with obvious pride that party activists 'voted and canvassed exactly as the strategists at national and local level planned. In the early days candidates were not allowed to canvass at all. In many rural constituencies in particular, the constituencies were divided among the candidates with mathematical accuracy and there were no breaches of the plan.'[1]

Carty,[2] too, has emphasised the desire of party leaders to build a strong, efficient, and enduring party machine, firmly anchored to the grass roots (the basic party unit was the parish cumann, which soon existed in every parish throughout the Free State) rather than the fleeting power of local influential figures. This development – facilitated by the fact that IRA commanders in general owed their charisma to their military office, rather than personal appeal alone – permitted Fianna Fáil to transcend the fissile tendencies encouraged by the Irish electoral system, to which practically all other political formations in Ireland at this time fell victim. Just to ram the point home, Fianna Fáil candidates were required to pledge that, in the event of their being elected to any public office, 'if called upon by a two-thirds majority of the National Executive of Fianna Fáil to resign that office, I shall immediately do so.'

Obviously, efficiency was not the only product of such an approach to organisation. Fianna Fáil's brand of democratic centralism greatly obstructed the operation of internal party debate. Differences of opinion, of policy, and of ideological outlook certainly existed, especially in the early days. But only indirectly could the party rank and file hope to influence policy or strategy, and dissident or critical elements were quickly neutralised without any real possibility of mustering significant support for their positions. Only at ministerial level were real political differences able to emerge and here, too, they were more often smothered than resolved under the veil of unanimity. Prager has commented upon the authoritarianism inherent in Fianna Fáil's politics from the outset; the individual's relation to political authority was mediated by a hierarchical authority structure and popular acquiescence by the rank and file to the vision of party leaders was such that 'political accountability extended no further than the élite's articulation of that vision.'[3]

Comment has frequently been forthcoming upon the lack of intermediate policy-making structures, the lack of accountability of party leaders to the general membership, the concentration of real power within the upper echelons of the parliamentary party, the failure of the annual Árd Fheis to develop as a real policy-making body, and the elevation of total obedience to the party leadership into a fundamental and inviolable principle of party membership. This last point obviously raises the question of the charismatic leadership, said to have been exercised by de Valera and to have been of such importance in securing his party's predominance. It has been argued that the social stratum most vulnerable to the appeal of the charismatic leader is the petty bourgeoisie.

> ... the [petty bourgeois] need for protection then becomes a craving for an individual *protector*, who will constitute and control an anti-bureaucratic part of the state machine; the petty bourgeoisie hopes to entrust its interests to such a populist leader, to whom it will have direct access, and to whom it will be able to appeal over the heads of capitalist officials.[4]

A similar method of leadership was predominant at all levels of Fianna Fáil. What the organisation developed was not simply a cult of de Valera, but a structurally anchored cult of leadership, which has been one of its most consistent features, and which concentration upon the relative qualities of successive leaders might well serve to obscure. We have already seen that the party was initially organised largely on the basis of local IRA commanders – often local charismatic figures who bequeathed to the party a method of exercising power which has been the object of numerous clientelist and brokerage studies. This structural orientation towards a particular method of the exercise of power is another facet of the legendary Fianna Fáil party discipline. Clearly, the party's inheritance of IRA power structures is of pivotal importance, and neither undue concentration upon the Sinn Féin model of organisation, nor careless assimilation of the IRA to Sinn Féin, really enlightens us much. Dogma, not discipline, was the predominant feature of the old Sinn Féin.

It is precisely the rejection of a dogmatic approach to politics which was the second major consequence for the new organisation of its anchorage in the mass of republicans who had not been active in Sinn Féin, or had tired of it. They were weary of the failed policy of no compromise and disgusted at the complete incapacity of Sinn Féin to defend their interests at a time of severe economic hardship. They had seen Sinn Féin flounder for want of any policy – political, economic, or social. It is scarcely surprising that the new party's lack of dogmatism should attract them; or that de Valera's abandonment of parliamentary abstentionism should provoke so little opposition, when the oath of loyalty to the British crown was transformed into an 'empty formula'.

This political pragmatism was personified by de Valera, whose ability to tactically manipulate his supporters by issuing 'firm statements followed by intricate qualifications'[5] was considerable; it went hand in hand with a conscious electoral orientation. This, too, marked a break with the Sinn Féin method of organisation, concerned as it had been as much with the administration of the affairs of 'the Republic' as with the winning of electoral contests.

Fianna Fáil was, from the beginning, totally electorally orientated. The party's ideals would be realised by winning a parliamentary majority; desired changes would be effected by the actions of a Fianna Fáil government. Repeated comments about the ambivalence of some party members towards the question of whether or not armed force still had a place in Irish politics, and whether the Free State should receive *de jure* or *de facto* recognition, has distracted attention from another fact worthy of mention: Fianna Fáil lacked any theory of society or of the state which might have remotely justified the hopes vested in its early radicalism by some socialist republicans. Its approach to the exercise of power was both parliamentary and paternalistic; it adhered to no concept of the progressive or gradual democratisation of the state apparatus (characteristic of social democratic parties of the time) and its understanding of the role of a political party never included the idea that a party ought to seek to democratise society in such a way as to reduce its own centrality. Accordingly, no attention was paid to questions of which internal organisational structures might facilitate fundamental alterations in the exercise of power in society – organisational questions inevitably centred on the question of greater electoral efficiency. No attempts were made to supplement, reinforce or check the electoral machine by the sort of auxiliary organisations which are again characteristic of working-class parties, both social democratic and communist. The cultural politics of the party involved the mobilisation of pre-existing convictions and beliefs and their imposition on new institutions. Admittedly, social bodies for members existed, most notably Craobh na Féinne (Irish language body), and music festivals were sponsored; Lemass and Boland told the 1929 Árd Fheis that 'everything should be done to counteract the tendency in recent years to concentrate exclusively on purely political matters, and members should realise that work done to foster the Irish language, games and customs was useful work for the Fianna Fáil movement.'[6] But the party lacked any concept of political power fundamentally different from that of its opponents. In the absence of any such theory of state power, thoughts of altering the structure of power floundered and were quickly abandoned. Much of the often naïve disillusionment with the failure of Fianna Fáil's republican radicalism stems largely from this fact.

The mobilisation of the electorate was the first task which the party set itself. Garvin has shown that the period up to 1933 witnessed a 'rapid and permanent rise in turn-out levels.'[7] This mobilisation of the electorate affected all areas of the country, but especially the east; not only were the small farmers and rural proletariat electorally mobilised during the 1920s so, too, was the Dublin working class, which had recorded low turn-outs at elections in the early 1920s. Moreover, working-class electoral politics in the city was at this stage dominated by independent candidates such as the renowned Alfie Byrne. This section of society, then, was prone to the appeal of any party which could accommodate sufficient of its needs within its political programme to offer some hope of social and economic amelioration.

By the end of August 1926, Fianna Fáil had already circulated a pamphlet on voter registration and a full check of the electoral register was under way by mid-September. Fianna Fáil recognised the importance of local government elections long before its opponents did; although the restricted nature of the property franchise might be expected to have adversely affected the party's fortunes, the experience gained in this field was used to build the organisation and to lay the ground for future parliamentary successes; for Fianna Fáil, the two inevitably went hand in hand.

In contrast with the severe financial difficulties of its predecessor, the new party seems to have been on a sound financial footing from the beginning. Although information on party finance is notoriously hard to come by, a number of observations may be made, even if some of the conclusions must of necessity be tentative.

First, the party did not hesitate to seek financial support from businessmen who might hope to benefit from its policies. Tommy Mullins has admitted that the party wrote to 200 or so 'wealthy friends' asking them for money; and Robert Briscoe[8] cheerfully recalls that collecting funds was easier than he had anticipated due to what he coyly terms 'the reckless generosity' of many such supporters. Reynolds[9] claims that businessmen in Wexford and Cork, attracted by the policy of protection, began supporting the party once it entered the Dáil. Indeed Gerry Boland is quoted by his son as bemoaning the influx of 'big subscriptions' from the early 1930s onwards.[10] What constitutes 'big' is, of course, open to endless dispute; and it seems likely, in view of the preceding comments, that this method of party financing was in operation from the outset. But it is certainly of interest that when a subscription of £500 was received from prominent businessman and one-time Cumann na nGaedheal supporter, Joe McGrath, in 1931, Boland's initial efforts to return the money were overturned by the Fianna Fáil National Executive on the insistence of Lemass. Henceforth the financial ties between the party and the business community were not in dispute.[11]

Boland's contention that this relationship must have gained a privileged position for the party's business backers where the formulation of party policy was concerned is supported by another veteran, Todd Andrews, who claims that 'heavy subscriptions to party funds have redounded to the benefit of the subscribers.'[12]

Also important initially, was the financial backing received from wealthy Irish-Americans whose taste for radicalism in any shape or form is questionable. De Valera had collected some £20,000 in the United States by 1927 and he visited that country in December 1927, and again for six months in November 1929, to raise funds and establish Fianna Fáil support committees.[13] A steady flow of money was available from the US from 1926 onwards from, inter alia, the American Association for the Recognition of the Irish Republic. The party's balance sheet, published in 1927, showed that, of its income of £30,402 2s. 5d. in that year, no less than £29,782 15s. 10d. came from abroad. Remarkably, a profit was actually shown in this year despite two elections.[14]

Further funds were made available as a result of the outcome of the so-called Sinn Féin Funds Case. When the New York Supreme Court decided in 1927 that money donated to Dáil Éireann in the early days of the national independence struggle should be returned to the original subscribers rather than to the Free State government, many of these American sympathisers with Irish republicanism gave the money to de Valera to be used for 'other national purposes'.[15] The money was used to buy new party headquarters and to launch a daily newspaper, the *Irish Press*, in 1931.[16] Significantly, business backing was sought for the launch of the paper and all of its directors, except de Valera, were wealthy businessmen.

Obviously, dependence upon the goodwill of successful Irish-Americans also had implications for the development of the party. Cronin has recorded how the IRA, following its move to the left during the late 1920s, found itself under severe pressure from its US financial backers. In fact, the IRA's financial support from America dried up and was not forthcoming again until after 1934, by which time the movement had effectively abandoned its flirtation with socialism.[17] It is unlikely that there was much significant difference between those sections of Irish-American opinion which financially backed the IRA and those which, in the late 1920s, backed Fianna Fáil.

The third main source of party finance would appear to have been the annual national collection. It is probable, however, that the real significance of the collection lay in its function as a form of party activity and a measurement of organisational strength. In 1927 the collection yielded about £2,000 at some 160–200 church gates in areas where the party was strongest. By the early 1930s, this amount had risen to about £5,000.[18] Even so, this seems a relatively small amount compared with the, admittedly impossible to properly estimate, sums which the party was receiving from the US and from business circles. The 1928 Árd Fheis was told that £30,000 had been raised through 'collections'.[19] There is no way of knowing how much came from businessmen or who donated. Given the estimates for church gate collections, the lion's share of the donations would seem to have come from other than the 'plain people of Ireland'.

The national collection did serve, however, as a catalyst of organisational expansion and consolidation. Returns were used by the leadership to assess the vitality of each region and weak areas were targeted; scarcely an Árd Fheis went by without detailed discussion of organisational problems.[20] It is interesting to note that Dublin was well-organised from the start and that the impetus for organising the rest of the country came from the capital.

Organisational success was immediate and impressive. By November 1926 the party had 460 cumainn; this had risen to 800 by the spring of 1927; more than 1,000 party units were operative by that summer. A team of up to 25 speakers was available on a more or less full-time basis to tour the country.[21] By November 1926 more than 400 public meetings had been held, with party speakers present. These meetings were used to mobilise supporters, present party policy, and serve as education classes.[22] As Dáil entry involved many of these party leaders in parliamentary life, a headquarters' team which included two full-time organisers was appointed to continue the necessary work. At a local level it was inevitably the TD or prospective candidate who became the organiser; or perhaps it would be more accurate to say that it was the local organiser who tended to gain parliamentary selection as many of the early Dáil deputies had been local or national IRA leaders, involved in party organisation from the outset. In any event, the predominance of the parliamentary party and its close personalistic ties to the mass membership ensured that 'Fianna Fáil, like many of its predecessor parties, understood itself to be more of a support organisation than a legislative or policy-making assembly.'[23]

Fianna Fáil's concentration upon party organisation was in sharp contrast to its opponents' behaviour. Many leaders of Cumann na nGaedheal maintained a haughty contempt for the whole business of mass mobilisation. Indeed, General Mulcahy, in later life, spoke of a deliberate attempt after 1924 to wind down the organisation in the country on the understanding that party branches were merely a hindrance to the government's work.[24] Cumann na nGaedheal, it seems, would succeed merely on the basis of its moral superiority. The Labour Party never proved capable of imposing upon its local cadres and politicians the discipline necessary to build an effective organisation, and was fatally hampered by the splintering of the trade union movement.

Fianna Fáil organisation was boosted by the launch of a weekly newspaper, *The Nation*, in 1927 under the editorship of one of the party's most consistent and shrewd populists, Seán T. O'Kelly. *The Nation* provided a valuable means of communication between members and between the party and the public, and an indispensable way in which to combat the propaganda of the overwhelmingly hostile established press. (Although it is interesting to note that, in contrast to the national press, many provincial papers were won over to Fianna Fáil between 1927 and 1932.) It also relieved the party of the potential embarrassment of sharing with the IRA the existent republican press such as *An Phoblacht*.

For Fianna Fáil, organisation was about the business of winning elections, and the business of winning elections was crucially linked to questions of policy and strategy. The experience of Sinn Féin had taught the proponents of the new departure precisely this lesson. Already in April 1926 – a month before the formal launch – a statement of the fundamental aims of the party was issued. The initial draft of this statement listed the party's aims as being:

1. To secure the unity and independence of Ireland as a Republic.

2. To restore the Irish language as the spoken language of the people and to develop a distinctive national life in accordance with Irish traditions and ideals.

3. To make the resources and wealth of Ireland subservient to the needs and welfare of all the people of Ireland.

4. To make Ireland, as far as possible, economically self-contained and self-sufficing.

5. To establish as many families as practicable on the land.

6. By suitable distribution of power to promote the ruralisation of essential industries as opposed to their concentration in cities.[25]

Even at this early stage there was manifest a tendency, which was to become more marked later, to place more emphasis on policy and less on nationalist rhetoric. The latter retained an important place in the party's arsenal – but no longer the sole, essential place; rather, as a back-up weapon with which to put rivals on the defensive and to consolidate a bloc of social forces attracted by various aspects of the party's programme. Soon, constitutional issues had been largely reduced to the single issue of the oath of allegiance, and so it was to remain until the party's advent to office.

The need to relate to socio-economic cleavages, and to come up with policies which could appeal to economically dissatisfied groups, was spelt out in an editorial in *An Phoblacht* on 11 June 1926. Under the title 'A new alignment needed? Organisation born of activity', this editorial castigated those who thought that the party's success could be guaranteed without relating to the everyday lives of 'the people'. In language reminiscent of Lemass's articles the previous year, the editorial urged the party to 'sectionalise' – i.e. to come up with policies and political rhetoric which would appeal to 'the peasant farmer and the wage earner' who stood to benefit from and would therefore support a programme based on complete separation from Britain.

At the party's inaugural meeting de Valera, having delivered himself of a sharp attack upon the oath of allegiance and pledged the party to 'peaceful reunification' concentrated upon economic and social issues, identifying himself and his party with James Connolly – founder of the Labour Party and 1916 martyr – thereby stealing Labour's clothes. He launched an attack upon unemployment, poverty and bad housing. Familiar themes of subsequent Fianna Fáil propaganda were aired – the promise of protection for Irish industry and the pledge that the 'ranches' would be broken up into small farms. And the finance for such sweeping reforms?

A loan would have been given, I believe, from the vast deposits which were held in our banks ... Even if it were not possible to get all the initial capital we required at home, I believe we could have gone to our race abroad and placed with them an additional loan of from twenty-five to fifty millions [of pounds].[26]

In other words, no action to reform the banking or financial institutions was proposed, and no real attention paid to the necessity of altering their patterns of investment (noises made in this direction on occasion by Lemass and a few others never came to anything). In the last analysis, the Fianna Fáil programme was to be financed by investment in Irish industry by wealthy Irish-Americans. In retrospect, the limitations of such a programme are obvious. But in the circumstances of the time, it was the promise of a new economic deal, and not its limitations, which excited the imagination and appealed to the social categories most in need.

De Valera took up another theme which was to become more marked later: a populist attack on the cost of state bureaucracy. Not surprisingly given the personal experiences of most republicans, his attack was focused on the cost of the army, police and civil service ('secretaries to secretaries to secretaries'). This was coupled with a pledge to reduce the number of Dáil deputies from 153 to 100 and to abolish the Senate. It is significant that the pro-Cumann na nGaedheal *Irish Independent* had run a series of articles attacking government 'waste', department by department, and that the cry had been taken up by the provincial press. Soon Fianna Fáil was linking the question of cuts in old age pensions to the allegedly high level of salaries paid to senior civil servants and TDs, and promising to restore old age pensions until the top salaries were cut.[27]

An information bureau was established with the purpose of advising cumainn on policy; of equal importance at least was to be its role in collecting facts and statistics on economic matters in particular, providing back-up service for Fianna Fáil TDs and 'issuing as speedily as possible for circulation among Fianna Fáil Deputies ... a précis giving all material helpful to the aims of the party or injurious to Cumann na nGaedheal (e.g. analysis of the Poor Law Commission Report showing distress in the country)'. Interestingly, in view of Fianna Fáil's subsequent failure to challenge the impartiality of the civil service, the Bureau was conceived of by its instigator, Frank Gallagher, as having another function:

both to those working on its staff and to those in receipt of its information the Bureau would be the nucleus of a training ground for a Civil Service with a National outlook on all branches of Irish affairs.

Those anxious to train in such a Department might be given the opportunity of an unpaid apprenticeship which would thus provide the Bureau with helpers at no cost and the country with young men and women trained to look at public affairs with Irish eyes.[28]

Notes for Speakers, issued by the party's Publicity Department, declared: 'Speakers should give wide publicity to those points in the programme of action set out in our printed leaflet, especially to the social and economic policy.'[28] Militant attacks on emigration went hand in hand with advocacy of protection. The process by which rural and urban working-class support was ascertained for Fianna Fáil's economic developmental strategy was underway.

So, too, were preparations for the party's first formal Árd Fheis, which opened in Dublin on 24 November 1926. This was, in many ways, simply a ratification of the policy statements which had been made at the May meeting and since. Attended by some 500 delegates, the Árd Fheis ratified an elaboration of the party's original policy statement which had been issued by the General Policy Committee earlier in the month and which pledged the party 'with a view to the realisation of [its] ultimate aims' to, inter alia:

> Develop the natural resources of the country, including its mineral wealth and sources of power, encourage native industries that minister to the needs of the people, and protect them by adequate tariffs;
>
> Establish a Tariff Commission independent of political and sectional interests to act as an Advisory Board to the Government, with power to publish its findings and recommendations for the guidance of the people, and to suggest safeguards so that the advantages of protection may be shared by the community as a whole;
>
> Encourage the creation of an Irish Mercantile Marine;
>
> Set about the reafforestation of the country on a national scale;
>
> Make a survey of the transport requirements of the country, with a view to facilitating internal communication and the equable distribution of commodities whilst utilising to the fullest extent native sources of motor power;
>
> Complete land purchase, break up the large grazing ranches, and distribute them as economic farms amongst young farmers and agricultural labourers, such as those at present compelled to emigrate.

In addition to this impressive list of commitments there was a pledge to help the ailing Gaeltacht communities by developing 'the fishing and other industries suitable to the Gaeltacht so as to enable the young native speakers to live at home.' Furthermore, there were pledges on protection of the rights of town tenants, and discussion of a state bank and a tax on native capital invested abroad. In other words, there was a continuous elaboration of the party's programme in a manner which was not at all vague and ambiguous, but calculated to facilitate the party's electoral penetration of Irish society.

The Árd Fheis reiterated opposition to the oath of allegiance, but irredentist rhetoric was at a minimum. Instead, a further attempt was made to woo working-class support with attention paid to questions of social welfare and health insurance. A commitment to full employment was given with the promise to provide 'employment in lieu of pensions for all pensioners under sixty years of age who are not otherwise unfitted for work.'[29]

The endorsement of pragmatism over dogmatism, the highlighting of economic and social policies which were felt to have practical appeal to disaffected groups in Irish society, and the concentration upon organisational efficiency and upon the construction of an electoral bloc comprising potentially fissile and antagonistic social forces, were all to be characteristic of the early Fianna Fáil as it sought to give concrete form to a political strategy which would carry it to electoral victory in 1932. So, too, were a deference to the rights of private property and a belief in both the capacity and the willingness of a 'patriotic' national bourgeoisie to deliver economic development and prosperity – given sufficient encouragement.

Notes:

1. K. Boland, *The Rise and Decline of Fianna Fáil* (Dublin, 1982) 21.

2. R. K. Carty, *Party and Parish Pump: Electoral Politics in Ireland* (Kerry, 1983) 103 *passim*.

3. J. Prager, *Building Democracy in Ireland* (Cambridge, 1986) 216–217.

4. G. Therborn, *What Does the Ruling Class Do When it Rules?* (London, 1980) 122.

5. T. Desmond Williams, 'De Valera in Power' in F. MacManus (Ed.), *The Years of the Great Test* (Cork, 1967) 33.

6. Quoted in B. Reynolds, 'The Formation and Development of Fianna Fáil, 1926–1932', Ph.D. Thesis (Dublin, 1976) 173–4.

7. T. Garvin, Nationalist Elites, Irish Voters, and Irish Political Development: a Comparative Perspective, *Economic and Social Review*, 8, 3 (1977), 172–9.

8. R. Briscoe, *For the Life of Me* (Boston, 1958) 227.

9. Reynolds, 1976, 139.

10. Boland, 1982, 62.

11. The private papers of Seán MacEntee contain copies of correspondence with numerous wealthy business backers throughout the 1930s, in particular, and receipts for some of the donations received. Amongst those donating were Johnston, Mooney and O'Brien (Bakers), Cahill and Co. (Printers), John Hughes and Co. (Tea Importers), University College Dublin Archives, MacEntee Papers P67/360.

12. T. Andrews, *Man of No Property* (Dublin, 1982) 251.

13. Lord Longford and T. O'Neill, *Eamon de Valera* (London, 1970) 247, 269.

14. Reynolds, 1976, 163.

15. S. Cronin, *The McGarrity Papers* (Dublin, 1972) 160–1.

16. Briscoe, 1958, 231.

17. Cronin, 1972, 160-1.

18. W. Moss, *Political Parties in the Irish Free State* (Columbia, 1933) 92.

19. Reynolds, 1976, 163.

20. Carty, 1983, 107.

21. Briscoe, 1958, 230.

22. Reynolds, 1976, 52.

23. T. Garvin, *The Evolution of Irish Nationalist Politics* (Dublin, 1981) 157.

24. R. Fanning, *Independent Ireland* (Dublin, 1983) 102.

25. Boland (1982, 36) adds a further aim – To carry out the Democratic Programme of the first Dáil – but this does not appear in de Valera's original policy statement.

26. See, for example, the resolutions passed by Fianna Fáil county councils in Cork, Galway, and Clare in August 1926 (National Archives of Ireland, Department of Finance, File No. S088/0004/26).

27. Quotations from 'Memo re information Bureau', submitted by Frank Gallagher (National Library of Ireland, Gallagher Papers, Ms. 18357).

28. National Library of Ireland, Gallagher Papers, Ms. 18357.

29. Quotations from Policy Committee statement (University College Dublin Archives, Brennan Papers, P50/1); for further comments see M. McInerney, *Eamon de Valera, 1882–1975: The Controversial Giant of Modern Ireland* (Dublin, 1976) 56.

3

Eamon de Valera: The Image and the Achievement

by Declan Kiberd

The widow of W.B. Yeats, as she sifted among his papers in the years after his death, remarked on her husband's many gifts, of which one in particular stood out. That was his extraordinarily developed sense, even in the course of a long tempestuous career, of how things would appear to those who had studied them in the future. Most people, even poets, live at the mercy of the immediate moment and are quite happy to do so, for, as Patrick Kavanagh once quipped, posterity has not printed its banknotes yet: but there are exceptions to this rule and Yeats was one of them. So also in the world of politics was Eamon de Valera. The long fellow of legend knew how to take the long view.

This may in the end turn out to have been one of his greatest strengths, but in the short term, even that prophetic power is being cited in evidence by his sharpest critics. Tim Pat Coogan's influential and highly readable books on Eamon de Valera and Michael Collins are bound together by a strong, overarching theme, which comes straight from the Chief himself. The final sentences of the Collins study quote de Valera as having said in 1966: 'It is my considered opinion that in the fullness of time, history will record the greatness of Collins, and it will be recorded at my expense.' Coogan's closing gloss ('He could be right') became the dominant thesis of the second book.

1966 was probably a double-edged year for de Valera, a symbolic reminder, as anniversaries so often are, of real progress and of much that remained unachieved. Contemporary accounts of his address commemorating the Easter Rising in that year record how some members of the 'youngest cabinet in Europe' shifted uneasily in their seats behind the old man as he reviewed the decades of progress and frustration: they were setting their sights on Europe and a vibrant consumer society. He had already warned of the potentially corrupting effect on national morale of the new television station (if it fell into the wrong hands): they couldn't appear on it often enough. To most of them, he probably represented a noble if somewhat antiquated ideal Ireland of saints and scholars: their future would be an island of silos and silicon.

In the years that followed, that fundamental split between the image of de Valera and the self-image of the emerging Ireland deepened. By the 1970s a young writer such as Neil Jordan would use the funeral of de Valera as background in a powerful short story, which spoke of liberation at last from the pull of the past (the same Jordan would, years later, make a film about Michael Collins). And so the theme was set. Poet Paul Durcan imagined de Valera as a cranky old puritan, who, when his spirit intervened in national life, came armed with repressive ordinances to young modern couples: 'Stop making love outside Áras an Uachtaráin'. Eventually the producers of a cabaret show, *Nighthawks* on RTE television, as if to confirm Dev's worst fears – presented him as a frozen old gent stored permanently in a refrigerator, who could be taken out from time to time for comical rap routines.

It was never quite clear, however, whether the *Nighthawks* sketches were simply another crude mockery of the dead man or a much subtler critique of all the clichés which were already congealing around his image. The killjoy of Durcan's poem was, for instance, light years removed from the actual de Valera who was known to knock back eight whiskies after a rugby match or to have spent much of his time in prison after 1916, learning and reciting one of the most ribald poems of the Irish language, *Cúirt an Mheán Oíche*. Those who had once groaned through Dev's disquisitions on the unfinished business up North, lived long enough to learn all about the 'return of the repressed', about the fact that the history which they had so conveniently forgotten, had quite inconveniently not forgotten them. The old man in the *Nighthawks* refrigerator was after all being preserved for occasional re-entry to national debate: the implication, if you thought about it, was that the stiff body could be unfrozen at any moment to make more telling interventions – an image from the past flashing forth at a moment of challenge and danger in the present.

If de Valera as a model figure were as empty an example as his detractors claimed, then why did they go on about him so much? Why had they to invest him with such symbolic import? And why, even today, do so many still talk obsessively about him? A recent article in the *Times Higher Education Supplement* of London, ran a Dev–versus–Collins debate: evidently, there are elements in the Murdoch press who would like nothing better than to see Irish intellectuals fight the Civil War all over again. And there appears to be no lack of volunteers to abet them in the task. The proper comment on such bogus theatrics was made by Bertie Ahern, in a fine speech praising the achievements of Collins at a function in the Shelbourne Hotel in June 1996. That will not prevent the likes of Geoffrey Wheatcroft and others from continuing to produce high voltage denunciations of de Valera in the British press, articles which are recycled with remarkable frequency in some Irish papers.

Underlying most of the critiques is a common assumption: that de Valera's Ireland, which lasted roughly from the 1930s to the 1960s, was a dark, drab land, which demanded an oppressive conformism, from which after an heroic contest the current generation of leaders had freed us, making today's country a vast improvement in almost every respect. There is no provinicalism in space quite like the provincialism of the present moment in time: in this version, we are all asked to believe that we, ourselves alone, are history's cutting edge, what it was all leading towards.

One element in this philosophy is the secular assumption that meaning dies with the end of a life: there can be no transcendent values that survive the death of the individual and those who act as if there can be are fools or dupes. Much of the debunking of Patrick Pearse and the rebels of 1916 comes from historians, who are quite baffled by the rebels' willingness to die for values which might transcend their own lives and times, by their ability to take the longer view. Most contemporary historians are actuated by no such belief and prefer to stress pragmatic questions of *realpolitik*. One of the reasons why Dev troubles them, is that he, most disobligingly, survived the 1916 experience to practice just the sort of *realpolitik*, which historians profess to admire in others, but somehow can never forgive in him, because he crossed it with the transcendent, 'otherwordly' ideals. The very intensity of the debate as to whether or not he 'choked' at Boland's Mills in 1916, might be attributed to the way in which it raises the question of a spiritual value which outlasts a man's death.

The first full-scale revisionist assessment of de Valera, Seán Ó Faoláin's Penguin study, is a tell-tale instance of much that was to follow, for it wilfully and consistently refuses to temper negative judgement by any recognition of the day-to-day constraints faced by a practising politician. Either Dev is to be judged as a visionary or as a fixer, but never as what he was, a fascinating mixture of both, an exponent of the 'both/and' philosophy of an Irish Ireland movement which sought the benefits of modernity and the liquidation of its costs.

Current televisual images of de Valera are summoned, of necessity for the most part, from black-and-white newsreels and framed by the colour-commentaries of sophisticates, whose main function in life is to remind people of just how far things have progressed (thanks mainly to them). The implication is that Dev can be used as the marker of a narrow-gauge nationalism which most Irishmen and women have abandoned with audible sighs of relief. In truth, much that was sacred to de Valera has been jettonised by the élites which replaced him. He wanted an Irish-speaking island, but today Irish speakers have to agitate for the civil right of dealing with the State in their own language. He defended rural values which are regularly mocked as touchstones of 'backwardness'. He asserted a principled neutrality which is currently being junked. The great newspaper organisation which he founded has expired, following a degrading period of being drip-fed by the owners of its major rival.

Given this litany of defeat and frustration, one might reasonably ask: why not leave de Valera's spirit to rest in peace? Why keep summoning it up? Why keep on raising the question which he seems to represent? The answer is that those who raise the question are part of a successful new Europeanising élite, who (in their few darker moments) are secretly haunted by much that he said. As a group these people are empowered, but, being Irish, they must pose as persecuted rebels, oppressed by the forces of darkness, which lurk (of course) around every corner. This is a trick which they learned, no doubt, from de Valera himself, who used it to perfection in the heroic decades of Fianna Fáil – a party which never found it difficult to sound like an opposition while holding the reins the government. Today, that trick has been deployed to some effect by the leaders of Democratic Left and their media surrogates, while Fianna Fáil, actually in opposition, tries to speak and to think of itself as 'the real government of the country'. The new élites, whether in government, opposition or the media, like to pose as occasional victims of barbarous intolerance (ritualised clashes with wild-eyed religious zealots bearing Gaelicised names feed the desired overall effect) while going about the work of modernising Ireland.

The name of an intellectual such as Seán Ó Faoláin has been much invoked in these debates as a liberal exampler, particularly in the years following his death, but most often by people (senior RTE figures, government ministers, 'star' columnists) who do not exist in the same kind of tension with their establishment as Ó Faoláin did with the rulers of Ireland in his day. Ó Faoláin is the 'liberal' hero because he bravely fought the grievous wrong of censorship, made himself into a cosmopolitan after an early and violent infatuation with nationalism, and thereafter devoted his life to defending the rights of the individual. Against these inspiring ideals, Dev's theories of frugal comfort, communal values and economic self-sufficiency can indeed sometimes seem narrow, backward, even somewhat anachronistic. In truth, there was much about the man which left him seriously open to such strictures: his patronising and restricted view of the role of women outraged many liberal nationalists from Dorothy Macardle to Mary Hayden; his desire to wish the complexities of an international economic order away seemed frequently puerile; and his verbal attacks on unionism may be said to have exposed nationalists to retaliation (of a more pragmatic kind), while offering no way forward.

All of these weaknesses are made much of in Tim Pat Coogan's study, *Long Fellow, Long Shadow* – and many others too. Yet, for all that, the man who emerges from its pages as another victim of historical revisionism may, in the fullness of time, be accorded a more positive verdict, even by the revisionists themselves. If the essence of revisionism Irish-style is a debunking of the myths of nationalism, then de Valera has some claim to being a seminal proponent of that movement. The old joke that Fianna Fáil was a 'slightly constitutional party' was intended to paper over an undeniable fact: that thereafter its members would devote themselves to legitimating and consolidating the 26-county state.

Fianna Fáil was perhaps slightly constitutional, but only in the way that a woman two or three months into a pregnancy is slightly pregnant. The condition was in fact irreversible: and the example given by Dev would be followed in due course by Democratic Left (the ferocity of whose clashes with Fianna Fáil may sometimes seem to arise from a joint fear of an underlying identity).

Moreover, as a framer of Articles 2 and 3 of the 1937 Constitution, de Valera may have been playing an abstract word-game about sovereignty, but these words offered the first *de facto* recognition of the orange state and, hence, the first unambiguous signal to Northern nationalists that they could be abandoned by future governments in Dublin. Far from constituting an imperial-style claim, the articles represented a major concession on Dev's part – too great a concession in the view of some nationalists at the time.

Ó Faoláin's assessment of de Valera might be described as unsubtle, since it took no account of the varying tugs on his sympathies as he wrote that constitution: it is in some ways a critique written by a literary man rather than by a student of political science. Coogan's study, though written by a more adept analyst of politics as the art of the possible, manages – for all its animus – to restore Dev's essential humanity to the portrait. For instance it has him mischievously suggesting that the rules of Gaelic football originated in Michael Cusack's experiences in the Blackrock College school yard. Since the yard was tarmacadamed, ground tacking was out of the question and so the tap-and-pass form evolved. Such an analysis, had Dev advanced it in public, would have made a mockery of the GAA ban on 'foreign' games.

He does appear to have panicked during the 1916 Rising (perhaps through the fear that might grip any man under stress, or through simple loss of sleep); but he also seems to have planned the protection of men under his command with meticulous care, casing the area around Boland's Mills during walks with his five-year-old son on the day before the event.

It may well be that the final truth about de Valera is to be found somewhere between the respectful and affectionate Tom O'Neill/Lord Longford biography and Tim Pat Coogan's energetic iconoclasm. If Dev is vulnerable to criticism, that is partly because he set such high ideals for himself as well as for others, ideals of a visionary kind which no politician in western Europe today seems willing to emulate. This led to inevitable conflicts between high theory and actual practice: he extolled family life while thousands of families were broken by emigration; he announced verbal republics even as real ones fissured; he spoke in a slow deliberate Irish as the Gaeltacht continued to decline.

Yet the problems faced by most other post-colonial prime ministers and presidents have proved generally intractable. The global economy which emerged in the mid-century was no respecter of national boundaries or of theories of self-sufficiency: and the unionists were so wedded to their siege mentality that they would have proved unresponsive to more generous initiatives. Coogan says of de Valera that 'self-righteous propaganda that stirred the pot of anti-British sentiment without adding anything fresh to its ingredients became his stock-in-trade': and he contends that a little magnanimity from the numerically stronger nationalities on the island might have gone a long way. A case can certainly be argued on these lines but it neglects a point which Coogan himself repeatedly made in powerful editorials during his *Irish Press* days: it is hard to achieve a *rapprochement* between two traditions when the very essence of one seems to consist in its triumphalist oppression of the other.

On the positive side in any final accounting must be listed real achievements, most obviously the creation of the party now celebrating its 70th anniversary, but also achievements which predated Fianna Fáil itself. Too little as yet has been written of de Valera's work in the post-colonial movement of the 1920s, but he played a crucial role in it at the time. The Ghadar Party – an organisation of Indian workers in the United States dedicated to the military overthrow of the British Raj – presented de Valera with an engraved sword and an Irish flag: and on 28 February 1920 he delivered a trenchant speech in New York at a meeting of the Friends of the Freedom of India. Taking courage from the American example, he reminded his audience of Washington's message to the patriots of Ireland: 'your cause is identical with mine', adding the inflection 'Patriots of India, your course is identical to ours'. He hoped that the ties which by then bound Ireland to the US might one day link Ireland to India; and, though the different conditions might call forth a variation in tactics, he urged immediate revolt: 'We in Ireland, comparatively small in numbers, close to the heart of Britain's imperial power, have never despaired. You, people of India, remote from her, a continent in yourselves, 70 times as numerous as we are, surely you will not despair.' From 1919 onwards the British authorities, in intelligence reports and cabinet minutes, recognised that if de Valera's case were conceded, the flames of revolt could be fanned in India, Egypt and elsewhere. It was even considered 'likely' that de Valera's New York speech had motivated such events as mutiny of the Connaught Rangers later in 1920.

This commitment to global decolonisation flowered in the genuinely independent foreign policy which won respect for Ireland at the League of Nations and later at the UN; the maintenance of neutrality protected most of Ireland from terrible bombing in the Second World War and, subsequently, made the Irish acceptable as successful UN peace-keepers. It may have also produced in de Valera and other Irish politicians a healthy scepticism about the abstract seductions of a fascism which gripped so many of Europe's 'Catholic' peoples. A generation tempered in the fires of anti-imperial struggle needed no Fanon or Sartre to tell of the links between the imperial mentality and the heady prospect of a 1000-year Reich.

Perhaps the most important lesson taught by de Valera was the one which he himself had learned from Douglas Hyde and the Gaelic League: the link between political and cultural nationalism. Hyde had argued that too many Irish political leaders of the nineteenth century had made the case for Irish separatism while at the same time throwing away the very basis of a separatist claim – the native language, games, dances, clothing, and entire culture. A freedom without these would, in his view, be hollow indeed. Yet the warning echoes of that hollowness were audible from the beginning: the young men in jail with de Valera after 1916 showed, according to Colm Ó Gaora in *Mise*, little interest in learning their own language or in studying its literature. They were far more keen on drilling and on mastering the use of arms 'to finish the job'. This was to be revealed as a major weakness not alone of the Irish movement but of many liberation movements elsewhere: for instance, Edward Said has often accused the PLO leadership of fetishising the use of arms and neglecting the cultural aspects of the struggle. All over the decolonising world young men and women extolled the tradition of the fight as a self-sustaining thing and forgot what it was that they were supposedly fighting for.

Now that cultural nationalism has come back into fashion again in figures such as Vaclav Havel, the time may be ripe for a positive reassessment of de Valera, recognising his strengths as well as his flaws. He may be revealed as less backward-looking than he seemed. The philosophies of frugal comfort and principled neutrality have found many echoes in the manifestos of Green parties and environmental groups of all over the world. The stress on communal values may have an unexpected appeal for a people jaded by uncontrollable individualism, whose townlands are racked by murder, robbery and sexual crime, much of it committed against the isolated or the elderly. Dev's willingness to address the diaspora as an intrinsic part of the 'Irish people' has been revived in recent years, after a number of decades in which a concerted attempt was made to reduce the concept, first to the 5 million on the island and, later, to the 3.5 million in the 26 counties. It is no accident that this shrinkage occurred in those very decades, after 1960, which are still extolled as years of enlightenment. It may well be that the globalisation of communication helped to bring de Valera's views on the diaspora back into consciousness. It seems certain that his ideas can still inspire our leaders: the presidency of Mary Robinson has taken up many de Valerean themes. Her campaign for it began with a video which depicted her dancing in slow motion at a village crossroads. Had the image appeared just a year or two earlier on *Nighthawks*, it would have been taken as a piece of pure parody: but in the context of her crusade, it showed that many of the images and ideas surrounding de Valera were, in all likelihood, about to be resuscitated. President Robinson has attempted, with great dignity and intelligence, to unite the individual rights for which Seán Ó Faoláin bravely stood with the communitarian world-vision of de Valera. The more fully she succeeds in this, the more likely are his detractors to quieten down and to take what is valuable in his legacy and try to build on it.

4

The Truth in the News

by John Garvey

Taoiseach Charles Haughey was in his office, bright and early, when the Department official arrived with the morning mail and the papers.

'There's a marvellous picture of you in the *Irish Press* this morning, Taoiseach,' he remarked as he unloaded his pile of correspondence. 'Have you seen it?'

Mr Haughey didn't even look up from his desk. 'What's wrong with it?,' he growled.

The official stared at him, somewhat bewildered. 'I didn't see anything wrong with it,' he replied. 'It's an outstanding picture. Your friend Colman Doyle took it, didn't he?'

Mr Haughey refused to be mollified. 'What page is it on?,' he asked, in a surprisingly challenging tone.

'It's on page three,' the official told him. 'Across six columns. They've given it a really big show.'

Mr Haughey looked up from his desk for the first time and caught the other man's eye. 'What page should it be on?,' he asked reprovingly.

It's a story that sums up the often testy relationship between the *Irish Press* and Fianna Fáil. As with friends everywhere who grew up together, there were imagined slights – sometimes by those who worked on the paper as well as by the party – accusations of disloyalty and a tendency to take each other for granted.

A six column picture or an editorial commendation in the *Irish Independent* or the *The Irish Times* was something to be cherished by Fianna Fáil. In the *Irish Press*, it was not just taken as the party's due – there were often quibbles that more could have been done.

The *Irish Press* was never a party organ, unquestioningly following the dictates of political masters, though some, with axes to grind, were eager to dismiss it as a 'Fianna Fáil rag'. It was, above all, a national newspaper, representing a distinctive, and at times, radical viewpoint, in contrast to the cosy editorial consensus that existed between D'Olier and Abbey Street, and which still exists, despite the occasional bout of shadow boxing by their blurb writers.

Inevitably, because of its origins, the *Irish Press* had a special relationship with Fianna Fáil. But it was a relationship based on shared ideals, not on subservience. The editorial backing at election times was not to be taken as a blanket endorsement. The paper saw itself as the party's friend – and, as friends do, it sometimes pointed out shortcomings, an exercise that, however well intentioned, is never popular.

Seen from the perspective of well over half a century, it is difficult now to imagine the sense of excitement generated by the first issue of the *Irish Press* on Saturday, September 5 1931. In today's world of marketing specialists and advertising gurus, the notion of launching a new national daily on a Saturday would be dismissed as ridiculous. But Eamon de Valera knew better.

He had raised the £200,000 launch capital from supporters in America and from 8,000 small shareholders at home – farmers, publicans, teachers, priests and housewives, who contributed in shillings as well as in pounds. His 'great enterprise', as he called it, was needed to provide a national voice for those who, as we used to say in Burgh Quay, remained with the republican side during the Civil War and were now victims of a conspiracy of silence by the media.

The William Martin Murphy-owned *Irish Independent* and the Pro-Unionist *The Irish Times* had opposed the 1916 Rising and supported the British authorities in the War of Independence. Now both were backing the Treaty in another cosy consensus which ensured the republican voice was not heard.

The *Irish Press* changed all that. The first issue, a 12-page broadsheet that, surprisingly, concentrated more on hard news than politics – the lead story was about a floods emergency in Dublin – might win no prizes for lay-out, judged against today's 'sophisticated' standards. But it was what the birth of the paper represented, rather than how it looked, which had the crowds milling around its offices, the former Tivoli Theatre on Burgh Quay, and much of the country on tenterhooks, as Padraig Pearse's mother, Margaret, pressed the button to set the presses rolling.

The first editorial set out the new paper's credentials. This was no Fianna Fáil house magazine or de Valera publicity sheet. 'Our service will be to the whole people,' it said. 'We are not the organ of an individual, or a group, or a party. We are a national organ, in all that term conveys.'

'We have given ourselves the motto: "Truth in the News". We shall be faithful to it. Even where the news exposes a weakness of our own, or a shortcoming in the policies we approve, or a criticism of individuals with whom we are associated, we shall publish it, if its inherent news values so demand.'

It was an impressive list of principles to nail to the mast for the maiden voyage. And *The Irish Times* and *Irish Independent*, which had refused to carry advertisements announcing the launch, were determined to make the voyage as turbulent – and as brief – as possible. Newsagents were encouraged not to stock it. The *Independent* went to court to prevent it being carried on the newspaper train. British manufacturers, who still controlled the Irish market, refused to advertise.

Despite all this, the *Irish Press* still prospered. The network of Fianna Fáil cumainn across the State, plus the 8,000 small shareholders, who provided a representative in almost every parish, ensured that. It also forged a link between the party and the paper which survived right to the end.

There was another reason for the success: Frank Gallagher, the first editor, who was still spoken of in hushed tones by Burgh Quay veterans some 50 years later. He was an ideal choice for the new paper, a man who combined rare journalistic flair with commitment to the cause.

As a reporter with the *Cork Free Press*, he had covered the historic Home Rule debates at Westminster. As a republican, he had joined the Volunteers after 1916 and later worked under publicity director Erskine Childers during the War of Independence.

At Burgh Quay, Gallagher was called upon to perform a daily miracle with limited resources. Some of his staff were new to journalism. Republican activist Paddy Clare, for instance, had turned up to watch the launch – and was recruited as a reporter. He stayed 50 years.

Despite the handicaps, the new editor produced a lively, radical newspaper that shook both the competition and the government of the day. One of his scoops so embarrassed the authorities that he was hauled before the courts. He refused to reveal his sources and was jailed for contempt, a penalty that enhanced his reputation and that of the paper.

He was an editor who believed passionately in good journalism. At this remove and in the light of today's media obsession with showbiz trivia, it is intriguing to read a memo he sent to the American news agency, United Press International, protesting about the type of coverage being provided. 'I hope,' he wrote, 'that we shall get some news of America other than what is now being supplied, namely an amalgam of gangster stories, divorces at Reno and prohibition raids.' When he resigned, after only four years as editor, it was, typically, in defence of the journalistic standards he had set. Economies which management deemed essential for the paper's survival would restrict its news coverage, he said, and quit.

It was a serious blow. But, as was to happen many times over the next half century, when penny-pinching attitudes drove some of Ireland's best journalists from Burgh Quay into the welcoming arms of the competition, new talents emerged to sustain the paper. Ben Kiely was one. So too were Brendan Behan, Patrick Kavanagh and Edna O'Brien, all regular contributors. Later, under the editorship of Tim Pat Coogan, David Marcus was to consolidate the paper's literary reputation with his unique New Irish Writing page in which many of today's major Irish authors, from John Banville – a former *Irish Press* chief sub-editor – to William Trevor, were published.

When I arrived in the mid-1960s, even the sub-editors' desk was a heavyweight division. Working alongside me was David Andrews, soon to move to affairs of state. Another sub-editor who worked in Features and drank pints with us in the now defunct Silver Swan, was also destined for higher things. These days he hands down judgements as Mr Justice Hugh O'Flaherty of the Supreme Court.

The Fianna Fáil influence at the paper was still strong. Taoiseach Seán Lemass was remembered as the best general manager the *Irish Press* ever had. He was a man who would make decisions, senior staff said.

Erskine Childers had done a stint as advertising manager. Now, as Minister, he was frequently complaining about his speeches being cut. Once, when speaking in his Monaghan constituency, he was reported only in the country and city editions. He got a northern edition – and complained. Next day the speech was run again in the country edition. By then he had returned to Dublin and missed it. So, incredibly, it had to be run a third time.

In the face of growing competition for readers, such indulgences could not continue. And so there were strains. They were compounded as the *Irish Press* tried to adapt to the changing attitudes of Irish society, as its rivals had already begun to do.

The Mary Kenny era at the paper is now regarded as a golden age of Irish women's journalism, and so it was. But at the time it provoked outrage among what was, despite the paper's early radicalism, a very conservative minded readership. In letters and phone calls they demanded to know what was happening to Dev's paper. It had not been founded, they thundered, to promote contraceptive train trips or bra-less feminists.

As our older readers became disenchanted, their sons and daughters – many now at university, thanks to Donogh O'Malley's free education scheme – were being weaned away from the family paper by a revitalised *Irish Times*. Once viewed as the paper of the Protestant minority, it had succeeded in broadening its appeal and catching the new mood of the country under the astute editorship of Douglas Gageby, an old Burgh Quay hand. It was a danger signal that, sadly, went unheeded at the *Irish Press*.

The arms trial and its aftermath, when emotions ran high, created extraordinary difficulties for the paper, caught in the middle of party divisions. It was now that Michael Mills established his reputation with solid, scrupulously fair reporting. Indeed, such was his reputation for fair-mindedness that he was later chosen to be the State's first Ombudsman – and by a Fine Gael-led administration at that!

Perhaps our most celebrated clanger was the infamous Haughey obituary, when the paper carried an extensive farewell tribute to the master of Kinsaley on the day he was expected finally to succumb to a leadership challenge. Instead, defying the pundits, he rose, Lazarus-like, from his political death-bed to leave Burgh Quay looking very sick indeed.

It was a serious mistake for a paper with the tradition and reputation of the *Irish Press*. But it was a mistake that stemmed, not from any ulterior motive but from the enthusiasm and inexperience of youthful executives, eager to get ahead of the competition.

Vivion de Valera, backbench Fianna Fáil Deputy and *Irish Press* editor-in-chief, was first in the firing line when the political flak hit the fan. He didn't have to read the paper, he once told me – though he did, meticulously – as he could guess from how ministers greeted him at the Dáil what they thought of that day's issue. He could be arrogant, obstinate and brutally dismissive of staff.

But he had a passion for fairness in reporting that reinforced one's belief in that 'Truth in the News' slogan. Some of the attitudes he expressed in private were surprising, to put it mildly. At the height of the Northern violence, he took me aside one day to explain how, as an Army man, he would 'pacify' South Armagh, my native place, then causing acute problems for Her Majesty's forces. It was a plan that, coming from a de Valera, amounted to political heresy. Next day he arrived in a rush to reassure me that his views were not to be taken as an editorial directive when writing about the North!

He was a one-man *Irish Press* management team, which meant that his death left an unfillible vacuum. There was no one qualified to take over, and no one with the authority to recruit the management expertise which the company now needed. As the old certainties about policy and direction began to crumble in a rapidly-changing Ireland, so did sales and advertising revenues.

Some critics blamed the collapse on editorial attitudes, that we had forgotten we were 'a Fianna Fáil paper'. Marketing experts claimed the exact opposite, that we hadn't shaken off the tag of being 'a Fianna Fáil paper'. It was an impossible dilemma, one that should have been resolved years earlier, as *The Irish Times* had successfully done from a much narrower base.

New printing technology was held out as the answer to our problems. But its introduction was badly handled, provoking a printers' strike which kept the papers off the streets for weeks. The *Irish Press* was last to return, but continuing production problems meant that in many areas it was late or didn't arrive at all. Even the most loyal of readers have a breaking point.

By 1990 the papers were in financial crisis and on the brink of closure, with the unions resisting a major redundancy programme. Bertie Ahern, then establishing a reputation as Mr Fix It in the Department of Labour, learned at first-hand just how sick Dev's great enterprise had become.

Somehow an 11th-hour reprieve was achieved. But the peace was short lived. Now a power battle broke out between the local management and its new American partner, publisher Ralph Ingersoll, which led to the public washing of Burgh Quay's soiled linen for months in the courts.

In the meantime, management had decided to turn the *Irish Press* into a tabloid. There were balloons and champagne to mark the changeover – but unlike that September Saturday in 1931, there were few in Fianna Fáil or elsewhere who felt a sense of excitement. They recognised, as we did, that this was more of a last-ditch gamble than cause for celebration.

The strategy was to concentrate on urban areas and attract young readers. Unfortunately, many of them had already been captured in the great British tabloid invasion while our traditional readers, particularly in rural Ireland, felt alienated by the new format. The paper that had changed Irish journalism – and Irish politics – was now struggling to find an audience.

In the angry summer of 1995, as the final curtain was being rung down, many in Fianna Fáil, the party which had inspired the paper's birth, marched with us to try to prevent its death. The level of public support and goodwill was heart-warming. But it was all too late.

In the end, a distinctive voice in Irish national affairs had been silenced through a combination of bad management and the harsh reality of marketplace economics. Dev's paper, in which so many people had invested their lives and their hopes, died with the loss of 600 jobs. But the ultimate loss to Irish national life remains incalculable.

5

Seán Lemass: A Man in a Hurry

by John Horgan

Our weapon to rally public support for our policy is the Fianna Fáil organisation. The future of Ireland depends almost entirely on the strength and vitality of our movement, and on the constancy of its members. By far the most important contribution to the nation's welfare and progress during this crucial period is being made by those who have devoted themselves to sustaining the strength and the efficiency of Fianna Fáil. Without them we could achieve little – with them there is no national purpose in which we will not succeed.[1]

In almost anyone else's mouth, words such as those just quoted could be fairly accused of oratorical flatulence, and indeed there is a touch of purple prose about them. But Seán Lemass, who uttered them close to the end of his active political life, had more reason than most to deliver them with passion and conviction. It was, after all, almost exactly half a century since he, together with Eamon de Valera, had taken the crucial steps to establish a separate organisation from Sinn Féin and use it as the basis for policies which were going to bring a critically important sector of the Irish electorate into the mainstream of Irish democratic politics and, within six years, into government in the new Irish state.

The foundation of the new party, in the wake of de Valera's defeat at the 1926 Sinn Féin Árd Fheis, has been well documented.[2] De Valera had decided to leave public life after his defeat: Lemass was the man who made him change his mind, and who convened the meeting at the old Sinn Féin offices to form the new party on Good Friday 1926.

It was a critical staging point in what had already been a hectic political apprenticeship. Lemass, by his own admission, had not even been interested in politics as such before the Civil War, and had not been a member of the old Sinn Féin organisation.[3] After the Civil War, he had thrown himself into the work of policy-making for Sinn Féin as a member of its key committees, but his interest in economics, which was even then apparent (he had spent much of his time in the Curragh internment camp reading omnivorously on this subject) was for a time taking second place to organisational work, especially in the capital. Even before the split in the organisation, Lemass's organisational abilities were noted, and he was Director of Elections for Pat Nash in his unsuccessful attempt to defeat Joe Devlin in West Belfast in 1924.[4] This was the same year in which – at his second attempt – he won a Dáil seat in a Dublin County by-election.

With the split in the organisation, there was no longer a ready-made membership to count on nationally, and Lemass, who became joint honorary secretary of the new party with Gerald Boland, had to play a major part in building it up, virtually from scratch. Initially he was pleasantly surprised to find out that the split at delegate level in Sinn Féin was not matched at the grass roots, and commented many years later that:

> the speed with which the Fianna Fáil organisation came into being, from
> a group sitting in Dublin to a nationwide organisation extending to every
> parish in the country, was quite phenomenal.[5]

Whether by accident or design, the personalities of the two joint honorary secretaries were admirably complementary. Boland who was 14 years older than Lemass, was like him a Dubliner (although born in Manchester, he was brought up here). He had been elected to the Dáil for Roscommon in 1923.

Initially, both shared the work of organising Fianna Fáil across the country. On holiday once, Lemass proudly pointed into a field in Donegal and said to his family 'That's where Fianna Fáil was founded in Donegal'.[6] Lemass bought five old Ford cars for five pounds each, to be driven by four other party organisers and himself. A fast and impatient driver, he cared little for the comfort of his passengers in his desire to maximise the party membership and its electoral base at this critical stage of its existence.[7] Once he arrived at an after-Mass meeting in Clara with one of his passengers, the future government minister Paddy Little, pouring blood from his nose after the car had hit a bad bump on its journey from Tullamore.

On another occasion Lemass, whose car had broken down, telephoned de Valera to explain his predicament, to be astonished by de Valera's accurate surmise that he had broken down just outside Portlaoise. 'How on earth did you know?' Lemass asked. 'I happen to know,' de Valera replied, 'that there's a long, straight, wide piece of road there, and that before that point it is very winding. I also know you and your impatience – and I know you could not resist slogging the old car.'

It was not long, however, before divergences in style between the two men became apparent. Lemass was – and remained for virtually all his public life – a man in a hurry. His brusque, no-nonsense approach worked well enough in the city, where the pace of life even in the 1920s and 1930s could be busy. It was in many instances ill-suited for the delicate, painstaking and always time-consuming task of talking to suspicious Sinn Féin stalwarts in far-flung corners of rural constituencies in an attempt to persuade them of the merits of the new organisation. After Lemass had trodden on a few sensitive toes his field of operations was, by mutual consent, increasingly confined to the urban areas – although he remained for a considerable time a speaker much in demand at venues throughout the country.

The reports of the two honorary secretaries to the annual Árd Fheiseanna, most of which are carefully collated in the Fianna Fáil Archives, provide vivid evidence of the nature of the organisational drive and of the energy which went into it. Although the reports were the work of both men, it is hardly fanciful to detect Lemass's sense of urgency, his drive for more and better organisation, between the lines. It is significant, for instance, that the report to the 1927 Árd Fheis, as well as issuing the customary warning that many of the 1,307 cumainn were in need of re-organisation, embodied a vision of the organisation as a two-way information system. It was not simply that the cumainn were expected to carry out orders from headquarters; they also had to 'pay special attention to the work of supplying the Teachtaí with reliable information concerning matters of local importance'.[8]

That Árd Fheis passed a resolution from a cumann in Lemass's constituency calling for a propaganda campaign throughout the cumainn in support of Irish industries, and specifically instructed local units of the organisation to make reports to headquarters on all factories closed in their area, detailing the date of closure, the reason for closure, the identity of the owners, the state of the machinery, the possibilities of re-opening it, and 'any other useful information'.

By now Lemass was also a party whip in the Dáil, following the party's decision to enter, and he was not above applying pressure through the Árd Fheis to make his task easier. Some TDs were apparently reluctant attenders, even then, and even in Fianna Fáil: the Fintan Lalor Cumann in Rathmines, also in his constituency, secured Árd Fheis approval in 1928 for a resolution that any TD who missed more than one third of the Dáil divisions in which he or she should have voted should be reported to all cumainn in the constituency concerned and should be ineligible for re-selection as a candidate.[9]

The same Árd Fheis instructed TDs, also on the basis of a motion from Rathmines, to visit every cumann in their constituencies at least once every six months. This may be thought of as a counsel of perfection, but for Lemass in particular it was evidently not an unwelcome burden, even though this was a year in which he visited both Northern Ireland and London as part of the organisational drive. Throughout his public life he was a conscientious attender at Comhairle Dáilcheanntair meetings in particular, and regarded it as an essential way of keeping in touch with grass-roots sentiment. He generally went to listen, not to give an oration.

Although enthusiasm was patent, the results did not always match up to expectations. By 1929, the number of registered cumainn notified to the Árd Fheis had declined to 703, and in spite of hectic activity at national level (the National Executive held 43 meetings in the course of the year), there was an increase in the number of cumainn in only five constituencies. Lemass and Boland, noting that in some constituencies growth of support for Fianna Fáil policies had actually been accompanied by a decline in party membership, warned grimly that this was 'due to known causes'.[10] In other words, if the cap fitted, wear it.

They also refined the organisational methods of the party, adopting a new system in Dublin, which was by now Lemass's personal bailiwick, by virtue of which prominent TDs would attend cumainn meetings in constituencies where there was, as yet, no Fianna Fáil member in the Dáil.

In 1930, the party took the risky step of requiring all cumainn to contribute a registration fee. The annual report for the year noted with evident relief that although the number of registered cumainn was now only 550, the more substantial drop which had been expected had not in fact taken place. Again, blame for the organisational shortcomings was placed fairly and squarely on the shoulders Lemass and Boland thought responsible: they were due to 'neglect or inefficiency' on the part of deputies and cumann officers.[11] The success of this disciplinarian approach was evident the following year, when the number of cumainn had increased by almost 50% to 759.[12] By 1932, at the end of Lemass's first tenure of office as joint Honorary Secretary, it had virtually doubled to 1,404.[13]

At this point, and for obvious reasons, Lemass disappears from the list of party officers on assuming his Cabinet post as Minister for Industry and Commerce, although he occupied the key position of Director of Elections, and headed the committee for the ratification of Dáil candidates at the 1933 election.[14]

The electoral difficulties of 1948 are reflected in declining cumann registration for 1946 and 1947. Evidently in view of the difficulty of the impending electoral task, Lemass was again co-opted to the National Executive – although not to his former position – on 1 December 1947 in the wake of Aodh de Blacam's resignation.[15] The following year, his evident popularity with the rank and file was reflected, as it was frequently to be thereafter, by his election at the head of the Committee of 15.[16]

During the 1948–51 period of opposition, however, Lemass's contribution to the party and its organisation and morale were made in a less direct form. This was through his work as managing director of the *Irish Press*, and not least through the highly successful launch of the *Sunday Press*. He always regarded his journalistic work – he was a prolific contributor of unsigned articles to the daily paper, but his style was a dead give-away – as politics by other means.

His major contribution to party organisation since the 1930s came during the 1954–57 period in opposition. His re-appointment as joint Honorary Secretary was signalled by a re-appearance of his basic message from 1927: the cumainn (now a satisfying 1,697 in number) were instructed to communicate to headquarters 'all information and views from their areas which are of political significance'.[17]

The following three years witnessed a whirlwind of activity which rivalled and probably even exceeded that of the earlier years. Boland was succeeded by Joe Groome. The annual cumann registration fee was fixed at ten shillings. By 1955, the number of cumainn had risen to 1,787, 152 different units of the organisation had received visits from a member of the headquarters team, the booklets 'Bealach Bua' and 'Coras Bua' had been prepared and distributed, and the Comh-Comhairle Átha Cliath had been founded.[18]

The latter organisation was Lemass's special creation, designed to improve the level of intellectual discussion of party policies (an objective in which, according to the organisers themselves, it was not always as successful as had been hoped). It also, perhaps not entirely by accident, served as a vehicle for many of the ideas of Lemass himself, notably his famous 'Clery's speech' a vision of the future which, despite or perhaps because of its somewhat unguarded optimism, became a rallying cry for the economic expansionism and organisational self-confidence which helped to propel Fianna Fáil back into government in 1951.

By 1956, although the number of cumainn had slipped slightly to 1,645 (still a record for a non-election year), Fianna Fáil's vote in by-elections was rising from just over 40% to just over 50%.[19] By 1957, although National

Executive meetings had by now almost halved in frequency (to 21 a year) the number of cumainn had risen to 1,728.[20]

The stark figures speak highly enough of Lemass's achievements during this period. They are fleshed out in a remarkable fashion, however, by the constituency files in the party archives for 1954–57. Lemass was active at every level of the organisational process – setting dates for meetings, providing policy advice to TDs as diverse as Donogh O'Malley (who wanted an assurance that plans for an oil refinery in Dublin Bay were not being secretly promoted by NATO), and Frank Aiken, to whom he supplied statistical information on economic development for use in public speeches. He sorted out rows, smoothed ruffled feathers, and created, or re-created, a political machine second to none in the country.

In all of this, he was assisted by an organisation committee of young people whose energy and commitment became a byword in the organisation, and ensured, in some cases, their eventual transition to ministerial or other office. As listed in the annual report, they were Kevin Boland, Stephen Ennis, C.J. Haughey, Anthony Hederman, Kieran Kenny, Noel Lemass, Brian Lenihan, Thomas O'Connor, Alec O'Shea and Eoin Ryan.

The result, when it came, was proof positive of the value of his efforts. With a net gain of only 14,000 votes nationally, Fianna Fáil had secured 13 extra seats, enough to put them – with the help of Independents – back into government.

With this, Lemass disappears again from the Honorary Secretaryship. The next time he was to re-appear as an office holder of the organisation proper is in the minutes of the National Executive for 22 June 1959, when, on Deputy Paddy Burke's nomination, he was unanimously elected President and Trustee of Fianna Fáil.[21]

Four years later, in his address to the party's Árd Fheis, he returned to a theme which he had first addressed, and in astonishingly similar terms, in his annual report to the party's 1927 gathering. On that occasion, he had urged that 'members of Fianna Fáil should endeavour to place themselves in positions where they can influence public opinion to support the policy of Fianna Fáil', and asked in particular that they should join organisations like the IAOS.[22]

Almost five decades later, the vision was still essentially the same, embodying a concept of the nature and function of the party which has been the subject of undying academic curiosity and never-failing political envy. As one sociologist wrote:

Insofar as the promotion of social solidarity militated against the politicisation of social conflict, it also acted against any possible break-up of the party's broad, cross-class coalition. To set one group against another would be to divide the party against itself. To mobilise the town against the country, or worker against employer, would be to undermine the very social solidarity upon which the party depended. It was in just such a context that Seán Lemass urged the incorporation of working-class interests in party policy in the 1950s and 1960s: no single social group could be excluded from the remit of the party.[23]

Seán Lemass put it himself in language to which his Fianna Fáil audience might have responded more readily. It was, in addition, worth recalling the context – the aftermath of the 1963 Budget, and the highly controversial turnover tax which had exposed not just the parliamentary party, but members of the organisation throughout the country, to a considerable volume of public and private criticism. Typically, he first of all admitted his share of the blame, and that of the party headquarters, for failing to communicate adequately with the grass roots of the party on this sensitive issue. Then he went on:

> [The] wider concept of democratic action is something which I ask all members of Fianna Fáil to propagate, and to urge within the vocational groups of which they are members, whether farmers' organisations, trade unions, or business or professional bodies. Whenever any action for the benefit of the group is being discussed, it is the member of Fianna Fáil who should be first on his feet to raise the question of the relationship between the proposed action and the national welfare, and its possible repercussions on the well-being of other citizens outside the group. The whole basis of Fianna Fáil's political philosophy is that the welfare of every citizen, and of every section, is interdependent, and can best be promoted within the ambit of, and in conformity with, a comprehensive national policy . . . The role of Fianna Fáil members in the growth of understanding and acceptance of a wider conception of democratic action and development should not consist only in organising political support for our Party, but also in securing understanding and acceptance of all its implications, throughout the whole national community.[24]

His opponents would have undoubtedly derided this as a cynical or desperate attempt to paper over the cracks, to maintain party unity against all the odds. Party unity was, indeed, becoming a more fragile plant by the year, but those who knew Lemass knew also that what he said on this and many other occasions, although undoubtedly crafted with an eye to its political effectiveness, was deeply meant. As the historical record shows without a hint of ambiguity, it was part of the political credo by which he lived. He could not, and would not, have done it any other way.

Notes:

1. Speech by Seán Lemass to the Cumann Seosamh Hudson Fianna Fáil, Dun Laoghaire, 26 January 1965. Text in NA D/T S 16272/G.

2. See especially Brian Farrell, *Seán Lemass*, (Gill and Macmillan, Dublin 1991). See also T.P. O'Neill's article on Fianna Fáil in the *Irish Press*, 26 May 1976.

3. NA 2B/82/116, File 6 (The Sinn Féin Funds Case file, 1943).

4. Communication from Francis McKay, Donegal, to author, 21 October 1994.

5. Michael Mills, *Irish Press*, 20 January 1969.

6. Family source. This was his initial meeting with Harry Blaney, Neil's father.

7. 'On the Tin Lizzie Trail with Seán Lemass' by Raymond Foxall, in the *Sunday Express*, 22 October 1961.

8. Fianna Fáil Archives (hereinafter FF) 700.

9. FF/702. It is difficult, in retrospect, to see how the promise – rather than the threat – of deselection could encourage errant TDs to mend their ways.

10. FF/703.

11. FF/704.

12. FF/705.

13. FF/707. This file refers to the 1933 Árd Fheis, and the Report indicates that the total number of cumainn then registered, at 1800, was an increase of 396 on the previous year, for which FF/706 does not give overall figures.

14. FF/707.

15. FF/715.

16. FF/716.

17. FF/721.

18. FF/722.

19. FF/723.

20. FF/724.

21. National Executive minutes, 22 June 1959, FF/345.

22. 1927 Árd Fheis, Report from Hon. Secretaries, FF/700

23. Philip O'Connell and David B. Rottman, 'The Irish welfare state in comparative perspective', in *The Development of Industrial Society in Ireland*, (eds. Goldthorpe, J.H. and Whelan, C.T.), (Oxford, the University Press, 1992) p. 406.

24. Speech to 1963 Árd Fheis, 19 November 1963. Text in NA, D/T S 9361 K/63.

6

Countess Markievicz and the Early Women

Introduction by Margaret Mac Curtain

The Fianna Fáil women who were founding members or supporters of the party in its early years were a remarkable group. They had taken leadership among a generation of women who had campaigned for the vote, who had elected to support the nationalist cause either by participating directly in Cumann na mBan, founded in 1914, or later taking part in the 1916 Easter Week Rebellion. In the aftermath of the Rebellion women were tireless in opposing conscription and their contribution to the Sinn Féin election and that of Countess Markievicz was full of determination. Whether the historian examines the testimony of Kathleen Clarke in her autobiography, or of Dorothy Macardle who devoted seven years to writing a book explaining from whence Fianna Fáil took its origins, *The Irish Republic*, or tests the sincerity of Maire Comerford in her unpublished memoir in the Belfield Archives, the overwhelming impression is that women of that generation who chose the political road had integrity, courage and intelligence. Having gone through experiences of losing friends, spouses and family as Margaret Pearse did, they remained remarkably free of bitterness and the recent studies of Mary Mac Swiney show her to be a woman who cared deeply about the future of republicanism but who was capable of turning her disappointment in a truly positive direction and pour her energies into an educational enterprise of distinction (see Charlotte H. Fallon, *Soul of Fire*, Mercier Press, 1986). This brings the reader to a perplexing insight, why are there not more studies of these women?

The scarcity of studies concerning the women who supported Fianna Fáil in its founding days certainly raises many questions. Among the first to note women in the 1916 Rising was R.M. Fox in his work, *Rebel Irishwomen* (Talbot Press, 1935). Fox's book is a small volume which focuses on women who worked for political freedoms as well as human rights in Ireland and abroad. Included are Maude Gone, remarkable for her activities in Irish nationalism, cultural revival, and the suffragist movement. Eva Gore-Booth (Constance Markievicz's sister) was involved in the suffragist movement, Irish nationalism and the Labour question. Maeve Cavanagh McDowell, Dora McGuire, Charlotte Despard and Mother Jones are singled out by Fox for their contribution as poets, nurses, labour leaders, human rights activists and, of course, Irish rebels. Those who took an active part in the 1916 Rising are Markievicz, Mary Mac Swiney, who was both a suffragist and a leader of the Cork Cumann na mBan, Grace Gifford who married Joseph Plunkett the day before his execution, Nora Connolly who walked 80 miles from Belfast to Dublin to reach the Rising, and Helena Molony who took part in the attack on Dublin Castle and became a high-profile trade unionist later. Since Fox's book only a handful of authors have explored the study of women in the Easter Rising of 1916 in the period between 1934 and 1996. Most have been interested in the dynamic figure of Constance Markievicz. All but one of the authors writing about Markievicz, or the women of 1916, were male but from 1969 onwards all who have written about that brilliant cohort were female. Moreover these women authors are very clear about their purpose in writing their narratives. Lil Conlon called her history of Cumann na mBan (*Kilkenny People*, 1969) a tribute to forgotten women who had played a part in changing history.

Margaret Ward writing *Unmanageable Revolutionaries* (the phrase was coined by Eamon de Valera) in the early 1980s explored the part played by women in the struggle for political power in Ireland against a backdrop of male power and in terms of an organised women's movement. In the following essay, Sari Oikarinen, a Finnish scholar, studies Markievicz in an ideological setting, that of cultural nationalism, what she terms 'the ideal-political field of Ireland'.

What is often forgotten is Markievicz's respect for constitutional politics and how she became a role model for her generation in espousing party politics in the party that seemed closest for her to republican aspirations of the 1916 idealists, in association with Eamon de Valera.

The Rebel Countess: Constance Markievicz

by Sari Oikarinen

In Irish history there is one figure who arouses feelings in people whenever her name is mentioned: Constance Markievicz. The countess who lived at the turn of the century (1868–1927) underwent a change from an upper-class woman into a rebel in a period of transition. At that time in Ireland the various ideas – nationalist, socialist and emancipatory – strove for the fulfilment of their own goals and tried to shape the form of the independent state that was gleaming in the horizon. What makes Markievicz so original and interesting is the way in which she attempted to join the varying goals together under one carrying principle, nationalism. She worked simultaneously in various organisations which had different views about Ireland.

Being a rebellious and colourful woman in the turmoil of Ireland's independence fight, Markievicz has awakened interest. There are altogether six biographies of her, most noteworthy of which is the work of Jacqueline Van Voris.[1]

The aim of Van Voris' work seems to be to restore Markievicz to her entitled position in Irish history and – as biographers usually wish to do – to cover her life as minutely as possible. Markievicz is portrayed as a kind-hearted and unyielding person who always remained loyal to both her ideas and friends.

The six biographies of Markievicz are, to a surprising extent, centred on the same citations from the same sources, correspondingly leaving some things out; in other words, they do not concentrate on interpreting the writings of Markievicz to a degree which I feel necessary in order to create an encompassing picture of her thinking and to break down the somewhat stereotyped picture of Markievicz. Male historians have not been interested in Markievicz.[2] Usually they seem to have regarded her as naïve or/and ridiculous. On the other hand, the women who have written about her have tended to emphasise her loyal and kind nature more than her thoughts. Furthermore, as often happens with a 'myth', Markievicz is regarded as thoroughly studied. The way she spoke and wrote has caused problems to researchers: why she acted or spoke in a certain manner or what her actions and views meant has often been neglected because of her colourful life, radicalism and propagandistic manner of expressing her thoughts.

Society Belle and Painter

Constance Gore-Booth, who was born into a wealthy Anglo-Irish family in 1868, dreamt in her youth of a career as a painter. While she was studying painting in Paris she met Casimir Dunin-Markievicz, a Polish count and painter, who became her husband in 1900. Their daughter Maeve was born a year after and the family moved to Dublin. There Markievicz got acquainted with cultural nationalist trends which had been sprouting in Ireland since the end of the nineteenth century. The renaissance of national culture was promoted on an organisational level especially by the Gaelic League, who wanted to create an Irish-speaking Ireland free from British influence. This ideology of 'Irish Ireland' originated from the research of ancient Gaelic culture and was fundamentally similar to other European nationalist movements in search of a national part.

Constance Markievicz was not satisfied merely with cherishing Irish culture; instead, in 1908 she joined Sinn Féin. Joining Sinn Féin meant a step away from the apolitical upper-class woman's life she had led although, the life of the Markievics' had already been in some terms unconventional as they both were painters. Behind Markievicz's change of direction lies, according to her own simplified explanation, the fact that she had read about the dead rebel leader Robert Emmet, and that had raised an immediate desire in her to join ranks with the nationalists.

Sinn Féin had radical republican members who acted in the secret society of the Irish Republican Brotherhood (IRB) as well. They carried on the tradition of rebellion, which had from time to time aroused violent uprisings against British rule. In Sinn Féin, Markievicz took sides with these radicals and befriended their leader, Bulmer Hobson. That she gained admittance in the governing bodies of Sinn Féin as early as the beginning of 1909 proves that she had some support in the field.

Being a member of Sinn Féin, Markievicz was also active in a small women's society called the Inghinidhe na hÉireann (Daughters of Ireland). As a member of this radical and nationalist group she began writing articles for their own paper. True to the idea she had adopted, she demanded Irish women take part in public actions, especially in national struggle, side by side with men. Advocating women's rights was not foreign to Markievicz, as she had already in her youth been a charter member of a society for women's suffrage. Her ideas, though, had changed to some extent: she now believed women's rights to be adequately secured only in an independent Ireland. As the suffrage societies were in close connection with the British sister societies, Markievicz was concerned that the British groups would lead Irish women off the nationalist track. Also, within Sinn Féin, which was relatively conservative in its attitude towards women's rights, Markievicz was one of those who kept the topic up. She wanted to lead women to the frontline of the struggle for independence so that they would, through internalising the fact that they were Irish, take part in the restoration of the lost free Ireland of the ideal past, where according to old Gaelic customs, women would not be banned from any areas of social life.

Not only women, but also the Irish youth had to be awakened. In 1909, Markievicz's idea to establish an organisation of young Irish boys as a counterpart to the British scout organisation became true. Na Fianna Éireann was an organisation whose objective was to raise the boys into future soldiers who had adapted the 'Irish ideology'. Besides the Irish language, history and various first aid and scout skills, the boys were taught the use of arms, including by Markievicz, who was one of the leaders. Along with a few Fianna boys she attempted to put co-operative ideas into practice on a farm, but that enterprise failed. In my opinion, for Markievicz, the co-operative idea was subordinate to the main question: Irish independence, the gaining of which could be backed up by co-operative ideas. It would also create a firm base for a self-sufficient and democratic future nation.

Similarly, Markievicz's growing emphasis on sacrifice, especially self-sacrifice must be noted and the meaning of it studied. The Fianna boys were to become soldiers: they had to be prepared to shed their blood for Ireland. The willingness to sacrifice, which had already been impressed on women, got a new dimension.

Furthermore, she felt that the hunger strike of the suffragettes in order to gain suffrage was a morally acceptable act: in her view the women held alive the rare and needed spirit of martyrdom.[3] Markievicz expressed the rebellious spirit she had shown with the Fianna boys on larger arenas as well. She was organising a protest against the King's visit in the summer of 1911 and urged people to show their insurgence in public. At that time there were contradictions within Sinn Féin especially concerning the means of actions. Although many radicals left the organisation, Markievicz stayed in it. She reacted strongly against all attempts that she felt were disrupting the nationalist camp.

'The Red Countess'[4]

Being acquainted with the socialist leaders James Connolly and Jim Larkin,

Markievicz was drawn into the new movement. In the autumn of 1913 she declared that Ireland now had three great movements: nationalist, women's and socialist. She regarded them as sharing the same core: fighting for human freedom. To Markievicz, Larkin appeared a nationalist on the same front, because Larkin wanted to found an independent trade union in Ireland. To Connolly, who founded the Socialist Party, socialism and national liberation were complementary, not separate issues: a socialist revolution was to be preceded by a national one, which was a prerequisite for the realisation of the workers' republic. In autumn 1913, Markievicz openly took sides with the labour movement goals in the lock-out in Dublin, during which she, for example, organised catering for the workers. She stepped to Connolly's side even more decidedly when she joined the Irish Citizen Army, which was formed during the lock-out to defend the working people. What did Connolly, and more generally the Irish labour movement policy, mean and offer to Markievicz? In my opinion, to Markievicz, Connolly's ideas meant complete equality between sexes. Furthermore, Connolly justified his demands by the ancient Irish society of clans, which was acceptable for Markievicz, too. For her socialism thus resembled the way that things were arranged in the ancient Ireland, as did the co-operative movement.

The commencement of the First World War hastened the rebellious plans of Irish separatists. Militarising had already begun before June 1914, with the Irish Volunteers organised before the end of 1913. The role of its women's organisation, Cumann na mBan, was to support men, to collect money for them and to provide first aid and maintenance. Markievicz criticized the Cumann because it decided to leave the political arena to men, but despite her differing opinions she helped Cumann with organisational and educational matters. The separatist stir culminated in the Easter Rising, which broke out in 1916 in Dublin. It was suppressed in less than a week. Markievicz marched along as an officer of Connolly's outnumbered Citizen Army. Her participation in the Rising, during which the foundation of the Republic of Ireland was declared, gathered the threads of the development begun in 1908. Markievicz was sentenced to death for her participation, but the death sentence was mitigated to life imprisonment because of her sex. She was pardoned in the summer of 1917, when remarkable changes were already taking place in the Irish political field. The weak Sinn Féin grew stronger and became more radical. The result of the parliamentary election in Great Britain, in which the Irish parties participated was a landslide for Sinn Féin in 1918. It was the first election where women were also allowed to vote. In the election the Sinn Féin candidate Markievicz became the first woman in history to be elected to the House of Commons. However, along with all other elected republicans, she refused to take her seat as a protest.

After being pardoned of the life sentence for her activities in the Easter Rising, Markievicz, in 1917, continued her work in many fields. She now worked in public in the republican Sinn Féin and as the chairwoman of Cumann na mBan she guided women to open political activity. The new strategy of the organisation – and of nationalist women generally – was to act independently in all sectors, in other words to take their place beside men, which was justified by the Easter Rising Declaration's idea of equality between men and women. Her conversion to Catholicism has traditionally been regarded as an essential factor of Irish nationalism. For Markievicz, it was presumably a complementary element to nationalism as well. But we have to bear in mind the many levels within the Catholic Church and to take note of the level at which Markievicz was attached.

Markievicz the Minister

Along with other significant Sinn Féin representatives, Markievicz took part in the work of Ireland's own shadow parliament Dáil Éireann, which was established in January 1919. She was appointed Minister for Labour and was the first woman in the world to hold this position. She held the post from 1919 to 1921. The activities of the Dáil were declared illegal in September 1919. Those years were a time of unrest and war and Markievicz was constantly in and out of prison. In the Dáil, Markievicz was nearly the only advocate of workers' rights. Labour gave its support to Sinn Féin, which it regarded as the best advocate of Irish people in the present situation. Under a moderate leadership, the labour movement concentrated mainly on strengthening the trade unions. This development could be seen as adverse to Markievicz's ideas about the role of the labour movement. After Connolly's death Markievicz's relations with the labour movement were indeed not unproblematic, because none of the leaders was keen on nationalism. Although her contacts and work in the labour movement especially after 1916 have remained nearly unnoticed, she was for example elected as honorary chairwoman of the Irish Women's Workers Union in 1917. Two groups, whose rights or position were not the primary concern of Sinn Féin were united in women workers. To Markievicz, they meant a necessary, if currently oppressed, resource, for whom liberation and freedom would be of prime importance. As a minister Markievicz had the opportunity to try to realise her aims and she made strong attempts to improve the living and working conditions of the poor and unemployed.

When the Anglo-Irish Treaty was signed after the war it meant the founding of the Irish Free State. The Treaty split the ranks of Sinn Féin. Like the radical republicans, Markievicz opposed the Treaty regarding it as traitorous. It did not provide full independence, which was her perpetual demand. It was a question of whether the goal had been reached or not. For Markievicz even the path was wrong, whereas many republicans took the path to be the right one, leading towards liberty. In the spring and summer of 1922, Markievicz was soliciting support for the republicans in the United States. After her return she took part in the war on the IRA's side, opposing the Free State, and went to prison once again. The Civil War caused bitterness which strengthened the decision of the defeated not to participate in the building of the Free State; the IRA carried on its activities. Markievicz remained a member of the IRA's women's organisation, the Cumann. She spoke and wrote against the Free State, trying to show that it was only a tool in the hands of the British.

In the Free State debates in the Dáil, Markievicz mentioned her goal to be the workers' republic advocated by Connolly. She vowed Catholicism into a third strand of that fabric in the pamphlet 'James Connolly's Policy and Catholic Doctrine' which she wrote in 1924. It illuminates her views of both Catholicism and Connolly's socialism, which she always considered to be based on Irish ideals. Markievicz defined it as 'James Connolly's socialism, and no-one else's' by which she obviously meant that it could not be evaluated solely on a socialist basis without paying attention to Connolly's personal views. According to Markievicz, Ireland's freedom for Connolly was not merely political freedom, which would leave the Irish both spiritually and materially enslaved by British ideals of civilisation and by the British capitalist system. Markievicz attempted to build a bridge between Connolly and Catholicism, along which the Irish Catholics could be made walk towards the ideal society which Connolly had outlined. Markievicz's views of socialism have been considered both emotional and naïve. On the level of theory of socialism this may indeed be the case. But one may well question whether it ever was Markievicz's goal to reach an 'orthodox' interpretation, or whether socialism – like Catholicism – meant a useful part of the grand national ideology to her.

In 1926, Markievicz joined Fianna Fáil, which Eamon de Valera had founded. She left Sinn Féin, which the year before had divided after the IRA had split from it. She was elected a member of the Dáil as a Fianna Fáil representative. The programme of Fianna Fáil strove for the unification of Ireland, the preservation of Irish language, land ownership and for the self-sufficiency of the Irish economy as well as traditional nationalist themes.

Two years before the birth of Fianna Fáil, Seán Lemass is carried shoulder high after a Sinn Féin by-election victory in Dublin, March 1924.

The first Fianna Fáil Parliamentary Party after the June 1927 Election.

Eamon de Valera and senior party members walk to Dáil Éireann. They were denied entry for refusing to sign the Oath of Allegiance, 23 June 1927.

Unveiling of memorial to Countess Markievicz in St Stephen's Green, late 1920s.

On horseback with Frank Aiken, 1930s.

Eamon de Valera signing autographs for young admirers, 1930s.

Being seen off to London by Seán Lemass and sons, Dr Eamon and Vivion de Valera, 1948.

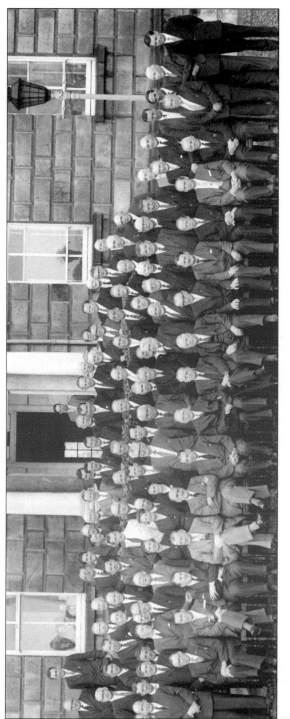

Fianna Fáil deputies and senators at Leinster House on de Valera's retirement, June 1959.

President Eamon de Valera with Seán Lemass and his government, 1965.

Eamon de Valera acknowledging the crowds from the Presidential Coach, mid-1960s.

Speaking his Mind: Seán Lemass with Cardinals Brown and D'Alton at a reception in the Irish Embassy to the Holy See, Rome, 1962.

With President John F. Kennedy on an official visit to Washington in October 1963.

Steps of Power: An Taoiseach Seán Lemass, with Ministers Lynch and Haughey en route to the Anglo-Irish Free Trade Agreement talks, 1965.

Jack Lynch after his election as leader of Fianna Fáil, November 1966.

Signing Ireland's accession to the EEC with then Minister for Foreign Affairs, Patrick Hillery, January 1971.

Bring Jack Back: On the 1977 General Election campaign.

The 1977 Fianna Fáil Cabinet.

With Jacques Chirac, late 1970s.

Jack Lynch in quiet contemplation.

Charles Haughey's first cabinet, 1979.

Markievicz died before she could take her seat in the Dáil, where she would have been required to take an oath to the British King. When Markievicz joined Fianna Fáil, she also resigned from the IRA's women's army, the Cumann. Thus it would seem that she had abandoned the idea of a violent uprising and had become an advocate of parliamentary action. It must be noted that Markievicz was always a supporter of representative democracy: for her democracy was both a means and an aim. Only the fact that the Irish MPs had earlier been part of the English system and that the members of the Dáil of the Free State swore an oath of allegiance to the British King had prevented her from joining them as an elected representative.

The Idealistic Rebel

Markievicz was an independence fighter, whose view of Ireland was based on a romantic picture of the national characteristics of ancient society. Compared to England, Ireland was small and poor, yet spiritually richer and its citizens more equal. Through passive resistance and cultural nationalism she wanted to create a readiness in the rank and file of the people for a violent rebellion. In that traditional rebellion, with waving flags and ultimate sacrifices, a republic of Ireland with all its national characteristics would be founded. The defects would then be remedied independently. In the past, she found the future. In the future awaited the equality between men and women, rich and poor. And in a way, her thoughts were from the future as well with their extensive equality.

Notes:

1. Jacqueline Van Voris, *Markievicz, Constance: In The Cause of Ireland* (Vermont, 1967.)

2. Apart from Seán Ó Faoláin, only Brian Farrell has written about her in an article ('Markievicz and the Women of the Revolution', in: Leaders and Men in the Easter Rising, Dublin 1916, F.X. Martin (Ed.), Norfolk, 1967). In history books she is usually mentioned only briefly or in a footnote.

3. Extract from her speech, *Irish Citizen* 5.7.1913

4. She was called that in the headlines of papers in Glasgow in 1923, when she started her propaganda tour in Scotland.

7

Squaring the Economic and Social Circles

by Joe Lee

Fianna Fáil emerged out of a civil war in which social and economic issues played only a subordinate role. The Civil War was essentially a legacy of the British connection, and a consequence of the Treaty diktat on the oath. There were social undercurrents, however, in determining which side people chose. The anti-Treaty side found disproportionate support among the men and women of small property. The very confused condition of the anti-Treaty mind after the Civil War, however, made it difficult to focus on social and economic issues. The anti-Treaty mentality was still rooted in pre-Treaty assumptions, where the national issue took clear precedence over material matters. Surprisingly good results in the 1923 general election allowed anti-Treaty Sinn Féin, still led by de Valera, to avoid an agonising reappraisal of its core values at that stage. It wasn't until the shattering failure of Sinn Féin in a cluster of ten by-elections in 1925 that it became clear that a doctrinaire refusal to operate within the Treaty framework was a recipe for electoral disaster. De Valera was a sufficient realist to draw the consequences by founding Fianna Fáil.

When Fianna Fáil not only emerged in 1926, but entered the Dáil in 1927, by however circuitous a route through the intestines of de Valera's conscience, it began to develop a social and economic policy rooted essentially in de Valera's image of the good society.

For de Valera, independence was a prerequisite for leading a full life. Independence was the core of personal identity as of national identity. That independence seemed to him best realised through the ownership of property. In a predominantly rural society, this meant the family farm was the cornerstone of independence. The family was, as his Constitution would phrase it in 1937, 'the natural primary and fundamental unit group of society',[1] and the ownership of the farm was the surest way of vesting that group with the capacity for independent thought and action. This meant that holdings must be small 'so as to get the greatest number possible of Irish families rooted in the soil of Ireland'[2] a sentiment reiterated in the Directive Principles of Social Policy in the 1937 Constitution, 'that there may be established on the land in economic security as many families as in the circumstances shall be practicable'.[3]

Although the age of the small farm now belongs to the past, it is easy to understand how he arrived at this version of his social ideal. De Valera was reared in an agricultural labourer's cottage on the Limerick–Cork border where strong farmers held the whip hand over labourers. An intelligent and sensitive boy could not but feel the humiliation of dependency. As far as he could, he was determined to remove both the economic hardship and the social stigma attaching to dependency of this type. The independence of the small farmer, retrospectively romanticised into an idyllic existence, offered a vastly preferable alternative to the ignominy of dependence.

Independence for de Valera was the essential foundation of a healthy society. But independence did not mean individualism as understood today – individuality, yes, but individualism in the sense of 'What I want, I get', no. Independence could be exercised only within broadly approved familial and communal modes of behaviour. Individual, family and society operated as a complex cluster of reciprocal rights and responsibilities. For de Valera, every right involved a corresponding duty. In this respect, he might be called the last of the great Victorians.[4]

His image of the family was as idealised as his image of the small farm. But that too is understandable in psychological terms. De Valera was, for practical purposes, an orphan. His mother sent him back to her family in Ireland at the age of two when she had to go out to work on the loss of his father. Conscientiously though the relatives exercised their stewardship, they could not substitute for his mother.[5] In a very human reaction, he idealised the family life he never had. That hurt lies behind the clause in the 1937 Constitution, that: 'The State shall endeavour to ensure that mothers shall not be obliged by economic necessity to engage in labour to the neglect of their duties in the home.'[6] While it was widely held at the time that a mother's main role was in the home, the formulation is de Valera's. On the one hand, no mother should find herself in the same position as his own mother when she was obliged to go out to work. On the other hand, the phrase 'neglect their duties' reflects an undercurrent of resentment at his own banishment back to Ireland. It was as if, despite his recognition at a cerebral level of the constraints of 'economic necessity', at an emotional level he still felt his mother was 'neglecting her duty' by going out to work even if she had no choice. It was not that de Valera did not have a high regard, in an abstract sort of way, for the rights as well as the duties of woman within his concept of society. Indeed, the Constitution 'recognises that by her life within the home, woman gives to the State a support without which the common good cannot be achieved',[7] an exalted claim indeed. This derived partly from his belief that the family, meaning in effect the mother, was the main educator of the child into the civic virtues. As he told the INTO in 1940:

> ... is é an teaghlach an scoil is túisce agus is bunúsaí. Ní féidir le haon rud a dhul ina ionad. Mura ndéanann an teaghlach an leanbh d'oiliúint chun umhlaíochta, chun ceansachta, chun comhoibrithe agus chun gnaiúlachta, is beag is féidir leis an scoil a dhéanamh. Ach má bhíonn a chion féin déanta ag an teaghlach le na tréithe sin a thabhairt chun críche, beidh ar chumas na scoile leathnú agus feabhsú ar an obair.

> (the family is the earliest and most fundamental school. Nothing can replace it. If it does not train the child in the principles of natural affection, obedience, mutual tolerance and cooperation, all those profound bases of human society, the school can do little, but if the family has carried out its great task of developing the character and social qualities of the child, the school can carry on that work in a wider sphere.)[8]

While the Directive Principles of Social Policy recognised that all citizens 'men and women equally, have the right to an adequate means of livelihood'[9] de Valera firmly believed that the mother's livelihood should ideally be within the home – and he tended to equate all women with mothers.

De Valera then had a clear, coherent, but highly idealised, image of the good society. But how was this society to be brought into being? Reality fell far short of the aspiration. Fianna Fáil could not bestow the vaunted independence of the small farmer on everyone – not even, in due course, on the small farmer.

But its general instinct lay in the direction of providing a safety net for the socially deprived, and of incorporating the poorer orders in the national family. This reflected genuine conviction as well as electoral calculation. The early years of Fianna Fáil government saw much social legislation, including the introduction of, or improvements in, unemployment benefit, old-age pensions, blind pensions, and even children's allowances in 1942. An active housing programme removed from Dublin the stigma of having some of the worst slums in Europe. The housing drive combined social, economic and political motives in a nice blend from a Fianna Fáil perspective. It led to genuine improvement in horrific housing conditions for families, provided employment for needy workers, profits for needy employers, and in due course subscriptions to a needy party.

The housing drive, and other social expenditure, had to be financed from a traditionally sluggish economy. Fianna Fáil's economic policy was designed to kick-start what it claimed to be a stagnant inheritance from Cumann na nGaedheal. This was not entirely fair to the efforts of the Cosgrave government during the 1920s. But it was true that the basic philosophy underlying Cumann na nGaedheal economic policy was that agriculture was the engine that would draw the economy in its train. However, agricultural-led sustained economic growth was virtually impossible in Irish circumstances. Firstly, prices would be determined by British policy, over which an Irish government could have little influence. Irrespective, therefore, of how efficient Irish farmers might become, the rewards would always be uncertain. Secondly, even in the event of flourishing agricultural exports, farmers were likely to spend the profits on imported goods, which would have the free run of the Irish market in the absence of protection. And if they saved the profits, they would deposit them in a banking system which would then invest them mainly abroad. What might be good for the farmer in the short-term might not be good for the country in the long-term. Fianna Fáil policy sought to conquer the fatalism underlying the assumption that Ireland was destined to remain dependent on agricultural exports for whatever economic development it might enjoy for the foreseeable future. It was not that Fianna Fáil was hostile to agriculture. But its agricultural ideal was the self-sufficient farm, not the export-led agricultural enterprise.

Fianna Fáil was also determined to foster an Irish industrial revival, through a protectionist policy, which would achieve economic self-sufficiency. To avoid the social evils of urbanisation, it sought decentralised industrial development, striving to achieve geographical as well as economic balance throughout the country.

The dynamic policy on which Seán Lemass, the long-serving Minister for Industry and Commerce, immediately embarked, reflected his unquenchable optimism, his boundless energy, and his impatience for results. He achieved striking success in the short-term. At a time of deep international depression, industrial employment increased significantly, whereas it would almost certainly have declined but for protection. While the rhetoric of self-sufficiency outraged most economic theorists (although not the greatest of all, Keynes) and indeed owed much of its emotional impulse to nationalist rather than materialist ideology, it was intellectually at least as plausible in the prevailing circumstances as any alternative. But it did suffer from severe limitations from the point of view of sustained growth.

The basic problem was that the home market was simply not big enough to enable firms to achieve the economies of scale which would make them sufficiently efficient to be able to export, and thus expand their operations. Protectionism had worked well for America and Germany in the nineteenth century because the home markets were big and expanding. Trying to achieve sustained growth, as distinct from a once-for-all jump, was much more difficult in Irish circumstances. For de Valera, protection was to some extent an end in itself. He believed that material wants should be limited and that 'frugal comfort' should suffice for the good life. Lemass did not share that ideal. For him, protection was merely a means to an end. That end was a competitive Irish industry, which would create enough jobs to end involuntary emigration, and duly lead to a reversal of the population decline that had, in his view, undermined both the economy and national morale since the Famine. But the differences between the de Valera and Lemass ideals were blurred by the outbreak of the economic war in the summer of 1932, which transformed protection from an economic into an ideological weapon, which for some years allowed it to be presented as desirable in itself, irrespective of the economic consequences.

The economic war, essentially political in origin, kept the temperature of Anglo-Irish relations at boiling point until de Valera negotiated a remarkably good deal in the Anglo-Irish Agreement of 1938. But the success of that Agreement did not disguise from Lemass the fact that the protectionist policy had largely achieved its objectives, and could not generate further growth, or jobs, at anything like the rate required to stem emigration. He had just begun to look around for alternatives when the Second World War drastically changed priorities. As Minister for Supplies during the war he worked desperately to bring in the imports he had worked equally desperately to keep out before the war.

His success as Minister for Supplies did not change the basic equation once the war ended. Although there could still be short-term employment gains, especially in food-related industries, sustained growth could be based only on exports. But firms could not grow unless they became more competitive, and it was hard to do that on the Irish market. How could the circle be squared? In addition, how could native industrialists, to whom Fianna Fáil had been good, and who in turn had been good to Fianna Fáil, be kept loyal to the party when protection was abandoned?

Seizing on the freedom for manoeuvre provided by the intellectual reorientation articulated in T.K. Whitaker's *Economic Development* in 1958, Lemass struck on an astute compromise between party political and national needs. He would, in the short-term, bypass Irish industry and buy in export capacity through inducing foreign firms to set up in Ireland for export purposes. Building on various tax incentive schemes, some of the Inter-Party Government initiative, he hoped that foreign firms would offer a model to Irish management and also create the breathing space in which protection could be gradually reduced, Irish firms be modernised through specific equipment grants, and a refurbished industrial base be created which would quickly allow Irish industry achieve sustained export growth in its own right.

The gamble partly, but only partly, paid off. Once the surge of the 1960s levelled out, it became clear that the hopes reposed in the capacity for rejuvenation of indigenous industry were exaggerated. Both under the Anglo-Irish Trade Agreement of 1965, and under the increased competition on the home market following entry to the EEC in 1973, much Irish industry wilted away. Today, foreign firms account for about three-quarters of all industrial exports. There are some encouraging signs in very recent years that native industry is at last beginning to record the type of export performance that Lemass hoped for thirty years ago, but it has taken a long time.

One of the ironies of industrial policy is that the Telesis Report of 1982, drawn up by Boston consultants, should have urged Ireland to become more self-reliant.[10] It must certainly count as some sort of Irish solution to an Irish problem to hire foreign consultants to tell us to rely more on ourselves. The clock had apparently come full circle since 1958, even if the purpose of self-reliance now was to be exports rather than self-sufficiency. We have become too dependent on foreign investment, and I suspect that Lemass would have no more clung to his new policy for any longer than he deemed necessary, any more than he clung to his earlier policy when circumstances changed. However, the very fact that it has proved so difficult for Irish industry to become internationally competitive does suggest the mountain that economic policy had to climb once the potential of protection was exhausted.

Since the departure of Lemass, Fianna Fáil has engaged in two major shifts in fiscal policy. The first was the expansionist course following Jack Lynch's election victory of 1977, identified in particular with Martin O'Donoghue, the second the fiscal rectitude following Charles Haughey's election victory of 1987, identified in particular with Ray MacSharry.

The 1977 initiative has been much criticised for having initiated a period of disastrous laxity in managing the public finances. The consequences were indeed unfortunate. But this should not divert attention from the fact that this was a bold attempt to anticipate the inevitability of rising unemployment unless dramatic pre-emptive measures were adopted. Unfortunately, the policy was based on the assumption that the strongest sectoral interests in the economy at the time would exercise self-restraint. That was an unrealistic assumption, and the country chose to live dizzily beyond its means for several years, until the inevitable *dénouement*, accelerated by the second oil crisis of 1979, occurred. The price would be paid for a decade to come, partly in higher unemployment than need otherwise have been the case – although it would almost certainly have been high anyway, as the O'Donoghue diagnosis rightly perceived – partly in higher emigration during the 1980s, and partly in lower growth as the Garret FitzGerald government, or at least the Fine Gael section of it, strove to cope with the consequences. Ironically, it was Fianna Fáil which would gain the main credit, after 1987, for reversing what were by then accepted as the misguided policies of a decade earlier.

A historic decision taken by the much criticised Lynch–O'Donoghue economic régime was to break the 153-year link with sterling when Ireland chose to enter the European Monetary System in 1979 and Britain did not. The advantages and disadvantages of the sterling link can be debated endlessly, and the fortunes of sterling continue to be highly relevant to Ireland, as the devaluation crisis following Britain's withdrawal from the ERM in September 1992 only too graphically confirmed. Nevertheless, the shift from sterling to the Deutschmark symbolises a historic shift in the psychology of economic policy-making.

That shift derived from membership of the European Union. It was already a defining moment in modern Irish history not only when Ireland entered the EEC in 1973, but when Lemass determined in 1961 that Ireland must seek full membership as soon as Britain decided to apply. The fact that the decision depended on Britain's, simply recognised the reality of existing Irish dependency on Britain. But the fact that as strong a nationalist as Lemass opted for the opening towards Europe indicated the more outward-looking elements in Irish nationalism had gained a decisive advantage over more isolationist impulses. Both were to be found in Irish nationalism, as in all other nationalisms, but Lemass saw no incompatibility between his ardent nationalism and membership of the European Community. Indeed, it was precisely his idea of nationalism that inspired him to conceive the opportunities offered by the Common Market as realising the dream of a vibrant, prosperous, self-confident Irish nation taking its equal place among the nations of Europe. Irish nationalism, as represented by Lemass at this juncture, adopted a far more constructive approach towards the idea of European union than did English nationalism.

A major difference between the Lemass growth strategy of the 1930s and his growth strategy of the 1960s lay in the role allocated to education. It says something for his popular impact that Donogh O'Malley's introduction of 'free' secondary education in 1966 remains the best remembered single initiative in Irish educational policy. There tended for a time to be a somewhat uncritical reliance on technological education, on the assumption that technology was so central to economic change that if one got the technology right, all else would follow as a matter of course, an assumption heavily influenced by American thinking, which failed to make adequate allowance for the different circumstances of the two societies. Important though high quality technological training was, and is, it only gradually came to be realised that the general quality of management and labour was also quite crucial, as human resources became more central to sustained growth than traditional natural resources as the service sector superseded the manufacturing sector as the main source of employment. Education is a subject highly susceptible to rhetorical posturing, a form of verbal gymnastics in which Fianna Fáil has rarely failed to hold its own. However, Fianna Fáil Ministers for Education, notably Mary O'Rourke, have sought to strike a reasonable balance between education as simply a tool for economic growth, and education as a basic requirement for a society that values a civic culture.

The rapid changes in education since the 1960s contrast with the more static approach of the previous generation. But insofar as the changes depended on extra finance, they probably had to wait on some economic expansion. De Valera was certainly not opposed in principle to adapting education to new requirements. He had stressed to the INTO in 1940 that: 'Locht mór ar oideachas is ea easpa na huanaíochta is ceart a bheith aige ar riachtanais an náisiúin dá dtagrann sé – is é sin, an ghnáth-chonair do chleachtadh tar éis i bheith fágtha ina dhiaidh ag an náisiún, cuspóirí atá spíonta do fhreastal agus faillí a dhéanamh in éileamh géar na nua-linne. Is móide an locht seo óir goilleann sé ní amháin ar shaol an duine ach ar leas an náisiúin. '

(Now, one of the greatest pitfalls in education has been the time-lag between its movement and the needs of the nation which it serves, its tendency to remain in conventional paths from which the life of the nation has passed, to continue to anticipate demands which are no longer made, while it ignores the urgent claims of new necessities. This danger is all the greater in that it affects not merely the life of the individual but the welfare of the nation.')[11]

The role of education in society was going to change significantly anyway after 1960, thanks to the arrival of television. Irish children today spend more time annually in front of the television than in front of the teacher. The education system no longer has anything like the role it once enjoyed, together with the family and the churches, as the main source of values for the younger generation. In fact, the education system is itself as likely to be a consumer of media values as a transmitter of independent ones. The fact that the dramatic economic changes from the late 1950s chanced to coincide with the arrival of the television age meant that Irish society would undergo exceptionally rapid cultural change in the following generation.

Economic growth is a solvent of inherited traditions in most cultures. But the initial response to the improved opportunities of the 1960s was in fact traditional. Population patterns responded as anticipated. Emigration rates fell sharply. So did age at marriage, while marriage rates rose sharply. The demographic decline of more than a century was rapidly reversed. Then an abrupt change in values occurred during the 1970s and 1980s, leading to spectacular changes in family formation. Marriage rates began to fall once more, age at marriage began to rise, and family size fell sharply, due to a combination of circumstances, including changing attitudes towards the role of women, with a rise in the proportions choosing either careers outside the home, rather than motherhood within it, or else striving to combine both, which meant reducing the number of children.

This in turn fostered greater receptivity to the individualistic ideology preached on the Anglo-American-Australian media popular in Ireland. And this in turn has led to new attitudes towards the family, reflected in the recent divorce referendum, a potentially disruptive issue for Fianna Fáil, where many party supporters still cherished de Valera's ideal of the family, and which was astutely mediated, in practical terms, by the party leadership, frantic to find a formula that would preserve party unity.

Although Lemass is often credited with virtually 'the second founding' of Fianna Fáil, given the extent of the changes that occurred under him, it may be argued that in certain respects, the age of Lemass is now as distant as the age of de Valera himself. For all of Lemass's obsession with economic growth, he was always adamant that it was not an end in itself, but merely a means to an end. That end was national regeneration, for which he had gambled his life, not only in the GPO, but in the Four Courts. He would never see 'involuntary' emigration, for instance, in contrast to some Ministers, then and later, as a solution rather than a problem. For all his adaptability to changing circumstances, Lemass dreamed his dreams. They were not of *enrichessez-vous* vintage. The patriotic impulse that inspired his restless energy, his determination to do things, largely died with him, or with his generation. Perhaps inevitably, politics would now become more a career than a vocation. Lemass is often called a realist and a pragmatist, as if the two were identical. A pragmatist he certainly was, in the sense of being willing to grasp at any policy that might achieve the goal of sustained growth that would in turn lay the basis for a vibrant national society. Whether he was a realist is a very different matter – in that the goals he set for that society may have been beyond its willingness.

It would be quite unhistorical to identify the bulk of the social and economic policies pursued by Fianna Fáil since the 1950s as the exclusive property of the party. A Fine Gael government would have taken similar decisions on most of the issues involved, given the fading away of the ideological differences between the two parties. It would, for instance, be quite wrong to attribute the opening towards Europe solely to Fianna Fáil, or even to Lemass.[12] Had Fianna Fáil, as the more self-consciously nationalist party, opposed entry to the Common Market, our European policy might well have taken a different turn. What is most striking about recent social and economic policy is the degree of consensus between the main parties. The broad similarity between them partly reflects the fact that they tend to rely for the bulk of their thinking on the same cadre of civil servants. But we take consensus too much for granted. Consensus doesn't just emerge. It has to be worked at. There are times when it may not be in the national interest. But it can certainly be argued that it has been in the national interest for the past decade. The various programmes of national recovery/progress since 1987, initiated by the Haughey government, and continued by Albert Reynolds, the consensus approach to labour relations adopted by Bertie Ahern, have generally served the country well even if unorganised interest, especially the unemployed, and the socially deprived in general, are still inadequately represented. Differences of personality, of style, and perhaps even of conviction, within parties are now often wider than differences between the main parties. It is in fact difficult to speak of any distinctive Fianna Fáil, or Fine Gael, social and economic policy at present. That is not necessarily a bad thing in present circumstances. Whether those circumstances will persist, and whether Fianna Fáil will respond any more adequately than other parties to the challenge of change, only time will tell. Maybe the promised, or threatened, review of de Valera's Constitution will give it an opportunity whether there is any longer a Fianna Fáil vision of the good society!

Notes:

1. Bunreacht na hÉireann (Constitution of Ireland), Article 41. 1. 1.

2. 'Aims of Fianna Fáil', *Press Statement*, 17 April 1926, in Maurice Moynihan (ed.), *Speeches and Statements by Eamon de Valera 1917–73* (Dublin, 1980), p. 131.

3. Bunreacht na hÉireann (Constitution of Ireland), Article 45. 2. 5.

4. S. Collini, *Public Moralists* (Oxford, 1991), esp. pp. 60–118.

5. For a particularly perceptive account, see Owen Dudley Edwards, *Eamon de Valera* (Cardiff, 1987), p. 24.

6. Bunreacht na hÉireann, Article 41. 2. 2.

7. *Ibid.*, Article 41. 2. 1.

8. Maurice Moynihan (ed.), *Speeches and Statements by Eamon de Valera in 1917–73* (Dublin, 1980),'The Primary School', pp. 426–7, 430.

9. Bunreacht na hÉireann, Article 45. 2. 1.

10. NESC, *A Review of Industrial Policy* (Dublin, 1982).

11. Moynihan, *Op cit.*, pp. 426, 430.

12. For a discerning discussion of the Irish approach to the EEC, see Miriam Hederman, *The Road to Europe: Irish Attitudes 1948–61,* (Dublin, 1983).

8

Jack Lynch: A Man Determined to do the Right Thing

by Frank Dunlop

It is a relatively short seventeen years since Jack Lynch stepped down as Leader of Fianna Fáil and resigned as Taoiseach in December, 1979. As Government Press Secretary at the time I have particularly vivid memories of the period immediately prior to his resignation – memories which have been dimmed in the interim, however short, but which were given renewed focus again in the preparation of this essay. Understandably, those who want to will put anything I write into the context of my working relationship with Jack Lynch between 1974 and 1979 when I was his Press Secretary in both Opposition and Government.

But notwithstanding this relationship I believe I can, however modestly, contribute something towards a balanced and objective assessment of the contribution which he made to modern Irish politics. Of course, the revisionists have already been at work and there are those who, if unchallenged, would gloss blithely over the period of Jack Lynch's leadership of Fianna Fáil as if it were something of a temporary arrangement instead of covering thirteen years in which he left an indelible mark on recent history, most notably in the context of Northern Ireland and not least in terms of electoral success. It was Liam Cosgrave who dubbed Jack Lynch the most popular man in Ireland since Daniel O'Connell. Ironically, it was Liam Cosgrave also who forced Jack Lynch's hand in the events of 1970 which had dramatic, and traumatic, consequences for Ireland and Fianna Fáil.

I first met Jack Lynch in early 1974. He had asked me to become his Press Secretary in February of that year and despite the strong advice of my immediate circle at that time, specifically in RTE, not to do so, I accepted and thereby began a unique 12-year insight into the somewhat arcane workings of the politics of both Opposition and Government. Having been a student of history and politics at UCD, I had a keen appreciation of the value of primary source material and so I decided to keep a diary. I kept up the practice throughout the time I served with Jack Lynch, Charles Haughey and John Boland and it is a salutary exercise now to revisit some of the events which, at the time of their happening, appeared of enormous importance, but which, in retrospect, apart from a few, were little more than pin-pricks in the map of recent Irish history.

In 1974 Fianna Fáil had already spent a full year in sulphurous resentment at being in Opposition. Most of the frontbench – ministers in the previous government – had never experienced Opposition and, apart from a wily few, were totally lost and remained so until about 1976 when Fianna Fáil's fortunes, both internally and in the country at large, began to undergo a sea change which was to culminate in the landslide victory at the polls in June 1977. The party's difficulties in coming to terms with the success of the Coalition Government under Liam Cosgrave and more particularly with the combined media presentation skills of their *bête noir* Conor Cruise O'Brien, and Maurice MacConghail, as Head of the Government Information Service, drove them inexorably into the cul-de-sac of transferred blame. The party's policies were not getting through because the media were conducting a love affair with the new Government. Alternatively, the Government had stolen Fianna Fáil's good ideas. Whether or which, something needed to be done before the creaking party organisation, which had been neglected down through the previous sixteen years of Government and which had barely survived the trauma of 1970, stopped working at all. To his credit Jack Lynch, having sniffed the wind, decided – or more accurately was finally persuaded by a small coterie of hard-nosed professionals – to act and he appointed a new General Secretary, Seamus Brennan, and myself to the new role of Press Secretary. However strange it may seem now in an age when spin-doctoring has become something of an eclectic science all political parties in the early 1970s saw no need to communicate in an inclusive way, with the media.

The residual, historic appreciation of the role of the journalist as a mere note-taker took some time to dislodge from the mental processes of men – almost exclusively men – who, if the truth were told resented the media deeply and categorised journalists politically in direct ratio to the type – hostility is perhaps a better word – of questioning to which they began to be increasingly subjected at that time.

This was the atmosphere – one of an expectancy of great deeds on the part of my new employers and a blindfolded enthusiasm on mine – into which I allowed myself to be catapulted at the tender age of twenty-five. It is difficult to replicate now the persuasive and charismatic effect that Jack Lynch then had on both an adoring organisation and on a public which, to a great degree, treated him as something of an injured household pet in need of constant solace and comforting. It will be recalled that despite the bone-chilling and nerve-wracking events of 1969 in Northern Ireland, combined with those of 1970 and the consequent turmoil within Fianna Fáil, he had only barely lost the general election in 1973. Having succeeded Seán Lemass in 1966 – his alleged reluctance notwithstanding – he became an almost immediate electoral asset, particularly in his natural and relaxed use of television on which he invariably appeared, to incredible political effect, as the soft-spoken voice of reason.

Having won the 1969 election it appeared inevitable that he would serve out an uninterrupted career as Taoiseach until he chose his own time to retire. This was not to be and in varying degrees, and at almost pre-set times, attempts were made to either persuade him to retire – on two occasions to the Park as President – or to dislodge him directly. None were to succeed and in November 1979, one full month before he actually resigned, he told me privately during the course of an official visit to the United States that he intended to resign in January the following year. The combination of infelicitous, off-the-cuff remarks at the Washington Press Club and events within the parliamentary party where, to all intents and purposes, he had lost control, forced him to change his plans and he decided to go in December in the full expectation that his chosen heir, George Colley, could ride out the storm and have a better chance of taking the leadership, and becoming Taoiseach than if the matter were allowed to fester over the Christmas period. The rest, as they say, is history.

It always struck me forcibly that Jack operated in the political arena exactly as he had done on the hurling and football fields. He was a tactical player who weighed up the odds and scored accordingly. Admittedly, the analogy can be taken to the ultimate, and accurately so in some instances, in that he was not averse to giving his opponent a jab of the hurley in the full knowledge that the referee was looking the other way. In my own case there was no need for a referee. Jack gave the jab when he considered it timely but only, in fairness, in circumstances where his patience would have been finally tested.

There has always been a debate as to whether Jack Lynch was a chairman or a chief. To me the answer is patently obvious. Jack was a chairman who delegated in the full expectation that the job, whatever it was, would be done. He did not indulge in the relentless pursuit of action. If it was done, well and good. If not there had to be a good explanation. This method of running a political party and a government inevitably led to accusations of semi-detached control and laziness. Neither was true but a perception which was impossible to dislodge and extremely difficult to contend with was successfully created. The truth of the matter of course is that Jack Lynch was a shrewd observer of human nature and was a consummate player of people. I recall one particular occasion when a special parliamentary party meeting was held to nominate a Fianna Fáil candidate for the Presidency in the aftermath of Cearbhall Ó Dálaigh's dramatic resignation as a result of remarks alleged to have been made by the then Minister for Defence. A succession of speakers at the meeting advocated Jack's candidacy on the basis, and not necessarily in this order, firstly that it was his due reward and secondly that it was the only way in which Fianna Fáil could win, if there was to be an election. Jack sat silently throughout all of this and the meeting broke for lunch at 1.00 p.m. At that time the main lunchtime news on RTE radio was at 1.30 p.m. and on his instructions, at 1.25p.m., I dictated a statement from him to RTE for immediate transmission. The statement was unequivocal. Under no circumstances whatever would he be a candidate for the Presidency, either on an agreed cross-party basis or as a Fianna Fáil candidate in an election. Having listened to the statement being broadcast on the radio in my office he then went home to Máirín in Rathgar for lunch. Meanwhile consternation broke out in the Dáil restaurant where the parliamentary party was lunching. As scheduled the meeting resumed at 3.00 p.m. and concluded at 3.02 p.m. when Jack said that having issued his statement he didn't see any need for further discussion! In one fell swoop he had flushed out those who wanted him to go, albeit allegedly as a reward, and likewise succeeded in frustrating their attempts by issuing the statement during the lunch break. I still have the statement in his own handwriting in my files to this day. He had written it during an impassioned plea to him from a backbencher to rest his laurels after dedicated service to the party and the country! It was noticed at the time that the backbencher in question, now sadly deceased, who was not noted either for his forensic advocacy skills or the finer points of English grammar, was speaking from a typed note of excellent syntactical quality.

Sadly, Jack Lynch lost his sure-footedness on a number of crucially important occasions when dealing with successive British Governments. He developed a good working relationship with Jim Callaghan but in reality it amounted to very little because Callaghan, like British Prime Ministers before and since – with the exception of Margaret Thatcher who hated them – took the Foreign Office bait. Jack's relationship with Ted Heath was particularly difficult. Heath evinced a mixture of rudeness and latter-day imperial boorishness that irritated the gentleman in Jack Lynch. The incident in Munich where, after a meeting between the two men, Heath instructed his spokesman to brief the media on how he had given Lynch a dressing down and advised him to keep his nose out of Northern Ireland infuriated him and rankled thereafter. Notwithstanding this, it was Lynch and Heath who together set the groundwork for the Sunningdale Conference and of course it was Heath, to the fury of the Unionists, who abolished Stormont. By the time Thatcher arrived Jack Lynch was in retirement mode. Even had he continued in office the relationship, in my view, would not have succeeded. Thatcher represented a type of politics that was alien to Lynch and the only meeting between them – at 10 Downing Street after the memorial service for Lord Mountbatten at Westminster Abbey – was not a happy one and was saved, surprisingly, by an unusually robust contribution by George Colley and an equally forceful, but extremely politically shrewd statement by Gerry Collins. Collins, in effect flushed out Thatcher on the vexed question of extradition and in front of her advisors exposed her lack of knowledge of the matter. Had both men not been present it would have been inevitable, in my view, that Thatcher would have scored heavily over Jack Lynch. This would have been a tragedy for a man who had more diplomatic and political skills than Thatcher ever had. Others, of course, may view matters differently but I believe that Lynch would have found the events in Northern Ireland throughout the 1980s, and Thatcher's handling of them, distasteful in the extreme and in truth, and probably would not have coped.

But this is unfair. Jack Lynch epitomised what many people probably would like, and certainly did like when he was Taoiseach, to see in their politicians – a successful sportsman, a transparently gentle man thoroughly grounded in the art of politics, fair and a shrewd observer of what would and would not be acceptable to the Irish public. But nothing is ever so simple. While possessing all of these laudable characteristics Jack Lynch led a broadly-based organisation whose leading lights when he took over ranged from the old guard such as Aiken, Ryan, MacEntee and Smith to the new generation such as Charles Haughey, Donogh O'Malley, Neil Blaney and Brian Lenihan. Lynch had to bridge both generations between 1966 and 1969 and displayed a steely determination prior to the 1969 General Election when he persuaded virtually all of the old guard to stand down, with the exception of Paddy Smith of Cavan.

There was an inevitable conflict in philosophies. The new generation, notably epitomised by Charles Haughey, wanted to move relentlessly forward and to build on the groundwork laid by Lemass. Lynch displayed a balancing prowess when he appointed Haughey to Finance, the job he himself held immediately prior to his election as Taoiseach. Charlie was given a free hand in developing the policies which he knew were needed and which had the added advantage of being populist. The relationship between the two was workmanlike – up to 1970 that is.

The relationship between Neil Blaney and Lynch was never comfortable and deteriorated to the point where Blaney was contemptuous, in both public and private, Lynch's Northern policy. The relationship with Brian Lenihan on the other hand was surprising. Lenihan, despite a carefully cultivated public persona which, on occasion, amounted to what could only be described as calculated buffoonery, was a singularly intelligent and well-read man who was deeply Christian and steeped in family tradition. But Jack found it difficult to warm to him, largely I suspect because of his close friendship with Charlie Haughey.

As to Donogh O'Malley there was a deeply-felt antipathy which inevitably would have flared into the open in 1970 had Donogh not died tragically. I recall asking Jack on one occasion about Donogh only to receive the cryptic response: 'He wore pink shirts'!

Perhaps the most fascinating relationship between any two politicians of the same party was that between Jack and Des O'Malley, Donogh's nephew who succeeded him in the by-election in Limerick East. Des arrived in the Dáil at a time when the difficulties in Northern Ireland were only faintly beginning and party unity was as sacrosanct as it was to remain until the repeated upheavals against Charlie Haughey in the 1980s were to destabilise the party to such an extent that it is only now that cohesion is once again something of an article of Fianna Fáil faith. In an unusual move Jack appointed Des O'Malley to the Whip's Office very shortly after his by-election success and from then on increased his dependency on him to an extent which surprised even those who had watched Jack Lynch's quiet progress through politics over a long period. The events of 1969 and 1970, together with the tough measures taken by O'Malley, including the Offences Against the State Act, bound the two men together almost inextricably – a situation which created its own impetus as the events of 1970 and thereafter unfolded. In his ideal moments Jack would have preferred Des as his successor but a pact between O'Malley and Colley meant that such a scenario was never to be. Des swore allegiance to George, George lost and thus the stage was set for the establishment of the Progressive Democrats whose immediate *raison d'etre* was an abiding dislike of Charlie's *modus operandi*. The irony of course is that one of Charlie's most successful governments was the coalition between Fianna Fáil and the Progressive Democrats.

So, it is almost a foregone conclusion that when historians bring their clinical skills to bear on Jack Lynch's political career, and particularly on his tenure as Taoiseach, they will almost inevitably hone in on Northern Ireland in all its aspects, both within Fianna Fáil and externally in the country. But were it not for his steady hand at times of grave danger, things might have gone terribly wrong.

Yes, there are, and will continue to be, arguments about Jack's decisiveness or otherwise in Government: did he react belatedly to events? how much did he know? how well-informed was he? and so on. These arguments are inevitable in circumstances where many of the participants are still alive and some of them remain in public life. But there will never be agreement on these issues and in a way it is even futile to attempt to arrive at such agreement. Suffice it to say that Jack Lynch's tenure of office was marked by some of the most dramatic events in recent Irish history – events which, no doubt, have already faded into the mists of time for most people and of which new generations know nothing and care less.

There is one other event which almost certainly will loom large in any historical evaluation of Jack's leadership of Fianna Fáil and that is the 1977 General Election. There are two things that must be said about his landslide victory in that election. The first is that despite the subsequent, and in some instances successful, rewriting of history, nobody refused the lunch. When the manifesto was published within 24 hours of the election being called, the game was already up and the late Frank Cluskey, in his own inimitable way, recognised that what was on offer was a tantalisingly successful package with which the Government couldn't hope to compete. And of course, though one would not think so nowadays when listening to the various pontifications on the matter, virtually every economic commentator fell with the 'pump-priming' stratagem which Martin O'Donoghue had persuaded Jack to adopt.

The second point will be equally thought-provoking for the revisionists. Fianna Fáil genuinely did not believe that they could win against the Cosgrave coalition. On the return journey to Dublin for the final rally, Lynch, weary after three weeks of relentless campaigning, reluctantly conceded that Fianna Fáil had only a small hope of success but admitted that 'we may barely make it'! Lest there be any doubt as to the accuracy of this, I can attest fully to it because I accompanied him on the journey. In the event he was the first to realise that a twenty-seat majority spelt trouble and thus it was to be on a constant basis until his departure in 1979.

The experience gained in working at close quarters with a Taoiseach of the status and qualities of Jack Lynch cannot be replicated. Jack Lynch's name evokes many pleasant and satisfying memories of working with a man determined to do the right and honourable thing for the Republic and of having, in whatever small a way, assisted him in doing just that.

9

From the Margins to the Mainstream: Fianna Fáil and the Women's Movement

by Yvonne Galligan

Social movements are complex political phenomena. Their emergence is often unheralded, their development is unpredictable and their demise is generally a very public affair. Nonetheless, social movements leave their mark on political processes. Social movement activity leads to a change in political agendas and a modification of institutional arrangements, reflecting the absorption of movement demands into the political system.[1] In 1971, the modern women's movement emerged into the public domain in Ireland. The effect of its demands for change on the Irish political scene is a good illustration of how a social movement can influence political change. In this essay, we look at how the political demands of the women's movement influenced and shaped Irish politics. We examine in particular its effects on Fianna Fáil. We conclude that the cumulative effects of two decades and more of feminist activity and pressure politics has shaped thinking within all the political parties, including Fianna Fáil, on questions of concern to women. In coming to this conclusion, we consider the context in which the women's movement was founded in Ireland. We look at demands for political and social change made by the women's movement from the early 1970s onwards. We will then examine the responses of the political parties to these issues on three levels: the political representation of women, institutional frameworks and the public policy responses of successive governments to women's demands.

Although the emergence of social movements can take political observers by surprise, they do not come about in isolation from the social and economic context of the time. It is important, then, in studying the women's movement in Ireland, to take the socio-economic context into consideration on the eve of the emergence of feminism. To all intents and purposes, Ireland in the 1960s was a conservative, traditional society. A strict observance of Catholic rites and teachings was practised by the population, the workplace was largely male, women's civic participation was minimal and their legal status significantly inferior to that of men. Yet, the economic modernisation process set in train by the Fianna Fáil government from 1957 onwards began to have a definite influence on the outlook of Irish citizens. Ireland began to open up to the outside world. Trade barriers were dismantled, growing economic prosperity raised popular expectations of a more modern lifestyle, and the communications revolution brought new ideas into people's homes. Concepts of individual rights, choice and freedom underpinning the civil rights protests in the US, and feminist activity in the US and Europe were introduced to the Irish public through the media. Changing attitudes towards the education of girls meant that young women stayed in school to finish their second level education and availed of a university education in increasing numbers. In some arenas, women began to question the appropriateness of the 'marriage bar' in the public service, which prevented them from remaining in the workforce after marriage.

Not surprisingly, the modernisation process led to a growing focus on social issues. One area of increasing interest was the civic condition of Irish women. This issue became of concern to the leaders of long-established women's organisations such as the Irish Countrywomen's Association, the Irish Business and Professional Women's Organisation and the Irish Housewives' Association. The politicisation of these traditionally moderate groups was influenced by their increasing participation in international women's networks where a debate on the status of women was taking place. This international discussion was brought to Ireland by the representatives from these groups. Along with members of other women's organisations, they embarked on a private study of the position of women in Irish society. The ensuing report was to lead to the first significant political initiative of an institutional nature in the area of women's rights – the appointment of a Commission on the Status of Women in 1970 by the Fianna Fáil administration of the day.[2]

The situation of women in society was not only of concern to organised women. Governments, too, were beginning to redress some of the more obvious gender-based legal discriminations. In 1957, the Fianna Fáil government passed the Married Women's Status Act, which enabled a married woman to sue her husband for damages. In the same year, Jack Lynch as Minister for Education, removed the ban on married women teaching in primary schools. In 1964, following a Supreme Court decision some years earlier, the Fianna Fáil government passed the Guardianship of Infants Act, which provided for the joint guardianship of children by their father and mother on an equal basis. In 1965, the Succession Act granted a wife rights of inheritance to the property of her deceased husband, ending the possibility of her being disinherited. The government decision to apply for membership of the European Economic Community gave an impetus to the need to address the situation of Irish women in employment, particularly in regard to equal pay and the marriage bar in the public service. So, we can see that the process of economic modernisation began to have an effect, albeit a modest one, on the social agenda of successive Fianna Fáil governments. Thus, social, economic and political circumstances were ripe for the birth of the new women's movement in Ireland.

The modern women's movement burst suddenly onto the public stage with its launch on Gay Byrne's *Late Late Show* on 5 March 1971.[3] For the first time, the situation of women in Irish society was openly debated and hotly contested in a public forum. The Irish Women's Liberation Movement activists published a manifesto of six basic demands around which they intended to mobilise public support. The issues – equality between women and men in pay, education, social welfare and the law, the demand for legal contraception and adequate housing for families – were not really new to the political arena. They were, in large measure, under consideration by the Commission on the Status of Women.[4] However, up to this point, the political debate on women's position had taken place in the rarified circles of government and leaders of women's groups. The emergence of the radical and non-conformist women's movement brought these issues to wider public attention and gave voice to a strong current of dissatisfaction among Irish women with their status in society.

Not surprisingly, the activities of the new women's movement sparked a lively public debate on women's rights. The discussion was assisted by the fact that the Catholic Church was campaigning at the time against a Seanad bill which sought to legalise the sale of contraceptives. The ensuing political conflict provided the new movement with a high profile and controversial issue around which to mobilise. In keeping with the pattern of social movement activity, women's movement activists embarked on a series of public and flamboyant acts of civil disobedience around this issue, the most famous being the 'contraceptive train' action. By taking a train from Dublin to Belfast to purchase contraceptives and returning with the illegal items, women's movement supporters placed a public spotlight on the ban on contraceptives in the Irish state. Other actions of a similar nature followed. The invasion of the front lawn of Leinster House by young women with children in prams singing

'We shall not conceive' is a further example of the colourful media-catching activities engaged in by the women's liberation movement. However, these modern feminists did not confine their activities to engaging in media-oriented demonstrations alone. They began to lobby for change in a conventional fashion. For instance, an article in *The Irish Times* of 24 March 1971 reported that:

> The Irish Women's Liberation Movement also gave details of its submissions to Mr George Colley, Minister for Finance, in relation to the forthcoming budget. These included demands for full sickness and unemployment benefit for widows paying the full national insurance contribution; a doubling at least, of the pension rates of widows and deserted wives; an increased tax allowance for working wives; the same tax allowance for widows as for married men and the removal of turnover tax and the proposed value added tax from the necessities of life: foods, basic furnishings such as beds and cookers and children's clothes.

In common with social movements elsewhere, the women's movement had no organisational framework to hold it together. It disintegrated in late 1971. However, from the ashes of the movement there grew a number of single issue lobby groups which were to develop into effective advocates of policy and legislative change. Groups such as AIM (which campaigned for the reform of family law), Cherish (dedicated to improving the legal and policy circumstances of single mothers and their children), the Women's Political Association and others took up where the women's movement stopped. In 1975, the women's movement re-emerged briefly as Irishwomen United with a more radical agenda for change. However, by the mid-1970s, women's groups with a specific political orientation were established and their views given consideration by decision-makers. The Council for the Status of Women, funded by government on a permanent basis from 1979, was recognised as the official representative of women's groups and consulted by government on women's issues. The AIM organisation developed a working relationship with decision-makers which assisted in the introduction of extensive reforms of family law. Other organisations, such as Women's Aid and the Rape Crisis Centres, had a more radical agenda than that of the 1971 women's liberation movement. The leaders of the Rape Crisis movement in particular developed links with political parties and government members. In the years following 1971, then, feminist activists had learned a valuable lesson about the Irish political system: change was most effectively brought about through conventional political means. This meant, of course, talking to politicians and persuading decision-makers of the need for policy reforms. Inevitably, party and government policies were influenced by the representations of pressure groups seeking changes in laws on the family, on violence against women and on the status of women in general.

The modernisation process which led to the development of identifiable feminist politics in Ireland did not bypass the political parties. The issue of women's political representation was one which elicited a clear political response. Fianna Fáil were first to prioritise the election of women to public office. In 1977, Jack Lynch indicated his support for the political representation of women by adding six women candidates to the Fianna Fáil list for the 1977 general election and by subsequently nominating three women to the Seanad. Indeed, Gardiner attributed the increased support of women for Fianna Fáil in 1977 as playing a significant part in the electoral success of the party.[5] Since 1977, elections have sought to appeal to the 'women's vote', with party election manifestos regularly including policies designed to attract women voters. The 1992 Fianna Fáil election programme, for instance, which contained specific commitments to improving the position of women in society is in marked contrast to the 1977 election manifesto which contained no mention of women or gender-related issues.[6]

However, if the parties were anxious to woo women as electors, they were less inclined to see them selected as candidates. While the numbers of women both selected and elected from 1977 to the present has shown an improvement on the representation of women prior to the 1970s, their electoral opportunities have been rather limited in the larger and longer established parties. Although the reasons for the under-representation of women in political life in Ireland is discussed elsewhere,[7] there appears to be a two-tier pattern in this area, with the older political parties offering less opportunities for the selection of women candidates than the newer ones. This is borne out if we look at the most recent candidacies for local and national elections. For instance, in the 1991 local elections – an arena where it is expected that women can enter more readily than national politics – 170 (13%) of the combined total of 1,315 candidates presented to the electorate by Fianna Fáil, Fine Gael and Labour were women. This contrasts with the newer political parties of the Progressive Democrats, Workers' Party and Green Party where 64 (25%) of 261 candidates were women. A similar pattern is evident in the general election of 1992, with the parties being split on an old–new axis. Of the total 255 candidates from the three older parties 33 (13%) were women while 28 (36%) of the 77 candidates from the newer parties were women. This suggests that there are institutional obstacles operating in the older political parties which militate against the selection of women. The older parties clearly have some catching up to do if they are to put into practice their commitment to the increased selection and election of women. Indeed, Fianna Fáil, with a base of 40% electoral support, has possibly more scope than other parties to improve its record in this area.

There is evidence that the party leadership in Fianna Fáil have become increasingly conscious during the 1990s of the need to present a woman-friendly image. The defeat of the party's popular and nationally-known candidate, the late Brian Lenihan, in the 1990 Presidential Election sent a shock-wave through the organisation and provoked a reassessment of party policies and strategies. This particular political cloud had a silver lining for women in the party, with a strengthened Women's Committee and a renewed attention to the participation of women contained in the commission on the aims and structures of the party. Current electoral strategy includes an emphasis by the party leadership on the selection of an increased number of women candidates. To date, the Fianna Fáil Women's Committee (recently renamed the National Women's Forum) and the National Executive, in common with Fine Gael, have rejected the use of quotas as a means of increasing women's participation in political decision-making. Instead, an affirmative action strategy is the preferred mechanism for bringing about equal gender representation.[8]

However, if the parties have been slow to respond to the demand for women's political representation, they have been somewhat more open to recognising gender as a specific factor in terms of political structures and to introducing policy changes which have redressed gender inequalities when in government. In both respects, governments have built on the foundation left by previous administrations. The 1973–77 coalition of Fine Gael and Labour, for instance, adopted the recommendations of the Commission on the Status of Women, which delivered its final report to the Minister for Finance, George Colley, in 1972. During the 1980s, Fianna Fáil governments did not appear to place as significant an emphasis on the institutional development of women's affairs as compared with the Fine Gael and Labour coalition administrations. In 1987, for instance, the Department of Women's Affairs was abolished, with the responsibility for equal treatment assigned to cabinet ministers on an individual basis. However, in November 1990, Charles Haughey gave the status of women a further institutional and political significance by establishing the Second Commission on the Status of Women chaired by Justice Mella Carroll. The report of this Commission, presented in 1993, has again formed a policy blueprint for political action. Although stopping some distance short of the 'femocracy' of the Netherlands, Irish politicians and administrators have, in the last twenty-five years, become increasingly sensitive to the 'woman question' in decision-making.

Aside from the agenda for change set out by the two Commissions on the Status of Women, other aspects of public policy have not been immune to the demands of feminist advocates of reform. Successive administrations have pursued different avenues of change, but the sum makes for a significant shift in public policy on women over the last quarter of a century. While Fine Gael and Labour coalition governments have focused on family law reform and introduced significant measures in this area, Fianna Fáil can point to its record on reform of the laws on sexual violence against women. From the early 1980s, Fianna Fáil showed a willingness to tackle this issue in both government and opposition. Indeed, the Criminal Law (Rape) (Amendment) Act, 1990, introduced by Ray Burke, stands as an important piece of legislation in this difficult and sensitive area. In the 1990s, one of the defining issues for all political parties, but particularly Fianna Fáil, was the X case. It was clearly an issue which united women of all political persuasions and, although the campaign was spearheaded by a coalition of women's groups, women as elected representatives found common cause with one another and with the broad consensus among women on this seminal issue of women's rights. The referendum outcome gave a clear signal to all political parties that women are a powerful political force and their needs require careful attention and incorporation into party policy agendas.

This lesson is one which Fianna Fáil, as the largest political party in the State, has absorbed over the years. An examination of party documentation in the 1970s and 1980s indicates a tension among party members at grass-roots level on gender-sensitive issues. A perusal of the cláir of Árd Fheiseanna during this period reveals calls for a removal of discriminations against women in public policy alongside demands for the retention of existing social policies such as the ban on contraception and the marriage bar.[9] Although this dichotomy was not completely removed by the 1990s, the tone of members' motions was more positive towards improving women's rights and the debate was more complex. The growing assertiveness of the Fianna Fáil Women's Committee during the 1990s has made a significant contribution within the party to bringing about an attitude of inclusion towards women and their political viewpoints.[10] National Executive members, on the whole, appear to have a greater record of openness to women's demands for equality than cumainn members, as the support for the introduction of equal pay and women on juries seems to indicate.[11] This acceptance and recognition of the 'woman question' in politics was recognised in 1993 by Albert Reynolds, who, in the course of his presidential address to the Árd Fheis delegates called for effective laws on violence against women and encouraged women's participation in decision-making arenas within the party and at national level.[12] Thus, at both élite and grass-roots level, the conditions appear conducive for women's advancement in policy and in representational matters. The women's movement has left its mark on all political parties, including Fianna Fáil. Although the received wisdom would position Fianna Fáil on the conservative end of the spectrum on women's issues, the evidence now suggests that the party appears willing to accept and act on a feminist agenda to an extent which would not have been thought possible in the 1970s.

So today as we approach a new millennium, what can Fianna Fáil do for the women's movement? There is no doubt, that whatever form future feminist activity takes, all political parties need to be conscious of the demands of women. Fianna Fáil, as the largest party in the State and with the largest number of women supporters, has a responsibility to be particularly attentive to women's concerns. The conservative outlook of the party may, as has happened in the past, sit uncomfortably with the political demands of women. Yet, Fianna Fáil has the potential to offer imaginative solutions to the challenge of women's demands. The party has a proud record of introducing far-sighted policy initiatives in the area of the economy and Northern Ireland. Individual Fianna Fáil ministers have a record of taking courageous policy decisions in many contentious areas. The conditions within the party appear to be conducive to tackling the 'woman question' in an equally imaginative and enlightened manner. This is the challenge for Fianna Fáil in the coming years.

Notes:

1. Russell J. Dalton and Manfred Kuechler (Eds) *Challenging the Political Order: New Social and Political Movements in Western Democracies* (Cambridge: Polity Press, 1990).

2. Yvonne Fitzsimons, 'Women's interest representation in the Republic of Ireland: the Council for the Status of Women', *Irish Political Studies*, **6**, pp. 37–52 (1991).

3. June Levine, *Sisters. The Personal Story of an Irish Feminist* (Dublin: Ward River Press, 1982).

4. Dr Thekla Beere 'Commission on the Status of Women: Progress Report', *Women in Ireland, Administration Special Issue* **23**(1), pp. 31–46 (1975).

5. Frances Gardiner, 'Political interest and participation of Irish women 1922–1992: The unfinished revolution', in Ailbhe Smyth (Ed.) *Irish Women's Studies Reader,* pp. 45–78 (Dublin, 1993).

6. The 1992 Fianna Fáil manifesto, The Six Point Plan for National Progress, p. 11 promised 'we will act swiftly on the recommendations of the 2nd Commission on the Status of Women. There will be a campaign for gender equity in education. The number of women on State boards will be doubled within four years. There will be increased funding of the Rape Crisis Centre. We will reform existing equality legislation in accordance with EC law to reflect our changing labour market. We will introduce a code of practice on sexual harassment.'

7. Yvonne Galligan, 'Women in Irish politics', pp. 207–26 in John Coakley and Michael Gallagher (Eds.) *Politics in the Republic of Ireland.* (Folens and PSAI Press, Dublin and Limerick 1993).

8. 'Participation, politics and policies', pp. 769–93 in the *Second Progress Report of the Monitoring Committee on the Implementation of the Recommendations of the Second Commission on the Status of Women* (Dublin: Stationery Office 1996.) (Pn. 2489). See also the Report of the Fianna Fáil Women's Committee, *Women in Politics and Public Life,* 1991, pp. 7–8.

9. Fianna Fáil Archives, FF/738–42 Árd Fheis Cláir 1972–77.

10. The revitalised women's committee have adopted a pro-active strategy towards women's inclusion in internal party policy debates. See the committee's *Five Year Development Plan*, 1990-95.

11. Fianna Fáil National Executive, Minutes, 12.1.1976

12. FF/756. Albert Reynolds, Presidential Address 1993, pp. 13–15.

10

Charles Haughey:
A Legacy of Lasting Achievement

by Martin Mansergh

Charles Haughey, the fourth leader of Fianna Fáil, was probably the most gifted and able politician of the post-independence generation. He led four administrations between 1979 and 1992. Over the course of a long Dáil career, spanning 35 years, and as a member of the Cabinet for about half that period, he developed a professionalism and a breadth of political interests that had few, if any, equals. While he was a much acclaimed minister in the 1960s, from 1970 on he had to surmount a succession of potentially destructive setbacks. At times, the extraordinary level of drama and controversy became part of a legend of survival, the excitement of which has sometimes distracted from his many real and lasting achievements. Now that he has retired from public life and the passion of most of his critics has largely subsided, the Irish people have had an opportunity to reflect on his legacy, and to see that it is, in so many areas, a highly positive one, that now commands wide respect.

Charles Haughey was born on 16 September 1925 in Castlebar. Both of his parents were from Swatragh in County Derry. His father was an officer in the Free State army, having been a prominent member of the Northern IRA in the War of Independence. His Northern parentage, and some school holidays spent with cousins in the North, gave him a vivid sense of the often bitter experience of Northern Nationalists from the early 1920s under Stormont. His father's army service and his own later service in the LDF and FCA during the Emergency and up to 1957 gave him a life-long attachment to and identification with the institutions of this State, of which he was enormously proud. In that respect, he shared certain attitudes in common with Liam Cosgrave, just as in a different way Jack Lynch and Garret FitzGerald were perceived as having much in common. After his father's retirement from the army, the family moved for a few years to a farm in Co. Meath, before settling in modest comfort in Donnycarney. His father was to suffer from a long and debilitating illness, which must have cast a long shadow as he grew up.

Charles Haughey forged ahead at school and college. He learnt for life, lines of poetry in Latin, Irish and English that would often emerge in impromptu banter, reflecting a more classical style of education that left even the better educated younger civil servants or politicians at a disadvantage. He has remained attached to St Joseph's CBS and to UCD, where he graduated in commerce. It was only after mature consideration in 1989 that he agreed to the creation of the new Dublin City and Limerick Universities out of the NIHEs, and he worked out with the Minister for Education Mary O'Rourke and the heads of universities an unprecedented expansion of third level places. One of his last acts as Taoiseach was to support the endowment of UCD with a magnificent business school at Carysfort, as so often in defiance of the begrudgers. He was also active in sport, notably winning a Dublin Senior Football Championship Medal with Parnell's in 1945. He remained loyal to the early ideals of the GAA, and because of that loyalty even as Taoiseach he resisted the invitations to internationals from the IRFU.

In May 1945, he first came to notice through being prominently involved in a counter-demonstration of UCD students outside Trinity on VE Day, when some Union Jacks that had been put out by Trinity students were burned. Some might choose to see in this as an early manifestation of anti-British sentiment, that was understandably still widespread in the aftermath of the independence struggle, the economic war, and the lack of any progress on a partition which was originally supposed to be temporary. But it was more a symptom of the pride in, and attachment of most people to, Irish neutrality, independence and sovereignty, that had been successfully upheld in the course of the Second World War, by a young, independent nation against enormous difficulties and sometimes heavy allied diplomatic pressure. Some days later, de Valera gave his famous reply to Churchill's jibes about Irish neutrality, after he had paid his diplomatic respects to the German Ambassador Dr Hempel, because he had behaved impeccably during the war, following the death of Hitler. Forty years later, disgusted by Mrs Thatcher's famous 'Out, Out, Out' rejection of all the constitutional options contained in the Report of the New Ireland Forum, Charles Haughey quoted from the broadcast exchanges the sentiment that de Valera turned back on Churchill, that all one could hope for was that a time would come when 'the tyrant would make some ghastly mistake,' to a visiting delegation of Tory backbenchers, who listened to him in stunned silence and who probably were unaware of the allusion. The tyrant was of course British misrule in Ireland over the centuries, not a specific Prime Minister, with whom, like everyone else who came into proximity with her, he had a sometimes productive but also chequered relationship.

Forty years after the war, as leader of Fianna Fáil, Charles Haughey agreed to an annual ceremony in July in memory of all those Irishmen and women who died in past wars, in service with the United Nations, including both those who fought for Irish independence and those who died in two world wars and other foreign conflicts. He also, with the slightly bemused help of the German Embassy, traced German pilots whose plane had been brought down over Inishvickillane, so that he could invite them back to the island.

Although when the time came, he exercised leadership with authority, and expected the traditional party discipline, like Parnell and de Valera before him, he was alternately accused of dictatorial tendencies, and, when he was not being 'dictatorial', vacillation. Yet he always left office with grace. He greatly admired American democracy, but also had an understanding of anti-imperialist sentiment, especially in the Arab world. As someone who in his younger days enjoyed foreign travel to places like the Mediterranean as a private citizen, he promised future Prime Minister Professor Andreas Papandreou in April 1970, whose independence and disregard for convention he later approved, that he would not holiday in Greece while the Greek Colonels remained in office. He developed a warm relationship with German Chancellor Helmut Schmidt, who was the very model of a modern and effective democratic leader, and later with President François Mitterrand, who combined the role of Head of State of a French Republic with a tradition of cultural grandeur going back to de Gaulle, the two Napoleons and the absolute monarchy. In 1990, Charles Haughey gave strong support as President of the European Union to German reunification, for which he was warmly thanked by Chancellor Kohl, turning a polite but deaf ear to obsessive complaints about the dangers of alleged German bullying from Mrs Thatcher. He respected Mrs Thatcher's professional ability.

But the statesman that he perhaps admired most of all was Mikhail Gorbachev, whom he credited with the transformation of Eastern Europe and its liberation from dictatorship through an unprecedented series of peaceful democratic revolutions, which would not have been possible in the past. His brief but memorable encounter for a few hours at Shannon with Gorbachev in March 1990 was one of the highlights of his international diplomacy. Though in domestic politics no socialist, it is nonetheless remarkable that most of the foreign statesmen with whom he formed an excellent relationship; Schmidt; Mitterrand, Commission President Jacques Delors; Bob Hawke, Prime Minister of Australia, a kindred spirit with whom he established a special rapport, and of course Gorbachev; all came from the left of the political spectrum. In general, they had more natural interest and empathy with Ireland than right-wing politicians, especially from countries with an imperial past.

After graduation, he formed a highly successful accountancy business that came to be called Haughey Boland, with Harry Boland, son of Fianna Fáil Justice Minister Gerry Boland. When certain people subsequently cribbed at his acquisition of wealth, they generally left his accountancy business out of the reckoning. Also anyone in a position to buy farmland or indeed any property before the 1960s close to the city were bound to see it markedly appreciate in value, something that could happen just as easily to a middle-class Labour politician. An old house, which needed a lot of upkeep and refurbishment, like Abbeville in Kinsealy, once the property of the Hon. John Beresford, builder of the Customs House and Commissioner of Revenue, and a house on which Gandon worked, could be picked up at a relatively modest cost in the 1960s, as few people wanted such properties. Abbeville provided him with a secluded residence, a superb house and grounds, where work and private meetings could be conducted, as well as fields for riding and even parking space for a helicopter. Charles Haughey experienced from certain elements in Irish life a deep distrust of the success that was achieved largely by his own efforts, as opposed to that achieved with the assistance of the comfortable connections that tend to come with inherited wealth or position.

He was drawn into Fianna Fáil at the end of the war by friends, and he was active in the North Dublin organisation. In 1953, he married Maureen, daughter of Seán Lemass, with the Taoiseach Eamon de Valera a guest at the wedding. They had four children, Eimear, Conor, Ciarán and Seán. His family have been a great asset and source of pride, as well as a support, a security and an anchor. His wife Maureen has rock-solid good sense. Eimear is a fine horsewoman, Conor a mining engineer, Ciarán runs a successful helicopter business, and Seán is a politician. Seán served as Lord Mayor of Dublin in 1989, taking precedence in certain situations over the Taoiseach, and undoubtedly the official letters of that time that began 'My dear Lord Mayor' and ended 'Yours sincerely, Taoiseach' are collectors' items.

Charles Haughey was elected to the Dáil on his third attempt in March 1957. His short maiden speech was remarkable in that it called for civil servants to play their part in a tremendous national crusade for economic recovery. It anticipated the role given very soon afterwards by Lemass to Dr Ken Whitaker, Secretary of the Department of Finance, to draw up a new strategy published in the 1958 White Paper on Economic Development that was to open the country to greater free trade, foreign investment and economic planning. In 1960, the year after Seán Lemass became Taoiseach, Charles Haughey was appointed to his first position as Parliamentary Secretary to the Minister for Justice, Oscar Traynor, who was in poor health, and from whom he took over the following year.

It was, as Minister for Justice, that he first had dealings with the Northern Ireland situation. When in February 1962 the IRA called off its border campaign, Charles Haughey issued a statement, saying: 'The partition of our country has been deeply resented by the great majority of Irishmen, but the foolish resort to violence by a few of them has been repeatedly condemned by all responsible people as conducive to the perpetuation instead of the abolition of the border.' He declared an amnesty for weapons handed in, and was prepared to release those willing to respect the Constitution. He also introduced the first extradition legislation, putting into domestic law the 1957 European Convention. For the first time extradition to the North was allowed for ordinary offences, and he expressed the hope that it marked 'the beginning of further beneficial co-operation in the administration of justice', both with the North and Britain. He was never particularly happy about extraditing those who were politically motivated, but he accompanied strengthening of the legislation in 1987 by significant safeguards, following a series of grave paramilitary actions. In a debate at the Queen's University, Belfast in 1962, he expressed pride in the State's treatment of its religious minorities and the absence of discrimination, at the time of the Second Vatican Council, when ecumencism was gaining ground, and before the deeper atavistic fears which that provoked in the North were fully evident.

Charles Haughey officially opened the new Garda Training College at Templemore in 1964. The early 1960s were the period when Ireland was most free from serious crime. As a result, he was the first Minister for Justice who was free to turn most of his attention to law reform. In this and all his subsequent offices, he had a talent for identifying and calling on the assistance of able collaborators, such as Roger Hayes, who subsequently worked for the Law Reform Commission. Charles Haughey *de facto* abolished the death penalty in 1963, and removed the discrimination against women in the matter of inheritance rights in the Succession Act, an achievement of which he was always very proud.

Charles Haughey was often able to detect the first stirrings of new movements, long before they became publicly apparent. From the early 1970s, his interest in ecology and the environment was a case in point, which was to culminate in the commissioning of the Green 2000 Report. Among male politicians, he was one of the first champions of women's rights. In March 1970, he was instrumental in the appointment of the immensely influential first Commission on the Status of Women under the chairmanship of Dr Thekla Beere. Their report effectively set much of the agenda for reform throughout the 1970s. As Leader of the Opposition in the 1980s, he was a keen participant in the Oireachtas Joint Committee on Women's Rights. In 1990, he appointed a Second Commission under Judge Mella Carroll. In 1979, he appointed Máire Geoghegan-Quinn the first woman Cabinet Minister since Constance Markievicz, and later made Mary O'Rourke Minister for Education. He also gave women like Miriam Hederman-O'Brien, Gillian Bowler and others the chair of important policy-making bodies and commissions. In 1980, on foot of a Supreme Court judgement, he established complete equality in the tax code for spouses. Even if the private man harboured somewhat more traditional attitudes to women, whose company by and large he enjoyed and they his, the public man strove to be a pioneer of women's rights in what had been a very male-dominated society.

In 1964, following the sudden resignation of Paddy Smith, he was appointed Minister for Agriculture. Charles Haughey was active and energetic, meeting the farm organisations, and negotiating better prices and outlets for their produce in the Anglo-Irish Free Trade Area Agreement. He entertained the Northern Ireland Minister for Agriculture Mr Harry West at his home as part of the Lemass–O'Neill exchanges. He was also instrumental in the introduction of the farmers' dole in 1965. But he also became embroiled in a prolonged stand-off with the farm organisations who picketed the Department of Agriculture and disrupted traffic over the price of milk. This perhaps did not help any chances of succeeding his father-in-law who suddenly retired in November 1966, when, like his rival and contemporary from school George Colley, he first put down a marker for his interest in the party leadership, which passed to Jack Lynch.

Charles Haughey, Donogh O'Malley (who introduced free secondary school education) and Brian Lenihan (who effectively removed literary censorship) – all young, able and thrusting Ministers brought on by Lemass, were sometimes referred to as 'the three musketeers' by the journalist the late John Healy, who socialised with them and wrote about them in his acute and witty

'Backbencher' column in *The Irish Times*. Their flamboyant style was far removed from the austere asceticism associated with the long de Valera era, and ironically is held against them by critics who in most cases have themselves strongly reacted against the ethos of de Valera's Ireland. The young bloods among Fianna Fáil Ministers did not hold much store by political correctness, and did not retire early to bed. Yet their dynamism, innovation and energy helped make Ireland dynamic and prosperous as never before in the 1960s. Close relations were developed not just with business but with the trade unions. Business funding was sought, as has since become the practice with virtually all political parties, though it was considered scandalous at the time. Yet philosophically, Charles Haughey believed that the new wealth should be used to improve social conditions, and that trade unionists would see their standard of living improve faster with Fianna Fáil policy programmes of economic development and social improvement than with the Socialist programmes of the revived and intellectually reinforced Labour Party. Who today can seriously doubt that he was right? In 1988, he privately considered the huge Lawson top-rate tax cuts that most benefited the wealthy in Britain as immoral. With considerable chutzpah he announced as Director of Elections in the 1969 General Election that Fianna Fáil would not be having a manifesto, as it had a Marxian ring about it.

The zenith of his early Ministerial career was reached under Jack Lynch as Minister for Finance, when he brought in four budgets. He was the last Minister for 25 years to run a surplus on the current budget, and also to cut taxes. It is little appreciated that later, as Taoiseach, he took a keen interest in, and worked intensively with, successive Ministers for Finance and officials on all Budgets and Finance Bills in 1980–82, and in 1987–92. He believed strongly in the power of the inexpensive imaginative gesture. He is famous for the introduction of the free travel scheme in 1967, which has enhanced the mobility and quality of life of old-age pensioners, adding a free television licence, and by other countries' standards, a generous free fuel allowance and later free telephone rental. As Taoiseach, in 1980–82, he gave three increases of 25% to old age pensioners, removing a large proportion of them from the poverty bracket, and he also supported Willie Bermingham's housing schemes to improve living and housing conditions of the elderly, in place of the administrative cost of Fine Gael's proposal of a £9.60 payment for the housewife.

In this early period, he became a patron of the arts, encouraging the first ROSC exhibition, and introducing in 1969 another unique measure the freedom from tax for creative writers and artists, which he supplemented in 1982 by the Aosdána scheme to provide income support to an independent group of 150 artists. His cultural adviser was the writer Anthony Cronin, friend of Patrick Kavanagh, Flann O'Brien, Brendan Behan and Samuel Beckett, and they had a very productive collaboration. Charles Haughey established the Irish Museum of Modern Art in Kilmainham. The new Government Buildings, opened in 1991, which is another of his monuments, was also filled with the best in modern art. He saved Temple Bar from destruction in 1987, and created a thriving cultural quarter there. In 1982, he removed VAT from books to the astonishment of the Irish publishing industry, which has never looked back since. But despite his great services as a patron of the arts, whose independence he respected, some tend to belittle him by reducing his achievements to that.

A keen hunting man, who exhibited at the RDS, he made earnings on stallion fees tax exempt, which is the foundation of the prosperity and worldwide reputation of the Irish bloodstock industry. One of the most fascinating aspects was his chameleon-type public persona. If part of him lived the life of the gentry, and another the islandman of the Blaskets, he had roots in Mayo, Dingle, Derry and Dublin simultaneously, and he never lost the common touch. Fianna Fáil dominated Dublin north of the Liffey while he was leader. He had a legendary reputation among his constituents for getting things done and problems fixed and for small acts of private charity. Nearly every day he was Taoiseach, certainly latterly, there were appeals for him to sort out at least half a dozen problems and difficulties all round the country.

Along with his 1970 Budget, he proudly produced a report outlining all the progress made by the country in the previous decade. At about the same time, he published the White Paper on our entry to the European Community. From the beginning Charles Haughey was a convinced European. He accompanied Jack Lynch on his tour of EC capitals in 1967. He believed EC membership was the key to the country's development, and that it was entirely compatible with pride in national sovereignty and identity, allowing us 'to break out of the disadvantageous, circumscribed position we have been in for centuries' and offering us 'a gateway to an entirely different world'. After he left Finance, co-ordination of negotiations shifted to the Department of Foreign Affairs.

At the end of the 1960s, the North erupted, creating huge policy dilemmas and problems of crisis management for a Government and a party that fundamentally believed in the peaceful reunification of the country. For Charles Haughey, whose parents were from the North, the street disturbances and attacks on Nationalist areas aroused strong feelings. Unlike Neil Blaney, he did not speak on the subject in public, though it has been suggested he had an important input in Cabinet into the content of Jack Lynch's famous broadcast of August 1969, particularly where he said 'The Irish Government can no longer stand by'. As Minister for Finance, he was given a key role in channelling token amounts of voted relief to the besieged Nationalist communities. Even the subsequently most respectable and moderate figures came looking for weapons to protect the community from further Loyalist incursions, and it was decided to establish field hospitals and a training camp near the border. The covert but authorised importation of small arms from the continent, which was the cause of the Arms Crisis, was stopped by the zeal of a senior civil servant in the Department of Justice against a background of armed action by radical Republicans within the State, possible British intelligence penetration, as well as the danger of misappropriation. The leader of the Opposition, who was tipped off by someone, precipitated the political crisis, which would otherwise probably not have happened. Whatever about some dabbling in troubled waters at the edges by marginal figures, Official IRA and later Workers' Party – inspired allegations that Fianna Fáil caused the split in December 1969 in the Republican Movement and spawned the Provisional IRA have not been substantiated by any serious historian who has written about this period.

Threatened with exposure about what had been happening, Jack Lynch dismissed two of his Ministers, and another two and a Parliamentary Secretary resigned. The effect on Charles Haughey and indeed on Fianna Fáil was shattering, especially when it was followed by an unprecedented public prosecution of former Ministers, and when that was unsuccessful, by a lengthy investigation by the Dáil Public Accounts Committee. Vindicated by the court, and treated as a hero by the more Republican-minded, Charles Haughey briefly challenged Jack Lynch, but the party closed round the Taoiseach. Unlike others, he did not quit, even though he was forced to swallow his pride and vote confidence in the Taoiseach. From then on, Charles Haughey, who had hitherto enjoyed a golden reputation, became deeply suspect to all those who disliked even constitutional republicanism, and it took some time to rebuild his career. Nationally, it marked the moment in the Northern crisis, where the

Republic decided to put its own safety first, and when it ceased for the best part of 20 years to engage with or try to exercise any private restraining influence over militant republicanism, not only for fear of contamination, but because the risk of misrepresentation of motives was so great. Memory of the Arms Crisis tied the hands of successive governments, which might otherwise have wanted to grapple more directly with trying to stop the violence much earlier.

Lying quiet, while Fianna Fáil remained in government, Charles Haughey was nevertheless much in demand by the party organisation. His reputation of outstanding ministerial ability stood to him in the barren years. In the company of PJ Mara, subsequently his genial Government Press Secretary, he toured the organisation and the country. When Fianna Fáil lost power in 1973, he became increasingly prominent and effective in the Dáil, brilliantly filleting the Minister for Posts and Telegraphs Conor Cruise O'Brien's proposal to rebroadcast BBC 1 as Ireland's second channel, and vigorously attacking the raft of new capital taxes including the wealth tax introduced by Richie Ryan. Public and party pressure brought him back to the Fianna Fáil Front Bench in 1975. He was never much enamoured with the political compromise of the Sunningdale Agreement, and fought responsibly alongside Des O'Malley the National Coalition's emergency legislation. In the 1977 General Election, he trounced Conor Cruise O'Brien, who had first challenged him in 1969, and who now lost his seat in the same constituency. He never forgave Charles Haughey for seeing him unceremoniously off the political pitch, and reducing him to the status of an outside commentator.

After the 1977 General Election, Charles Haughey was appointed Minister for Health and Social Welfare. Though it was known that he disapproved of the expansionary economic policies introduced by Martin O'Donoghue, Minister for Economic Development, he used a large share of the increase in public service numbers to expand and modernise the health services in an unprecedented way, including provision of free hospital care for all, and to plan new regional hospitals. He took on the tobacco companies by introducing the first legislative controls on tobacco advertising and sponsorship, which succeeded in limiting and reducing tobacco consumption. He also had enacted the first family planning legislation, following the defeat of the Coalition's measure, with the reluctant acquiescence of the Catholic Bishops, and in careful consultation with all the Churches and other interests. In a phrase he was not allowed to forget, he described the medical prescription of contraceptives for '*bona fide* family planning purposes' as 'an Irish solution to an Irish problem'. In fact, the legislation, which was subsequently further improved on in stages, by his successors, was a monument to his skill as a legislator in steering a careful course between liberal and conservative opinion. Careful consultation with a wide range of parties and attempting to build a consensus, which would take account of other religious views, was also his approach to the pro-life amendment, following a perhaps rash commitment first given by Garret FitzGerald in the lead-in to the 1981 general election, and which Charles Haughey at least felt honour-bound to fulfil. The problems created by a relatively liberal formulation of an essentially conservative demand became more apparent after the 'X' case in 1992.

The economic effects of the second international oil crisis in 1979, an apparent lack of content and direction in Northern policy faced with aggressive security demands by new British Prime Minister Margaret Thatcher following major atrocities in August 1979, and the loss of two by-elections in the Cork heartland of the Taoiseach in November, led to growing pressure for an early change in leadership, pressure which was to cause deep and lasting resentment. When Jack Lynch brought forward his retirement after the European Council that he presided over in December 1979, there were two contenders, George Colley, supported by nearly all members of the Government, except Ray MacSharry, then Colley's Minister of State, and Michael O'Kennedy, who declared for Charles Haughey, whose main support came from the backbenchers. Charles Haughey was narrowly elected to the consternation of many of his opponents inside and outside the party, not least because he was perceived as likely to be strong and effective. On nomination, he was subjected to a searing and typically sanctimonious attack by Garret FitzGerald in the Dáil, who accused him of having 'a flawed pedigree', a metaphor redolent of snobbery. While Charles Haughey sought to conciliate those in the party who were opposed to him, by including most of his opponents in the Cabinet (with the exception of Martin O'Donoghue, as well as prominent supporters like Ray MacSharry, Albert Reynolds and George Colley, the Tánaiste and Minister for Energy), quickly made it clear that his support would only be conditional. During his first three years as leader, Charles Haughey had constantly to look over his shoulder, and in 1982–83 he confronted and overcame an unprecedented series of three frontal attacks on his leadership. As for the media, its attitude was summed up in an *Irish Times* editorial which said that he would have to be twice as good as anyone else even to stand still, because of several circumstances in his background. In other words, he had quite literally to live up to a double standard in the media.

An overheated economy, suffering from rapidly rising inflation, high deficits on the budget and balance of payments, and rising unemployment, with industrial unrest on a massive scale, posed a serious challenge. In a famous broadcast in January 1980, Charles Haughey warned the country that it was living beyond its means and that it was imperative to have industrial peace. He did restore a measure of industrial peace, working closely with trade unions and employers, with whom he concluded a second National Understanding, but at a price. The onset of vicious international recession, coupled with the unpopularity of rising unemployment in advance of an election, with Jack Lynch's hostage to fortune in 1977 that if it exceeded 100,000, the Government would not deserve to be re-elected still ringing in people's ears, led to a decision in mid-1980 to substitute a policy of trying to tide over recession for a policy of fiscal rectitude that had to be postponed. In the climate of the time, a dose of Thatcher-style monetarism would have been deeply unpopular. In January 1981, a major investment plan for the modernisation of infrastructure such as roads and telecommunications, the importance of which Charles Haughey passionately believed in, using EU loans and subsidy funding, which he saw as the justification for Ireland's EMS participation without Britain, was introduced. The most controversial decision was the building of Knock Airport, backing the vision of Monsignor Horan and running the gauntlet of the mockers of Dublin 4, on 'the foggy and boggy hill' later conjured up by Jim Mitchell. The plan staved off deep recession for another year, but at the price of a spiralling level of borrowing, exacerbated by the political need to pacify various pressure groups in the run up to the third no-holds-barred competitive auction-style election. For many years previously a bad practice had emerged of regular and often large supplementary estimates towards the end of the year, and this would have been and was the position again in 1981. If Fianna Fáil had won the general election in 1981, there is little doubt that Charles Haughey would have had to tighten up the public finances considerably, which is what he originally wanted to do, and *he* would have done it without shaking economic confidence to its foundations.

The most important of his achievements in the 1980–81 period was the forging of the Anglo-Irish framework. While not departing from the broad policy position of previous Irish Governments, he nonetheless declared his belief that Northern Ireland was a failed political entity, that must be looked at in the total context of relations between the two countries. Encouraged by the British Foreign Secretary Lord Carrington's resolution of the Rhodesian situation, he politically wooed Mrs Thatcher, presenting her with an Irish

Georgian silver teapot at their first summit in May 1980. To help resolve the tense first hunger strikes, she came to Dublin Castle with her senior ministers in December. Phrases like 'the totality of relationships', bringing about peace, stability and reconciliation, recognition that Irish unity would only come about by agreement, and the commissioning of studies that would include institutional structures characterised an initiative that for the first time envisaged the two Governments as partners. Out of this was later to develop the more North–South oriented Anglo-Irish Agreement of 1985 concluded by Garret FitzGerald with Mrs Thatcher, and all the other joint initiatives since, specifically the British-Irish Parliamentary Body established in 1990. However, this approach even initially ran into a lot of Unionist opposition, with controversy about its constitutional implications, if any, while the compromise settlement of the first hunger strikes by Republican prisoners in the North also broke down.

The second hunger strikes led to a number of deaths both before and after the June general election, the election of two H-Block candidates in the border constituencies, and the loss of power to Garret FitzGerald. Garret FitzGerald was highly regarded by the media, and had put forward an apparently ambitious tax-cutting plan offset by a lot of small print, which had to be rapidly abandoned, as his Fine Gael–Labour Coalition Government moved in precisely the opposite direction, raising taxes to meet the deficit.

Garret FitzGerald went on an economic crusade, in which Fianna Fáil's economic record since 1977, which was certainly open to criticism, but even more its intentions, were absurdly exaggerated and extrapolated to justify the swingeing tax increases introduced by the Fine Gael–Labour Coalition, instead of more obvious and less damaging reductions in the alleged overspending of their predecessors. He certainly ignored his own and his party's role in popularising deficit-financing in the early years of the National Coalition. He established the problem of the deficit in the public mind, but where tackling such problems effectively ought to raise confidence the opposite result was achieved between 1981 and 1986.

Charles Haughey blossomed as a ruthlessly effective and aggressive leader of the Opposition. With the collapse of its tax reform platform and a badly-launched constitutional crusade, which alienated those who were proud of Ireland's record as an independent country and who resented any comparison with the record of Unionists in Northern Ireland, the first Fine Gael-Labour Coalition only lasted seven months. So began the extraordinary and fateful year of 1982, which saw two general elections. Charles Haughey would have been willing to form a new administration without a general election, something that did not happen till late 1994, but attempting to communicate that to President Hillery was subsequently represented by FitzGerald as something reprehensible and was used by him with devastating effect to damage Brian Lenihan's candidature for the Presidency in 1990. The February 1982 election was no more conclusive than the June 1981 one, with the parties remaining very close to each other in strength, and leaving Fianna Fáil two seats short of an overall majority. Fianna Fáil was able to form a Government only with the support of Tony Gregory, on the basis of an elaborate but much needed programme of inner city renewal, and of Sinn Féin the Workers' Party, whose deputies leapt over the balustrade of the press gallery in the Dáil in order to be able to vote for Mr Haughey. This was only after the first of three internal challenges, the first led by Desmond O'Malley, had been overcome, for which the alleged double-voting of an agent in the constituency had perhaps been a catalyst.

The 1982 Administration, though it had some achievements to its credit, was dogged by ill-fortune. Rapidly deepening recession threw a deflationary budget off the rails, and occasioned the loss of SFWP support, as the Government finally turned away from any remaining Keynesian illusions. In the interregnum, the British Government had launched an internal initiative for an assembly opposed by the SDLP, and it was clear that the hopes for progress via the Anglo-Irish route of 1980–81 had waned. The Falklands War, which Charles Haughey, reasserting the principle of neutrality, decided to oppose internationally, following the controversial sinking of the *Belgrano*, reduced Anglo-Irish relations to freezing point, as Mrs Thatcher's political survival depended on her ability to win the war. Overnight, the thrust of British policy towards its remaining possessions had moved from one of decolonisation by degrees to a neo-colonial one, severely reducing the scope for movement on Northern Ireland. Relations thereafter were correct, but never very cordial, even though as President of the European Community in 1990 he sought to avoid her being isolated by the other member States. Despite this, to judge from her memoirs, she had a higher regard for him than for FitzGerald, with whom she concluded the Anglo-Irish Agreement. There were positive economic initiatives, notably an agreed reduction of special pay claims, and an ambitious plan *The Way Forward* for putting the economy back on the rails, which combined a continuing development thrust with fiscal retrenchment. The issue in the televised debate between Charles Haughey and Garret FitzGerald in the general election of November 1982 was whether the economic crisis was best tackled by reducing current expenditure or whether there was further scope for increased taxation. Between 1982 and 1987 Fine Gael and Labour opted for the latter, with the recovery delayed for four years as a result.

Confusion over the arrest of a murderer found bizarrely in the flat of the Attorney General was blamed on the Taoiseach, and as the Government seemed increasingly shaky, a further challenge, this time laid down by Deputy Charlie McCreevy, who was able to muster the support of 22 deputies in all, led to another damaging challenge to Mr Haughey and the resignation of two ministers opposed to him. The minority Government fell in November on a confidence motion. But in the subsequent general election held in the most inauspicious circumstances, Charles Haughey managed to contain the defeat and keep Fianna Fáil the largest party a nose ahead of Fine Gael, retaining 45% of the vote. The revelation shortly after the change of government that the telephones of two journalists had been tapped with the legal authorisation of the Minister for Justice Mr Seán Doherty caused the biggest crisis in Charles Haughey's career, and brought him to the brink of resignation. But the hounding of the media was so intense and excessive, that he was given time by his party, and there was a strong surge of grass-roots support back in his favour. Against all media expectations, he survived his third vote of confidence. Thereafter, his leadership was for a long time reasonably secure.

Neither Garret FitzGerald nor Charles Haughey gave each other much quarter, though Charles Haughey always stood with the Government in moments of national crisis. He dominated the Dáil from the Opposition benches, and excoriated the ineffective economic policies that failed to lift the Irish economy out of the quagmire of debt, redundancies, recession and soaring unemployment. While prepared to play his part in committees, he would not let this take away from the Government's responsibility to govern. He scorned the liberal agenda that distracted from economic management, and likened the premature plunge into the divorce referendum to the charge of the Light Brigade, admonishing the Taoiseach that 'responsible political leadership is surely about the successful attainment of objectives, not about rushing erratically into crushing defeats'. While Garret FitzGerald saw politics as being about ideas and shaping public opinion, Charles Haughey regarded it as being about securing tangible changes and improvements.

He worked with Garret FitzGerald, John Hume and Dick Spring in the New Ireland Forum, in redefining and updating the shared agenda of Irish nationalism. However, in so doing, he resisted the excessive encroachment of revisionist ideology. While initially attracted to the idea of joint sovereignty, he came down in favour of the unitary State as the best solution. While his trenchant reassertion of democratic Republicanism, in tones that had not been heard since the days of de Valera were treated with impatience by the Government and by many commentators, he secured the flank of Irish democracy against the incursions of militant Republicanism, at a time that Sinn Féin was growing rapidly in the North, while at the same time he was beginning to build an ideological bridge towards them, which would be a valuable building block in the peace process.

From October 1983 to June 1985, Fianna Fáil swept the board in by-elections, the European Parliament and local elections. Two collective decisions were costly. Somewhat against his better judgement, Fianna Fáil decided to oppose a minor liberalisation of the family planning laws in 1985, in the hope of seeing a repetition of the revolt which had defeated the Government on the wording of the Pro-Life Amendment. But the price for what was seen as opportunism was a good deal of hostility among the liberal media and much of the urban middle class and the labelling of Fianna Fáil as a conservative party. The neutrality over divorce was much more defensible. The second costly decision was the initially hardline opposition particularly to the constitutional aspects of the Anglo-Irish Agreement, which was strongly supported by most other Irish nationalist opinion, North and South. The two decisions precipitated the formation of the Progressive Democrats, and the defection of a small number of Deputies, which arguably was to deprive Fianna Fáil of an overall majority in 1987.

During the 1980s, Irish neutrality, Europe and foreign policy were a lively source of debate. Professor Patrick Keatinge once quipped that Irish neutrality was a debate between Mr Haughey in Government and Mr Haughey in Opposition. While deeply committed to Europe, and recognising that this could eventually have defence implications, as spelled out in the Maastricht Treaty, he was also conscious of the strong anti-nuclear feelings of people, especially during the early Reagan years. He addressed UN Special Sessions on Disarmament. He also spearheaded political opposition to Sellafield. He recognised that European integration to be attractive had to be accompanied by substantial EU funding to enable Ireland to compete. On this basis he secured ratification of the Single European Act in May 1987, and signed the Maastricht Treaty, with safeguard protocols or clauses recognising Ireland's independent foreign policy tradition. In 1987–88, working closely with President Jacques Delors, he oversaw the negotiation of £3 billion in funding from 1989–93, which made all the difference following a period of budgetary deflation. In all his EC and national programme negotiations he was greatly assisted by Pádraig Ó hUiginn, Secretary of the Department of the Taoiseach, one of the most accomplished of all Irish civil servants. In diplomatic and Anglo-Irish negotiations, and in Cabinet, Dermot Nally was his mentor. His politically most experienced adviser in the early 1980s was the late Pádraig Ó hAnnracháin, former private secretary to Eamon de Valera and head of the GIS under Seán Lemass.

The Fine Gael–Labour Coalition, which had seen its majority vanish, crumbled in January 1987. Fianna Fáil swept back in the general election, with a clear and substantial lead over its nearest rival, Fine Gael, though again, the support of Tony Gregory was needed, this time without any deal, and the conditional support of another party, Fine Gael, under Alan Dukes, who developed the Tallaght Strategy to justify their position. The lack of an overall majority, which continued to disappoint Fianna Fáil followers, inclined Charles Haughey towards caution in naming his Cabinet.

This time he was determined to make no mistake on the economy. March 1987, indeed, was the decisive turning point in Ireland's economic fortunes. The resolute action over the next two years in cutting public expenditure by an unprecedented amount, slashing borrowing, while securing a basis of a broader consensus with the support of the Social Partners, business, trade unions and farmers in the Programme for National Recovery, has laid the basis for 10 years' strong and consistent economic performance. Benefits have included low borrowing, lower real debt, low inflation, lower interest rates, rapid export growth, a balance of payments surplus, industrial peace and above all, a sustained growth in employment to new record levels. At the same time, Charles Haughey launched a series of development initiatives, such as the International Financial Services Centre, the National Treasury Management Agency, the revival of tourism, forestry and aquaculture, and, less successfully, the beef industry.

His Northern Ireland policy was, first of all, to implement and honour the Anglo-Irish Agreement, as an obligation in international law, where the major achievement was new fair employment legislation, secondly, to explore the possibility of negotiating a broader new agreement with the Ulster Unionist Party, and thirdly, to see, particularly post-Enniskillen, if there was any realistic basis, on which the Provisional IRA might be persuaded to renounce violence. The initiative *vis-à-vis* the Unionists eventually bore some fruit with the commencement of the 1991/92 talks, belatedly resumed in June 1996. He conducted a courteous diplomatic minuet with James Molyneaux at a distance. Some of the origins of the current peace process lie in the contacts between Charles Haughey and Father Reid of the Clonard Monastery in Belfast, two authorised secret meetings between Fianna Fáil and Sinn Féin in Dundalk in 1988, and the first draft of the joint declaration which he prepared with the SDLP leader, John Hume, in the autumn of 1991, and which he spoke about to John Major on his first visit to Dublin as Prime Minister in December 1991. The initiative was handed on to his successor Albert Reynolds, leading eventually to the Downing Street Declaration and the IRA ceasefire of August 1994. He was determined to use the International Fund for Ireland and EU funding to create something lasting and worthwhile with a high profile. The linking of the Shannon-Erne Waterway, through the rehabilitation of an old disused canal, has attracted many visitors, and made a major impact on some of the border countryside.

In 1989, spurred by a number of minor Dáil defeats, his final effort to win an overall majority backfired, forcing him to try and form a first Fianna Fáil Coalition with the Progressive Democrats. He succeeded in bringing the party with him with considerable skill. Even though the PDs contained many of his old party rivals and critics, he strove to make the Coalition work. Direct taxes were cut. A lot of reforming social legislation was passed right through from 1987, with new laws abolishing illegitimacy and rape, and on judicial separation. He succeeded through political lobbying with President Reagan and Congress in Washington in persuading them to regularise and thereby transform the position of the undocumented Irish newly arrived in America. He also concluded a second National Programme, for Economic and Social Progress, early in 1991.

In 1990, he conducted a highly successful European Presidency, with two summits in Dublin Castle, and with an important agenda covering: association agreements with the new democratic states of Eastern Europe, the integration of a united Germany into the European Community, movement towards the Maastricht Treaty and political, economic and monetary union, closer political relations with the United States, the encouragement of the peace process in South Africa following the release of Nelson Mandela, without prematurely lifting EU sanctions, together with the Dublin Declaration on the Environment, shortly after he had helped Mary Harney ban smokey coal to clear smog from Dublin. During the Presidency he went North to address the Institute of Directors about the potential of North–South economic co-operation against the backdrop of the European Single Market, with a small group of people demonstrating from a nearby rooftop, including Ian Paisley and Peter Robinson. The EU Presidency was probably the zenith of his political career. In this whole period, 1987–92, he won the deep respect of all who worked with him, especially in the public service, for his professionalism, his grasp of issues, and his immense political skill, notwithstanding the occasional withering acerbities or probing dialectical debates.

The unexpected loss of the presidential election, after he reluctantly acceded to PD demands for the dismissal of his old friend Brian Lenihan from the Government, and the more indifferent showing in the 1991 Local Elections made the party begin to turn towards the succession, in advance of the following general election. His closest ally, Ray MacSharry, had gone to Europe as Agriculture Commissioner, where he made an outstanding impact. Albert Reynolds, then Minister for Finance, was well placed, as was Bertie Ahern. In the autumn of 1991, a succession of alleged scandals in the commercial world, without any real political connection, were nonetheless linked by Opposition and media in an atmosphere of mounting hysteria to the alleged aura surrounding the leadership of Charles Haughey. People waiting for too long in the wings became impatient. His position became weaker, although he counter attacked vigorously, fragmenting the unity of the Workers' Party in the process. Another internal challenge was made with again twenty-two voting against him as in October 1982. A controversial and in one case aborted re-shuffle, following the dismissal of the ministers who opposed him in the vote, including Albert Reynolds, even though it allowed him to promote some younger talent, robbed him of the fruits of victory. Even in this difficult and trying period, he continued to do much vital work, signing the Maastricht Treaty, and overseeing the 1992 Budget. But as he prepared for a planned and dignified departure, new controversy over what had happened in 1982, in relation to the phone-tapping of journalists, including a new version of events put forward by Seán Doherty, brought his time as Taoiseach, sadly, to a sudden close, despite always a vigorous rebuttal. But as if the Irish public realised the unique qualities of the Taoiseach that they were losing, there was a great outpouring of public tributes. Passing on the baton on 11 February 1992, he quoted from *Othello:*

I have done the state some service; they know't.
No more of that.

With that he embarked upon an active but politically dignified retirement, carrying out from time to time low-key public and charitable functions, and generally acting the opposite of those former leaders such as Mrs Thatcher and

Dr FitzGerald who continue to make constant public interventions. Ireland lost one of its greatest and most exciting parliamentarians, who loved the cut and thrust of the Dáil, who would readily stand in for question time for his ministers. Sometimes Opposition members would taunt him in the hope that he would say something memorable about them. As he was wont to say, there were performances on occasion, 'when even the ranks of Tuscany could scarce forbear to cheer'. Charles Haughey's contribution to Ireland will long continue to be honoured, as the fruits of his work continue to be enjoyed. As he said on one occasion, echoing the inscription to Sir Christopher Wren, '*Si Monumentum requiris, circumspice*'.

11

Fianna Fáil on the Highwire of Foreign Policy

by Eunan O'Halpin

Introduction

This chapter explores the evolution of Fianna Fáil's approach to foreign policy issues since its foundation.[1] While the themes underlying the party's approach to external relations issues have remained constant – the ending of partition by peaceful means, the vindication of national sovereignty, staying out of other peoples' wars, ensuring that independent Ireland would not be used to harm Britain's interests, the search for a just international order in which the rights of small states are recognised equally with those of great powers, a vague hostility to European colonialism and a general sympathy for self-determination as a defining principle in state formation throughout the world – the process of policy formulation has undergone a sea change.[2] Where once 'the Chief' ordained and the party obeyed, policy now emerges mainly through advisory channels within the party organisation, through committee work in the Oireachtas and the European Parliament, and through dialogue with increasingly organised single issue pressure groups concerned with a galaxy of problems in areas such as human rights, Third World development, and civil and military nuclear proliferation.[3]

Two other introductory points must be made. Firstly, any discussion of Fianna Fáil's policy outlook is complicated by its sheer success as a party of government. This presents the difficulty of untangling the mesh of party, national and administrative influences which have moulded external policy during the total of 47 years when Fianna Fáil has enjoyed office. Secondly, external relations seldom figure high on the Irish electoral agenda. The record suggests that not even the Northern Ireland issue has been a significant factor in the competition for votes between Fianna Fáil and the other major parties, although Fianna Fáil has been prone to losing votes to fringe republican parties and to independents in sensitive constituencies when emotions are running high, as happened with the H-Block candidates in 1981.[4] During its stints in opposition, the party has generally concentrated its energies on the articulation of policies directed towards the overwhelmingly domestic concerns of the electorate. With a few partial exceptions – those in June and September 1927 and in February 1932, where constitutional and economic relations with Britain were, together with radical social policies, at the core of the party's campaigns for office, and that in 1948 when Clann na Poblachta briefly filched some of Fianna Fáil's anti-partition clothes and votes – election campaigns have focused on strictly domestic policy issues.[5]

Fianna Fáil and External Policy 1926–48

A recent study of the party's first decades comments on 'the culture of the early Fianna Fáil, with its emphasis upon party unity, iron loyalty to the party and its "Chief", and its own form of democratic centralism'.[6] This otherwise fanciful comparison between the sanguinary party management tactics of Joseph Stalin and those found in Fianna Fáil contains a grain of truth in respect of external policy. For over 20 years, Eamon de Valera exercised an unchallenged pre-eminence in the formulation and expression of party policy on every aspect of external affairs including partition, Anglo-Irish relations and the State's relations with the wider international community.

The explanation for this is rooted in the party's origins. Fianna Fáil was founded by republicans who had come to see the political futility of denying the legitimacy of the new Irish Free State, who recognised the impracticability of winning Irish unity by force, and who opted for the parliamentary over the military route to political power and to the eventual achievement of an all-Ireland republic. It was evident both from the painful experience of the Treaty split and from the post-Civil War vicissitudes of the republican movement that internal discipline, unity of purpose and clear leadership was a prerequisite to any significant political progress.[7] This de Valera provided partly by gathering the most sensitive and contentious threads of policy firmly into his own hands. The party's more recent history suggests that his instincts were sound: no questions have been more divisive than Northern Ireland and Anglo-Irish relations, matters which prompted the 1970 Arms Crisis and the formation of two breakaway parties, and which proved Jack Lynch's downfall in 1979.[8]

While some expressions of alarm and impatience were heard at Árd Fheiseanna and elsewhere between 1927 and 1931, de Valera encountered no significant opposition to his generally cautious line on partition and Anglo-Irish relations. Todd Andrews' recollection that 'Dev presided at the [national executive] meetings . . . indeed, for all practical purposes Dev was the executive because his rulings were never questioned' is largely borne out in the party's surviving records.[9] In opposition, Fianna Fáil naturally deprecated the considerable diplomatic achievements of the Cosgrave government both in the progressive redefinition of relations with Britain and in the establishment of a distinctive Irish voice at the League of Nations.[10] De Valera was to be the beneficiary of his opponents' successes in both areas after he took office in March 1932, because he inherited the constitutional, administrative and legal means by which to advance his own very different external policy goals.

De Valera and External Policy 1932–38

In March 1932, de Valera consolidated his hold on external policy by becoming Minister for External Affairs as well as President of the Executive Council. He held the External Affairs portfolio for 16 unbroken years. Seán MacEntee recalled that 'as Minister for External Affairs, de Valera was responsible for formulating that policy and you did not challenge that policy unless you had very strong grounds for doing so ... Nobody ever formulated foreign policy except de Valera. Make no mistake about that. He might have listened to advice from Joe Walshe [the Secretary of External Affairs] but de Valera "had the last word".'[11]

According to MacEntee de Valera himself said that he 'did not put down on paper what his policies were going to be. He always said: "If you write something down people know what you're going to do ... are warned and may be in a position to stop you. So always keep your policy under your hat".'[12] For more than 20 years, in office and out of office, that broad brimmed black hat enveloped all external affairs. This presents difficulties for anyone seeking to probe developments in de Valera's and his party's policy positions as distinct from those of the (then) Department of External Affairs, because official records contain little in the way either of detailed exposition of the minister's views, or written directions from him to his department. The problem is compounded by the fact that, with the notable exceptions of Frank Aiken, Sean MacEntee and de Valera himself, the first generation of senior Fianna Fáil politicians left no personal papers for researchers to work on. Most seriously of all, over 20 years after his death, and contrary to his wishes, the bulk of de

Valera's voluminous papers remain closed. Until this crucial collection is finally available in its entirety, historians writing on any aspect of Fianna Fáil's management of Anglo-Irish relations and all other external affairs up to 1948 do so in the frustrating knowledge that vital evidence lies inaccessible, though secure, in a Franciscan house in Killiney.[13]

To the surprise of many, there was no clear-out of civil servants when de Valera took office: he relied on those officials who had served the Cosgrave regime.[14] This demonstration of confidence in the political impartiality of the Civil Service set an important precedent; it also facilitated continuity in the management of foreign affairs. This was particularly evident in respect of the League of Nations, where de Valera made a considerable impact internationally precisely because he eschewed narrow advocacy of Ireland's case against Britain. Instead, he repeatedly outlined the dilemmas of small states in a world increasingly threatened by military aggression which the League seemed unable to contain. His involvement at Geneva also resounded to his credit at home: he was 'the first leader of [independent Ireland's] government to realise and exploit the domestic political advantages of foreign policy'.[15] While he grew increasingly pessimistic about the League, he ensured that Ireland observed both the letter and the spirit of its resolutions. The most striking instance was Ireland's adherence to the League's sanctions against Italy in 1935–36, despite considerable political and clerical sympathy for a fellow Catholic state supposedly bent on a civilising mission, in fact conducting a barbaric war of conquest.[16]

De Valera was to find bilateral diplomacy a more fruitful ground for advancing the State's interests. Within days of taking office, he told a British official that there was 'no question of an immediate settlement [on partition]... although the issue stood at the back of everything it had to be left out of account so far as immediate relations with Great Britain were concerned'.[17] Other demeaning aspects of the Treaty of 1921 could, however, be addressed through judicious action. Between 1932 and 1936, and despite sustained British objections, he succeeded in the meticulous demolition of dominion status as defined in the 1921 Treaty quite legally and while observing the forms, though emphatically not the spirit, of membership of the British Commonwealth.[18] In December 1936 he excised the Crown entirely from the Constitution, restricting it through the External Relations Act to 'a defined place with limited functions in the external field' held at the pleasure of the Oireachtas.[19] The consequences for the State's external standing were, as de

Valera anticipated, clearly beneficial; the extent to which he put the likely impact of the changes on Northern Unionist opinion into the scales, given his declared belief in an eventual peaceful ending of partition, is not known.[20]

In parallel with his onslaught on the Treaty settlement, de Valera honoured his campaign pledge to retain land annuities payable to Britain. This precipitated what quickly became know as the 'Economic War', and it facilitated the operation of Fianna Fáil's policy of industrial development through protectionism.   The wisdom of this extended dispute with the State's predominant trading partner remains a matter for debate: what cannot be doubted is that de Valera exploited the potentially damaging conflict brilliantly, consolidating the party's electoral position despite the hardship caused to Irish agricultural interests, and providing his more republican-minded followers with a 'war' against the old enemy which bolstered national pride without costing a drop of blood.[21]   This also had the unintended consequence of intensifying diplomatic exchanges between the British and Irish governments from 1935 onwards. The search for agreement on the irksome trade dispute opened the possibilities of a wider political settlement. With the glaring exception of partition, much was achieved in the spring of 1938 when the ending of trade hostilities was tied into a broader Anglo-Irish agreement.[22] Britain relinquished her Treaty rights to the use of a number of Irish ports for naval operations, as well as her entitlement 'in time of war or strained relations with a foreign power' to demand additional naval, air and communications facilities required for coastal defence. This made Irish neutrality in a future war involving Britain, established policy since 1921, for the first time militarily plausible just as such a war was looming.[23] In return de Valera, who unlike most republicans, had long grasped of Britain's strategic concerns about her Atlantic security and had tried to address them in 1922 with his Document Number Two, reiterated that Irish territory would not be used to harm British defence interests. This declaration was soon followed by the first arrangements for what became very extensive covert security collaboration.[24] The 1938 agreement proved a remarkably good bargain. It allowed Ireland to shelter under Britain's defensive umbrella without tying her to anything more than an informal security pact which served the State's own internal security interests.

Fianna Fáil and the Politics of Neutrality 1938–49

De Valera's policy was clear in September 1939: Ireland would stay out of war unless dragged in, and would resist aggression from any quarter. Attempts to use Ireland to harm British interests would not be tolerated: the draconian Offences against the State Act had already been passed in response to the IRA's renewed declaration of war on Britain and its 's-plan' bombings in England.[25] Public and political support was virtually unanimous, based on fear of the consequences of modern warfare, knowledge of the State's utter defencelessness, and the antipathy of a substantial minority towards Britain.[26] The views of the latter were chillingly expressed by the veteran Fianna Fáil TD Dan Breen to his party colleague Bob Briscoe, a Jewish immigrant who was understandably pro-Ally:

> I hold the old Irish view and that one is very plain and simple and it has not changed ... "you can't serve Ireland well without a hatred for England". This is old, but it is as true today as when it was first spoken ... The Germans and the Italians are not the people that murdered and robbed my people for 700 years. It took your good English friends to do that and they continue to do it.[27]

For about a year after the collapse of France, Ireland was a likely target for invasion by either set of belligerents or by both. In the event, neither Hitler nor Churchill came. Churchill did, however, make a sudden and ambiguous offer of possible post-war unity in return for Irish participation. Even if sincerely meant, there was no guarantee that Northern Ireland would acquiesce, and de Valera declined to be drawn in.[28] Ireland stayed neutral, despite further pressure from both Britain and the United States: indeed, a reaction against that pressure may partly explain de Valera's attachment to all the formalities of neutrality, culminating in his notorious visit to the German Legation to express his condolences on Hitler's death. Given Germany's savage treatment of neutral states, and what the government well knew by 1945 about her hideous achievements in mass extermination, this was, arguably, one gesture of independence too many.[29]

Neutrality had its costs. Censorship, condemned even by one devout Fianna Fáil supporter as 'inelastic and unintelligent', operated with a rigidity unmatched in other European neutrals, suppressing debate about domestic politics and restricting the flow of war news.[30] Neutrality also unavoidably reinforced partition, it inevitably damaged Anglo-Irish relations and, more surprisingly, it weakened Irish influence in America, where Roosevelt had been an impatient critic of what he regarded as Irish myopia and selfishness. Finally, what had been a largely pragmatic policy, underpinned by the political imperative to demonstrate true independence but sustained by all manners of profoundly unneutral covert collaboration with the Allies, has retrospectively been portrayed as an approach mysteriously based on moral considerations.

For whatever reason – self-satisfaction, insularity, exhaustion – the de Valera government's post-war foreign policy performance was inconsequential and reactive. Partition remained as intractable as ever, a fact which Seán MacBride's Clann na Poblachta party briefly exploited.[31] In 1946 Ireland found herself punished for neutrality when admission to the UN was blocked, not by the British or the Americans but, ironically, by the Russians (who until June 1941 had themselves done all they could to help Hitler).

Marshall Aid, the fuel which fed the fires of economic regeneration throughout western Europe, was accepted only grudgingly at the behest of External Affairs, and without any clear idea of how it might be productively used.[32] The unexpected outcome of the February 1948 election denied Fianna Fáil even the pleasure of spending it.

From Self-Absorption to European Integration 1948–1973

The Fianna Fáil leadership availed of their years in opposition from 1948–1951 principally to take a rest from the burdens of office. De Valera travelled widely abroad in order to denounce the evils of partition, an exercise primarily designed to protect Fianna Fáil's republican flank at home. He was also a polite though somewhat sceptical attender at the inaugural meetings of the Council of Europe. The Fine Gael Taoiseach John A. Costello's sudden announcement in Ottawa in 1948 that the government intended both to declare Ireland a republic and to leave the Commonwealth took Fianna Fáil as much by surprise as it did Costello's own Cabinet colleagues, but de Valera's criticisms had perforce to be directed at the chaos surrounding the decision, in Joe Lee's words 'a shambles from start to finish, perhaps the most inept diplomatic exhibition in the history of the State', rather than at the more substantive issues.[33] A year later, the Costello government adduced partition as Ireland's reason for refusing to join NATO, again a policy position which de Valera could not unduly criticise but which he might well have been able to avoid adopting had he been in charge. The party's next stint in office, from 1951 to 1954, saw Frank Aiken take over as Minister for External Affairs, but there were no great initiatives either on partition or on wider foreign policy. Ireland was finally admitted to the United Nations in 1955 under the second Costello administration, which also had to deal with the first consequences of the IRA's 'border campaign' in 1956. By then the complacency and insularity of the 1940s had been succeeded by despair at the country's economic prospects. Fianna Fáil's return to office in 1957 brought no immediate relief, although within the Civil Service and in the wider policy community – the trade unions, business organisations, the farming bodies – wheels were already turning which were to produce a transformation in the country's economic fortunes.[34] This involved the reorienting of the Irish economy from protection towards free trade, together with the encouragement of foreign investment in Irish industry and conscious efforts to join a European trading bloc. *The First Programme for Economic Expansion* provided the impetus for economic regeneration, but the State's newly acquired ambition of becoming a member of an enlarged European Common Market had to await British entry. During the negotiating process in 1962, the Taoiseach Seán Lemass, stated that Ireland recognised that membership of an integrated Europe would ultimately entail defence and security, as well as economic obligations. This suggested that in certain circumstances partition might no longer be an impassable obstacle to joining in the collective defence of Western Europe, and that Lemass saw military neutrality as a contingent rather than an absolute principle. It also reflected the high economic and political value which Fianna Fáil now placed on European integration.[35]

It is significant that the impetus for this sea change in thinking about the nature of economic independence, the need for involvement in a multinational trading bloc, and the possible attenuation of neutrality came from the Department of Finance, not from External Affairs. Aiken's preoccupations lay in the UN, where Ireland's promotion of the Nuclear Non-Proliferation Treaty, and its support for communist Chinese membership, marked it out as an independent actor in Cold War terms, reflecting the concerns of small states and sympathetic towards the newly emerging ex-colonial nations of Africa and Asia. The decision in 1961 to send an army detachment for UN service in the Congo demonstrated a new willingness to accept some of the more hazardous and painful obligations as well as the rights of membership of the international community.[36]

The economic success of the Lemass era notwithstanding, membership of the EEC became Ireland's long-term foreign policy goal for security as well as economic reasons – despite its high standing with the Irish public, the UN during the Cold War remained an institution strong on the rhetoric of international peace and justice, but an ineffectual guarantor of states' rights. Once Britain decided to re-apply to the EEC, the Fianna Fáil government willingly followed. While Fianna Fáil by now saw distinct political as well as economic advantages in EEC membership, the latter were the ones pressed in the successful 1972 referendum campaign on EEC entry. So, far from threatening national sovereignty, EEC membership would strengthen the Irish economy and would accord the country a greater voice in European affairs.[37] It would also have the effect of lessening Ireland's trade dependence on Britain, although optimists also saw it as contributing to the attenuation of partition as national borders gradually lost economic significance.

One national problem which had refused to go away in the 1960s was partition. In January 1965, Seán Lemass took the country by surprise by travelling to Stormont to meet Terence O'Neill, the prime minister of Northern Ireland. Shortly afterwards, and at Lemass's prompting, the Nationalist Party abandoned its boycott of the Stormont parliament. He must have hoped that his personal initiative would presage a transformation in North–South relations, but many in Fianna Fáil saw it as an ill-judged gesture by a Dubliner who, despite his unimpeachable republican credentials, had never really grasped the depth of Northern Catholic alienation or understood the bitter impact of partition on the people of the Border counties.[38] So far from marking the beginning of a new era of constructive engagement, these exchanges produced no long-term results save to weaken O'Neill's position in his own party. Three years later, the North boiled over, and Ireland still endures the consequences.

Fianna Fáil and Foreign Affairs 1973–96

Fianna Fáil's approach to European policy since accession has been generally consistent. In government, the party has been a proponent of greater European integration, always provided that appropriate attention is given to Ireland's particular economic and social needs. Fianna Fáil MEPs have, like other Irish representatives, adjusted to the unusual milieu of the European Parliament in different ways: while some have concentrated their energies on policy areas of immediate concern to Ireland, others have become involved in broader issues of human rights, the strengthening of democracy in developing countries and the search for a more equitable distribution of power and resources between the First and the Third Worlds.

In government, Fianna Fáil promoted the operation first of European Political Co-operation (EPC) and since 1992 of a Common Foreign and Security Policy (CFSP). The one significant exception to this came in the wake of the Argentine invasion of the Falkland Islands in 1982, when the government joined its fellow EC countries in supporting the British position only with obvious reluctance. Fianna Fáil's strong though apparently uncoordinated reaction to the subsequent sinking of the General Belgrano, while it echoed public outrage at the great loss of life, made diplomatic sense only if framed as one element in a broader Irish policy that all EC states should aim quickly to relinquish their residual colonial holdings. That was not the case. While there was some silent sympathy for the Irish position amongst many other EC member states, where continued support for Britain mostly arose from the logic of EPC rather than from popular enthusiasm for her cause in the South Atlantic, in London, it was, naturally, viewed simply as a piece of atavistic Brit-bashing. Anglo-Irish relations took one of their periodic nose-dives.[39]

In opposition Fianna Fáil on occasion called for greater defence of Irish interests in Europe, and during the debate on the Single European Act in 1986, the party aired some doubts about the diminution of national sovereignty which that measure entailed. Once back in government, however, such reservations evaporated. Indeed, in December 1991 Fianna Fáil negotiated the far more radical Maastricht Agreement and campaigned vigorously for its acceptance in the consequent referendum in 1992. That referendum was largely dominated by wild claims about Maastricht's implications for military neutrality, anxieties which have since spread to Irish participation in UN operations involving the use of military force.[40] Neutrality remains an issue dogged by distortion on which Fianna Fáil, in common with other political parties, has appeared to haver, although it was a Fianna Fáil Minister for Foreign Affairs who announced the country's intention to apply for observer status at the Western European Union, and a Fianna Fáil Taoiseach who in 1993 argued that traditional neutrality had died with the Cold War and should not impede wholehearted Irish involvement in new European security structures designed to preserve peace.[41]

Conclusion

Fianna Fáil has been the dominant party in the formulation of Irish foreign policy since 1932. Its performance has been characterised by a combination of pragmatism and aspiration: partition has always gnawed at the party's heart even as its head has concentrated on the consolidation of the 26-county state's political and economic independence. A leading Irish political scientist has recently rather grudgingly ascribed its enduring electoral appeal to its capacity 'to perform somersaults on sensitive issues ... but still retain control of a populist political agenda'.[42] Fianna Fáil has, certainly, never been averse in opposition to striking more dramatic rhetorical poses on foreign policy issues than it adopts when carrying the burdens of office, but that is the way of electoral politics. The suggestion that it is uniquely opportunist in this only holds good, in foreign as in domestic affairs, for as long as no one examines the policy records of the other major parties. It is not necessary to probe very far into history to find far more astonishing gymnastic feats than Fianna Fáil's occasional wobbles on the high wire of neutrality. In 1948, a Fine Gael Taoiseach stood his party's defining policy on its head with his decision to declare a Republic and to leave the Commonwealth. Fine Gael's two partners in the present strongly pro-European integration Rainbow Coalition government originally opposed EEC membership root and branch, while in its previous incarnation Democratic Left was, as recently as 1990, still wedded to the nostrums of ultramontane Stalinism as the solution to all national and international ills.[43] Furthermore, two Labour TDs who proclaimed their intention in June 1992 of voting 'No' in the Maastricht Treaty referendum soon afterwards overcame their objections to the European integration process sufficiently to accept office in the Reynolds/Spring coalition government. The only member of Fianna Fáil to vote against the measure in the Oireachtas was, by contrast, expelled from the parliamentary party for his pains. In comparison with its political rivals, therefore, Fianna Fáil's foreign policy development since its foundation appears a model of almost Fabian consistency of purpose. Alone of all the mainstream political parties it adheres to the same aim it set itself in 1926, the achievement of Irish unity by peaceful means. Holy grail or will o' the wisp, that remains its core objective in the conduct of external relations.

Notes:

1. The terms 'foreign policy' and 'external policy' used here include Anglo-Irish relations and Northern Ireland issues, Article Two of the Constitution notwithstanding. Northern policy since 1969 is dealt with in Chapters 10 and 12.

2. For an examination of Fianna Fáil's first decades see Richard Dunphy, *The Making of Fianna Fáil Power in Ireland 1923–48* (Oxford: 1995) and Chapter 2 in this book.

3. For discussion of recent developments in Oireachtas treatment of foreign affairs, see Patrick Keatinge, 'Ireland's Foreign Relations in 1992, 1993, 1994', in *Irish Studies in International Affairs*, Vols. 4, 5 and 6 (1993, 1994 and 1995), and Eunan O'Halpin's 'Irish Parliamentary Culture and the European Union: Formalities to be Observed', in *National Parliaments and the European Union*, Philip Norton (Ed.) (London: 1996), pp. 124–35.

4. J.J. Lee, *Ireland, 1912–1985: Politics and Society* (Cambridge, 1989), p. 506; Patrick Keatinge, *The Formulation of Irish Foreign Policy* (Dublin, 1973), pp. 258.

5. For a concise discussion of developments in Anglo-Irish and in Anglo-Commonwealth relations arising from Fianna Fáil's victory in 1932, see Nicholas Mansergh, *The Unresolved Question: the Anglo-Irish Settlement and Its Undoing, 1912–1972* (London, 1991), pp. 282–3.

6. Richard Dunphy, *The Making of Fianna Fáil Power in Ireland 1923–1948* (Oxford: 1995), p. xvi.

7. John Bowman, *De Valera and the Ulster Question, 1917–1973* (Oxford: 1982), pp. 94–108; interview with the late Dr CS Andrews, June 1982; CS Andrews, *Man of No Property* (Dublin: 1982), pp. 230–1.

8. These were Aontacht Éireann and Independent Fianna Fáil. They were principally associated respectively with Kevin Boland, who resigned from the Cabinet at the time of the Arms Crisis, and Neil Blaney, who had been dismissed from office. For a trenchant exposition of his reasons for leaving Fianna Fáil in the wake of that embroglio, see Kevin Boland, *The Rise and Decline of Fianna Fáil* (Cork: 1982). On the immediate causes of Mr Lynch's ouster, see Eunan O'Halpin, 'Anglo-Irish security co-operation since 1969: a Dublin Perspective', *Conflict Quarterly* **10** (1990), 5–24.

9. Bowman, *De Valera and the Ulster Question*, pp. 94–108.

10. Keatinge, *The Formulation of Irish Foreign Policy*, p. 79. On the Cosgrave Government's successes in Commonwealth affairs, see Mansergh, *The Unresolved Question*, pp. 260–78. On its considerable achievements at the League of Nations, see Michael Kennedy, *Ireland and the League of Nations, 1919–1946* (Dublin, 1996), pp. 18–162.

11. Dermot Keogh, *Ireland & Europe, 1919–1948* (Dublin, 1988), p. 69.

12. The late T.P. O'Neill, quoted in Bowman, *De Valera and the Ulster Question*, p. 341.

13. See Chapter 13 in this book.

14. Andrews, *Man of No Property*, p. 119. Although a small number of former officials dismissed in the 1920s for refusing to swear allegiance to the Free State were reinstated and given posts abroad, they were not otherwise favoured. With one embarrassing exception, they performed without blemish. Keogh, *Ireland & Europe*, pp. 38–9.

15. Kennedy, *Ireland and the League of Nations*, pp. 167–243; Keogh, *Ireland & Europe*, p. 41.

16. Keogh, *Ireland & Europe*, pp. 57–60.

17. Peters to Batterbee (Dominions Office), 14 March 1932, quoted in Bowman, *De Valera and the Ulster Question*, p. 118.

18. Brendan Sexton, *Ireland and the Crown, 1922–1936: The Governor-Generalship of the Irish Free State* (Dublin, 1989), pp. 128–170.

19. Mansergh, *The Unresolved Question*, p. 294.

20. Bowman, *De Valera and the Ulster Question*, p. 122.

21. Bowman, *De Valera and the Ulster Question* pp. 190–96; J. Peter Neary and Cormac O'Grada, 'Protection, Economic War and Structural Change: the 1930s in Ireland', *Irish Historical Studies*, xxvii, No. 107, pp. 250–66, (1991).

22. Bowman, *De Valera and the Ulster Question*, pp. 160–4.

23. Eunan O'Halpin, 'The Army in Independent Ireland', in *A Military History of Ireland* Thomas Bartlett and Keith Jeffery (eds.), (Cambridge, 1996), pp. 416–8.

24. Document Number 2 provided de Valera with perhaps his worst parliamentary hours. See The Earl of Longford and Thomas P O'Neill, *Eamon de Valera* (London, 1970), pp. 172–9.

    For a clear indication of the development of republican thinking on the legitimacy of Britain's defence concerns about Ireland, compare the 'Message to the Free Nations of the World' issued by the Dáil at its first meeting on 21 January 1919, and 'Document Number Two' put forward by de Valera for ratification by the second Dáil on 4 Jan. 1922, both reproduced in Dorothy Macardle, *The Irish Republic* (1st Edn, London, 1937; Corgi Edn, 1968), pp. 850–1 and 886–91.

    Eunan O'Halpin, 'Intelligence and security in Ireland, 1922–45', *Intelligence and National Security* 5(1), 64–73 (1990).

25. Gerard Hogan and Clive Walker, *Political Violence and the Law in Ireland* (Manchester, 1989), pp. 177–8.

26. For the confidential views of opposition leaders, see the minutes of the Defence Conference established in June 1940. These are in National Archives of Ireland, S. 11896.

27. Breen to Briscoe, 18 April 1941, NA, DFA, p. 40.

28. Lee, *Ireland* 1912–1985, pp. 249–50.

29. Longford and O'Neill, *Eamon de Valera*, p. 411.

30. Liam C. Skinner, *Politicians by Accident* (Dublin, 1946), p. 175; Donal O'Drisceoil, 'Moral Neutrality: Censorship in Emergency Ireland', *History Ireland* (2), 46–50 (1996).

31. Bowman, *De Valera*, pp. 264–6.

32. Keogh, *Ireland & Europe*, pp. 201–5.

33. Longford and O'Neill, *Eamon de Valera*, pp. 434–5; Keogh, *Ireland & Europe*, p. 210.

34. The most recent analysis is in Gary Murphy, 'The Politics of Economic Realignment: Ireland, 1948–1964' (unpublished Ph.D thesis, Dublin City University, 1996).

35. Patrick Keatinge, *A Singular Stance: Irish Neutrality in the 1980s* (Dublin, 1984), pp. 24–7.

36. Patrick Keatinge, *The Formulation of Irish Foreign Policy*, pp. 32–3.

37. Patrick Keatinge, *A Singular Stance*, pp. 24–9.

38. Mansergh, *The Unresolved Question*, p. 344; Seamus Brady, *Arms and the Men* (Wicklow, 1971), p. 28.

39. Patrick Keatinge, *A Singular Stance*, p. 82. My own view is that public outrage at the loss of life on the Belgrano might more rationally have been directed at the Argentine naval authorities, who played with fire and suffered the consequences.

40. Michael Holmes, 'The Maastricht Treaty referendum of June 1992', *Irish Political Studies* 8, p. 107 (1993).

41. Patrick Keatinge, *Ireland's Foreign Relations in 1992*, 71–2.

42. Review by Paul Bew of Dunphy, The making of Fianna Fáil, *Irish Political Studies* 11, 194–5, (1996).

43. What is now the Democratic Left party has its roots in Official Sinn Féin of the early 1970s. Richard Dunphy, 'The Workers' Party and Europe: Trajectory of an idea', *Irish Political Studies* 7, p. 22–3, (1992).

12

Albert Reynolds:
Delivering the Impossible

by Martin Mansergh

'The fox knows many things. The hedgehog knows one big thing.'

So wrote an ancient Greek poet, as cited by the political philosopher Isaiah Berlin in an essay on nineteenth century Russian thinkers.

Albert Reynolds, the fifth Fianna Fáil leader and Taoiseach, will be remembered, above all, for his decisive role in the Irish peace process and for bringing about the IRA ceasefire of 31 August 1994, after 25 years of armed conflict in the North that cost over 3,000 lives and caused many more permanent injuries.

Albert Reynolds was a successful businessman before becoming a politician. Born in Roscommon in 1932, and educated, like Ray MacSharry, at Summerhill College, Sligo, he started his working life with Bord na Móna and then CIE. He continued to take an interest in the welfare of both companies. As Taoiseach, he was especially keen on the project for a new peat-burning electricity station in the Midlands and in ensuring the inclusion of the Sligo railway line for modernisation with EU funding under the second National Development Plan.

But he was soon seeking greater outlets for his entrepreneurial drive, and became involved in organising dances and arranging for bands to play at them. That world has been poignantly evoked in William Trevor's *The Ballroom of Romance*, but Albert Reynolds was at the business end of it. No doubt, the huge number of deals that he negotiated and the type of poker-playing that was often involved in the process influenced his approach to the more complex task of political negotiation and deal-making subsequently. One of the biggest concerts he organised took place in the Ulster Hall in Belfast. His later business career in a branch of the meat processing industry also brought him into contact with businessmen of a Unionist background, whom he regarded as

Charles Haughey on the 1981 General Election trail.

Standing Together: with Margaret Thatcher at a summit in the early 1980s.

Touring the west with Máire Geoghegan-Quinn and Mark Killilea, February 1982 General Election campaign.

The unveiling of the de Valera monument, Ennis, Co. Clare, October 1981.

Patron of the Arts: with the artist Robert Ballagh at an exhibition of landscape art in Dublin, September 1984.

With Mikhail Gorbachev at Shannon Airport, March 1990.

Sharing a joke with the late Cardinal Tomás Ó Fiaich, Irish College, Paris.

Albert Reynolds in relaxed mood as Taoiseach.

With John Major at 10 Downing Street at the signing of the Downing Street Declaration, 15 December 1993.

Returning to an all-party welcome at Leinster House after the 15 December 1993 signing of the Downing Street Declaration.

Partnership for Peace: Taoiseach Albert Reynolds with Gerry Adams and John Hume at Government Buildings seven days after an IRA ceasefire was declared on 31 August 1994.

At the 60th Árd Fheis, RDS, 1993.

Greeting Ógra Fianna Fáil delegates at the National Youth Conference with Ógra chairman, Mícheál Martin, Wexford, 1993.

Youthful Leader: Bertie Ahern (centre), the then chairman of Ógra Fianna Fáil, training for the Dublin marathon, October 1981.

Meeting some young friends at Merrion Square on Sunflower Day, 1995.

Addressing the Forum for Peace and Reconciliation with Fianna Fáil deputy leader, Mary O'Rourke TD and Executive Deputy President of South Africa, FW de Klerk, November 1995.

Acknowledging the applause for his first presidential address, Árd Fheis, RDS, November 1995.

With US President Bill Clinton at Leinster House, November 1995.

Meeting the Dublin Fianna Fáil's Women's Forum.

Organisers of the 1984 National Women's Conference: Mary Hanafin, Ann Ormonde, Ita Greene, Kate Hayes, Mary O'Rourke and Eileen Lemass.

Acquaintances Renewed: the late Brian Lenihan chatting with delegates at an Árd Fheis, early 1990s.

hard-headed and pragmatic, their political attitudes mainly influenced by the present economic advantages of the Union, including the large British subvention, so long as it lasted.

His business career, which was broadly successful, nevertheless had its ups and downs, sometimes with changing partners. He acquired first-hand experience of the difficulties faced by the small Irish entrepreneur, in dealing not just with the tax office but with the whole range of State authorities. He was consequently sympathetic in government to reducing red tape, and was hostile to endless public discussion with no action which he called 'paralysis by analysis', when criticising the tendency of the FitzGerald-led 1982–87 Coalition to engage in a seminar style of government tending to inertia. He understood at first-hand the impact of the 1992 currency crisis on sections of domestic industry primarily oriented to the British market. C & D Foods in Edgeworthstown, one of the few domestic manufacturers and exporters of pet food, now run by his son Philip, has created sustained employment for around 200 people in manufacturing, and he was one of very few in politics that could make that boast. The network of County Enterprise Boards created in 1992 was intended to fill the gap in State support for the local entrepreneur with a good idea, where the more glamorous multinational was perceived to be the main focus of attention of the State agencies. He also instituted the Taoiseach's Business Linkage Awards, designed to bring greater interaction between the multinational and indigenous sectors. He pushed through the 1994 tax amnesty, which raised about £240m, on the pragmatic grounds that it would raise substantial money for the State with some continuing benefit of a wider tax net, but also because it gave businessmen and the self-employed a final chance to put their tax affairs in order.

For a time, he also owned a local newspaper, the *Longford News*. This gave him an eye for the snappy headline and the message that could be conveyed by a photo. He was never slow in the publicity department, and in his early days in politics even the most seasoned politicians were amazed at the amount of personal coverage and photo-opportunities that he succeeded in generating locally at election time.

He came from an area, Longford–Roscommon, where traditional Republicanism was strong. In 1970, he regularly attended the Arms Trial in Dublin. But his understanding of Republicanism was always a pragmatic one. He did not believe that IRA violence in the North ever made sense, nor was he consciously influenced by revisionism either. As a minister, he was involved in North–South economic cooperation. Privately, he would have favoured a more pragmatic response to the Anglo-Irish Agreement in 1985, though he later avoided the approach of going over the heads of Unionists. He was sometimes praised by the then Taoiseach Garret FitzGerald, no doubt, to annoy Charles Haughey. Generally speaking, in Charles Haughey's day, the leader or the Taoiseach was the principal spokesperson on the North, and other ministers or colleagues rarely spoke on the subject, an exception in Albert Reynolds' case being the Seán Moylan Commemoration, when he was Minister for Finance. So there was little track record to inform expectations when he became Taoiseach.

In 1962, he married Kathleen Coen, who was from Ballymote. They had a large and happy family with two sons, Philip, running the family business and Albert now working as a banker in Wall Street, and five daughters: Miriam, a solicitor and taxation specialist; Emer, in personnel management; Leonie, a barrister; Cathy, a business executive and Andrea, an accountant. Kathleen was, and is, very close to Albert, a friend, partner and confidante, as well as a wife. Albert worked long hours, even when at home, and so they always enjoyed their sunshine holidays together abroad. His daughters took it in turn to provide an escort for him as Taoiseach at functions, particularly when his wife, who was recovering from a serious illness, was not able to attend.

In 1977, at the comparatively late age of 44, he was elected to the Dáil for Longford-Westmeath, ousting a sitting Fianna Fáil Deputy at convention. He campaigned on local issues, and largely ignored the 1977 Manifesto, of which he would later be very critical. By 1979, the Lynch Government was facing into serious difficulties. Albert Reynolds was one of Charles Haughey's key supporters for the leadership, seeing him as the best person to provide a firm, businesslike approach to government.

In December 1979, Charles Haughey appointed Albert Reynolds to be Minister for Communications, in charge of the Departments of Transport and Post and Telegraphs, only two and a half years after his entry into the Dáil. He rapidly made an impact as a dynamic and successful minister, who was able to get things done. Taking the plans prepared by his conscientious predecessor Pádraig Faulkner for the modernisation of our very underdeveloped telephone system, he set in train a billion pound programme of investment, which has probably made the single biggest difference to our competitiveness and particularly our attractiveness as a location for manufacturing industry and international services. With the encouragement of Brian Lenihan, who was Minister for Foreign Affairs, he had the Maynooth railway line reopened for commuter traffic at minimal cost. When he became Minister for Energy in

1982, he took the Whitegate Oil refinery into public ownership as an alternative to its abandonment at a bargain price, and he saw to it that the Dublin–Cork gas pipeline was constructed for a fraction of the original estimated cost. He drove such a good bargain for the supply of Kinsale Gas to the North, that Mrs Thatcher afterwards repudiated it, some time after Fianna Fáil had left office.

In Opposition in the mid-1980s, he went back to his business interests while remaining on the front bench. At Árd Fheiseanna and Ógra Fianna Fáil Conferences, he tended to finish with a barnstorming style of oratory, second only to Brian Lenihan. In 1987, he was appointed as Minister for Industry and Commerce. He has always represented Ireland well abroad, especially when speaking as one businessman to another. He enraged the oil companies in July of that year, when, after studying their various free gift packages, he instructed them to lower their petrol prices by 10p per gallon at the pumps. He was not long enough in that office to arrange a sale of Irish Steel to a German company Korf AG. In all these matters, he trusted his own business knowledge and judgement, and was not solely dependent on the advice of officials. He was a person who liked to get his information and to form an opinion through wide sounding and discussion. Sometimes to the distraction of his private office, who often had difficulty in tracking him down, he was the epitome of what Micheál MacLiammoir once called his one-man show, 'I must be talking to my friends'.

By far the most controversial episode of his period as Minister for Industry and Commerce in 1987–8 was his role in first unfreezing then increasing export insurance cover to Iraq, from which two companies Goodman International and Hibernia Meats were the principal beneficiaries. The Fianna Fáil Government of 1987 were determined to balance financial stringency by strong economic development policies. The Goodman Group, with which the previous Fine Gael–Labour Coalition had also a close relationship, had formed an ambitious plan for the development of the beef industry, which was welcomed and promoted by the incoming Government. But they were also pressing for renewed export insurance cover, a scheme dating from December 1982, which had been temporarily halted in 1986, because of concerns about repayment in the circumstances of the continuing Iran–Iraq War. International comparisons show that most Western countries were increasing their export cover to Iraq in the 1987–9 period. In promoting such exports through insurance cover, Albert Reynolds was following his own hunch, not more cautious official advice. It subsequently turned out that some of the meat for export came from intervention and was not even domestically sourced, though he did not know this at the time. But despite this dilution, increased beef sales to Iraq still contributed a sufficiently dynamic multiplier effect to drive cattle prices to their highest level to date in November/December 1988. Domestic competitors began to complain, and by early 1989 Goodman became engulfed in political controversy on more than one front, mainly on account of his alleged closeness to Charles Haughey, despite the fact that he had worked very closely with individual members of the previous Fine Gael–Labour Administration, as the Dáil was reminded in May 1991. Albert Reynolds' ministerial successors, Ray Burke and Desmond O'Malley, took steps to limit or reduce what they considered to be over-exposure. Cattle prices dipped considerably, when, as a combination of the Gulf War and animal health scares, Middle Eastern markets were largely cut off in 1990–1. The courts have yet to determine what the State's exposure on the policies actually amounts to.

In November 1988, when Ray MacSharry was appointed Ireland's EC Commissioner, Albert Reynolds took over as Minister for Finance. As minister, he was the beneficiary of the severe cost-cutting in the estimates from 1987 to 1989, and he used the scope to start reducing rates of personal taxation in the 1989 to 1991 budgets, including the 1992 budget, for which he did some of the preparatory work. The standard rate of tax was reduced from 35% to 27%, and the top rate from 58% to 48%. Despite this, he had little time for the gung-ho 'radical' tax reform policies of the PDs, the main beneficiaries of which would be the upper income earners, and he regularly crossed swords with the chairman of the Progressive Democrats, Michael McDowell, who could not wait to get back into the Dáil. Albert Reynolds believed in the maintenance of essential services, and in 1989 regarded the depth of the health cuts as out of keeping with the spirit of Fianna Fáil. In the first half of 1990, he presided over the Council of Finance Ministers as part of Ireland's EU Presidency. During an informal council at Ashford Castle, much headway was made in establishing the criteria for participation in economic and monetary union, the so-called Maastricht criteria. It was at this time that he forged a friendly relationship with John Major, then Chancellor of the Exchequer, who was shortly to become British Prime Minister in November 1990.

Albert Reynolds was not enamoured with the formation of a coalition with the Progressive Democrats, following the loss of four seats by Fianna Fáil in the 1989 General Election, even though with Bertie Ahern he was one of the negotiators with the PDs of the Programme for Government. In a party speech that autumn, he described the coalition as 'a temporary little arrangement'.

Relations between Charles Haughey and Albert Reynolds cooled, as the latter made himself the standard-bearer of those in the party who believed that under another leader Fianna Fáil could still win an overall majority and govern alone. Against a background of slower growth in the economy, the atmosphere deteriorated sharply in the autumn of 1991, with a succession of business and financial scandals that were being associated, albeit with little justification, with Fianna Fáil. There were very difficult and tense negotiations with the PDs over the renewal of the Programme for Government. Some young Fianna Fáil TDs put down a motion of no confidence for the parliamentary party, and when Albert Reynolds and certain other Ministers and Ministers of State felt they had no option but to support them, they were dismissed. There was little obvious political or ideological difference between the two camps. It was more a difference over what was best for the party at that time, in mid-term preparing for the next election. The motion, which mustered 22 votes, was heavily defeated, but after a controversial reshuffle in which one nominee Jim McDaid, at PD insistence on account of his presence at an anti-extradition rally outside a Court, was dropped, Charles Haughey's position remained no stronger. In some ways Albert Reynolds was fortunate to be on the backbenches for the following few months, as his wife Kathleen was shortly afterwards diagnosed as having cancer, and he was with her to support her over a critical period.

In January 1992 there was little confidence among Charles Haughey's opponents that he was about to step down. At the age of 59, Albert Reynolds did not have time on his side. In addition, Ray MacSharry's term as EC Commissioner was due to end in 12 months' time. Seán Doherty's new claims about the telephone-tapping of journalists in 1982, implicating the Taoiseach in it, though vigorously contested, were the catalyst for Charles Haughey stepping down when the PDs would no longer support him (though they rapidly began to regret his more accommodating style). There were two principal contenders for the leadership, who the previous autumn had been regarded as allies, Albert Reynolds and Bertie Ahern, though the latter had remained loyal to Charles Haughey, as well as Michael Woods and Mary O'Rourke, who also announced their intention to run. Bertie Ahern, who had the support of most of the ministerial office holders, and who was undoubtedly the preference of the outgoing Taoiseach, was not able to count a majority, and stood aside. Albert Reynolds, with the support of most of those who had remained on the backbenches throughout the Haughey era, then won an overwhelming victory.

Attempting to put a decisive line under the recent past, his inclination in most things was to do the opposite of his predecessor. Where Charles Haughey had been criticised by some of his own supporters for attempting to conciliate his opponents, by keeping most of them in Cabinet when he became leader, Albert Reynolds ruthlessly jettisoned experienced ministers and junior ministers who had benefited from the reshuffle of November 1991, in favour of those who had supported the No Confidence motion of the previous November, as well as the most prominent of those who had been left out in the cold during the previous thirteen years. For example, David Andrews replaced Gerry Collins in the Department of Foreign Affairs, Pádraig Flynn replaced Ray Burke at Justice, Máire Geoghegan-Quinn who had not been in Cabinet since 1987 but had been Minister for European Affairs became Minister for Transport. Noel Dempsey, the most outspoken of Charles Haughey's backbench critics, became Chief Whip. Dr John O'Connell achieved his long-term ambition of becoming Minister for Health. Charlie McCreevy became Minister for Social Welfare, where his attempts to adopt a more rigorous approach earned him much left-wing opprobrium. Mary O'Rourke, who had been a successful Minister for Education, but who was also Albert Reynolds' constituency colleague, was surprisingly demoted from Cabinet, and accepted, not without some soul-searching, a junior ministry, with responsibility for Labour and Consumer Affairs, where she made her mark. Bertie Ahern, with the look almost of a lone survivor straggling in shell-shocked from the front, remained Minister for Finance. John Wilson, a very experienced figure, became Tánaiste. During the early settling in period in 1992, Pádraig Flynn acted as mentor in conjunction with Tom Savage of Carr Communications. But the Government Press Secretary, Seán Duignan, from RTE, one of politics' most perceptive observers, was his closest and most faithful companion, and has left a lively account of his experience. The Government as a whole had a strong midlands and western component, with a Cabinet Minister from County Cork in Joe Walsh, who became Minister for Agriculture.

In his press conference after being elected leader on 6 February 1992, Albert Reynolds outlined three priorities. The first was to work for an end to the cruel Northern conflict, particularly in the light of the appalling atrocities of the previous few weeks. The second was to boost the economy and employment suffering from low growth caused by an international recession. The third was to create a modern society, progressive, enlightened and socially caring, a promise of a more liberal and less authoritarian approach both to social problems and to the whole conduct of government.

Events did their best immediately to sabotage the last aspiration, also cutting short any potential honeymoon that Albert Reynolds might have enjoyed. Within two days of taking office, he was confronted by a furore over the case, which had arisen during the *de facto* interregnum, of a suicidally disposed 14-year-old girl. She was a victim of child abuse, who had been restrained by an injunction, sought at the initiative of the Attorney General, to stop her from travelling to Britain to have an abortion, under the terms of the Pro-Life Amendment. While there were different opinions as to whether the Attorney General Harry Whelehan could have avoided acting as he did, Albert Reynolds had to cope with the political fall-out. While his own initial instincts would have been conservative (without being reactionary), in the course of a short period he became thoroughly familiar with the problem. He had a growing appreciation, particularly in the light of his wife's illness, that it was not at the margins a purely black and white issue, especially in medical terms, and that the overlapping moral, legal and medical concepts were not necessarily coterminous. In the end, the State, most unusually, funded the costs of a private appeal against a judgement that it had sought, which resulted in the Supreme Court deciding that in certain very restricted circumstances such as this a termination was consistent with the law and the Constitution. This created a furore on the other side, which was to have an impact for the rest of the year both in the context of the Maastricht referendum and three referendums in November on the right to travel, the right to information and the right to life. In the process, Albert Reynolds stood up to intense political pressures, dismissing Mr Justice O'Hanlon from the Presidency of the Law Reform Commission for outspoken comments on the abortion issue that have tended to be confessional in tone, and removing the whip from Senator Des Hanafin who was not happy with the watertight character of the Maastricht referendum and the protocol negotiated the previous December to protect a legal status quo that now seemed less certain, when he could not support Government legislation in the Seanad.

The Maastricht campaign took up most of the spring and summer, with the Taoiseach placing considerable emphasis on a new round of EU funding, expected at that time to provide abut £6 billion for infrastructural and employment programmes. High-minded Europhiles and indeed their opponents denounced the appeal as crude. But the result was again a resounding 'Yes', by 69% to 31%, despite the initial defeat of the Maastricht Treaty in Denmark two weeks earlier.

In the autumn of 1992, the Minister for Justice Pádraig Flynn produced a White Paper on marital breakdown, which for the first time committed the Government to holding a referendum on divorce after further underpinning legislative measures were put in place. There was further liberalisation of the law on contraception, which was not carried to its logical conclusion until the subsequent Fianna Fáil/Labour Government. A formula was worked out for a substantive referendum on abortion, which made an explicit and arguably invidious distinction between the life as opposed to the health of the mother. It fell between two stools, pleasing neither conservative nor liberal opinion, and particularly not most women's groups, and was defeated in the midst of the November election campaign. The lesson was learnt, when Máire Geoghegan-Quinn as Minister for Justice came to liberalise the law on homosexuality, a change that Albert Reynolds was most reluctant about, in a straightforward manner without discrimination, establishing a common age of consent at 17, a more liberal law than exists in the UK or the North. The referendum on the right to travel and the right to information passed, the latter still causing some difficulty for the party in Opposition in early 1995, when it came to be given legislative effect. While the course towards liberalisation had already been accepted by Fianna Fáil in government since the late 1980s, with enlightened social legislation on rape (including acceptance of the concept of marital rape), the abolition of illegitimacy and legislation on judicial separation, Albert Reynolds did give significant further impetus to the process. It was largely completed for the time being with the passage of the divorce referendum in 1995, with official Fianna Fáil support in Opposition and courageous leadership from Bertie Ahern, albeit with a wafer-thin majority.

While Albert Reynolds did not have the same keen interest in the arts as his predecessor, he was nonetheless supportive. He had a particular interest in films, and commissioned the study, which Michael D. Higgins as Minister for Arts, Culture and the Gaeltacht with the Taoiseach's support used to create the incentives that put Ireland on the map, as far as film-making was concerned.

Economic recovery was underway domestically when the currency crisis hit, triggered off in part by the strength of opposition Europe-wide to the Maastricht Treaty and the economic factors that in part underlay that opposition. Ireland, which had been very comfortable in the European Monetary System following British entry, was dealt a body blow, when on a black September day sterling was forced to devalue and quit the system. Pressures intensified on weaker currencies, culminating in an attack on the French franc the following summer, when the fluctuation bands were widened almost to the point where they lost much of their meaning. For four months, the financial authorities in Ireland fought a vigorous rearguard battle to protect the value of the currency, which soared above sterling, reaching about 109p at one point. But it was better to fight and lose than not to fight at all, though Albert Reynolds felt privately like Margaret Thatcher that in the long-term one could not buck the market. Eventual devaluation was possibly delayed by the political uncertainty of a general election and the lengthy interregnum before the formation of a new government. For once, however, all turned out for the best, as plunging interest rates following a substantial but well-judged devaluation ushered in the strongest and best sustained period of economic growth this country has yet experienced, averaging 6–7% of GNP per annum. In 1994, Bertie Ahern achieved the first current budget balance since Charles Haughey in 1967. Inflation remained very low, and exports, tourism and inward investment were buoyant. Employment was rising sharply, unemployment was falling, and substantial tax cuts in the 1994 Budget helped underpin a third National Programme, for Competitiveness and Work. In December 1994, no outgoing government had ever handed over to their successors an economy in which virtually all indicators were pointing so strongly in the right direction.

Politically, the Beef Tribunal loomed over 1992, with the focus of attention switched from Charles Haughey's role in approving the IDA-backed Goodman plan for the development of the beef industry to Albert Reynolds' role in approving insurance for beef exports to Iraq. Albert Reynolds on becoming Taoiseach was determined not to suffer any more ultimatums from the Progressive Democrats. Indeed, on one or two occasions he pushed decisions through against Progressive Democrat opposition. However, in the witness box in the Tribunal, in July, the Progressive Democrat Leader Des O'Malley described Albert Reynolds' ministerial decisions on export credit insurance as 'foolish, reckless and grossly unwise', which in the context of Coalition relations constituted an unprecedented attack, indicating the depths to which relations had sunk. While not sufficient to break the Coalition there and then, because it related to previous events and did not directly impugn the Taoiseach's integrity, Albert Reynolds bided his time till he appeared in the witness box.

In the meantime, the Supreme Court turned down the Tribunal's request for details of Cabinet discussions, laying down in the most trenchant terms their absolute confidentiality. While this was warmly approved of by the Taoiseach, it was felt by his critics to be at variance with the promise of more enlightened government. It has been suggested that Harry Whelehan's position as Attorney General, shaken after the 'X' case, was consolidated by his emphatic victory on Cabinet confidentiality.

The Taoiseach's appearance before the Tribunal was unprecedented, and something which he had considerable misgivings about. His evidence, no doubt after he had been weighed down by the best legal advice, was stilted and defensive, and lacked the free-flowing spontaneity, which is his more usual characteristic. More crucially, he described Des O'Malley's evidence to the Tribunal as 'reckless, irresponsible and dishonest', and doggedly declined to retract or modify the stark meaning of the statement. Making as he thought a not unusual political charge, and firmly convinced that the figures on the State's liability vindicated him, a matter on which the courts have still to adjudicate, he did not seem to appreciate, by whoever had cynically advised such a macho response, that this was bound to bring down the Government, which after some last-minute hesitation on the part of the Progressive Democrats it did.

The following general election was a nightmare. Fianna Fáil as in 1989 was blamed for causing an unnecessary election. The Taoiseach repeated a particular four-letter word in an interview, that on other occasions has caused neither John Major nor Bill Clinton the slightest difficulty, but it brought down the wrath of *The Irish Times* in one of its periodic fits of morality. The brief honeymoon with the Irish media that was a result of increased openness, including weekly briefings with the political correspondents, that had tended to get bogged down on issues relating to abortion, was well and truly over. Albert Reynolds, unlike his predecessor, was disposed to take legal action against newspapers, with considerable success, whenever his integrity was impugned. But for all his efforts he was unable to resist being transformed within the space of a few months by Fianna Fáil's long-standing critics into being in effect a Haughey Mark Two. At the end of the election, the final phase of which featured a strong counter-attack against a surging Labour Party, Fianna Fáil was down to 68 seats and dipped to 39%, the first time the first preference vote had fallen below 40% since the late 1920s. But Fine Gael also suffered a bad setback. Yet out of disaster was to come one of Albert Reynolds' greatest triumphs.

After the election there was little choice but to accept that Fianna Fáil had lost, and that it was up to others to try and form a government. The Fine Gael Leader John Bruton behaved as if his idea of a Rainbow Coalition with Labour and the Progressive Democrats was already a *fait accompli*. Labour in response, having won 19% of the vote and 33 seats, went off to construct a common platform with Democratic Left, which Labour then sent to other parties. Fianna Fáil was prepared for the paper and had its response ready, which winged its way back to Labour within a few hours, before serious negotiations with Fine Gael and the Progressive Democrats had a chance to get underway. All this had been carefully planned and concerted by Bertie Ahern with the Taoiseach's full approval and backing. The Fianna Fáil response made it clear that a coalition with Labour would be a partnership, unlike anything that had gone before, and indicated Fianna Fáil's openness and responsiveness to a great number of Labour ideas, such as the third banking force. Many in Fianna Fáil had long been aware of the political compatibility of Fianna Fáil and Labour, who had been allies back in 1932, and Brian Lenihan, who had little reason to love the PDs, had openly advocated this during the election campaign.

Over the weekend, the Taoiseach went to the European Council in Edinburgh to participate in negotiations on the size of the new Structural and Cohesion Funds. To everyone's astonishment, he was able to announce, on the assumption that Ireland's existing share was broadly maintained, that Ireland would receive £8 billion in Structural and Cohesion Funds from 1993 to 1999. Subsequent negotiations were to reduce that headline figure nearer to £7 billion, and while critics were to stress the embarrassment of the climbdown, the funds are and were still very important and represented a major achievement, and are even today an endless source of recycled ministerial good news announcements. Albert Reynolds remains confident that the actual sum that will be received in the end will be around £8 billion.

With that success under his belt, Albert Reynolds returned to Dublin, met Dick Spring, and was able to convince him that a Fianna Fáil–Labour partnership government was a serious proposal, despite some limited opposition in Fianna Fáil. Serious negotiations ensued, resulting in the most comprehensive and impressive Programme for Government yet seen. The new Government comprised nine Fianna Fáil members and six Labour ones, with Dick Spring establishing an Office of the Tánaiste as well as taking over Foreign Affairs. Unknown to the public, Albert Reynolds had also briefed Dick Spring confidentially and in some detail on his secret Northern peace initiative.

127

When he took office in February 1992, Albert Reynolds regarded the continued killings in the North after more than twenty years as an affront to humanity. He resolved at his first meeting with John Major to try and bring that violence to an end. He reversed the long-standing habit of seeking a political settlement first, in the hope that it might bring an end to violence. Charles Haughey briefed him on the state of his initiative with John Hume. Albert Reynolds pushed on the drafting work on what he publicly called 'a formula for peace', which addressed some of the stated reasons for the conflict, such as recognition of the right of national self-determination, which had to be consistent with the principle of consent as contained in the Anglo-Irish Agreement. A key element was also the willingness of the Irish Government to establish an Irish Convention or Forum, in the context of an end to violence. He worked from the beginning in close understanding with John Hume, and met from time to time the intermediary between John Hume and Gerry Adams, Fr Alex Reid of the Clonard Monastery.

Given his age, Albert Reynolds did not expect even in the most favourable conditions to be Taoiseach for a long period. He was more concerned to achieve something substantial than to stay in office for its own sake. He sometimes said that he did not care if he were the shortest term Taoiseach ever. The usual 'prudential' calculations did not apply when he decided that it would be justified to renew direct contact between a member of his office and Sinn Féin in order to pursue the peace initiative further, from the autumn of 1992.

The general election result threatened to cut the whole initiative short, as Sinn Féin saw little point in pursuing it with a Rainbow Coalition. The formation of the Partnership Government gave it a renewed and enhanced lease of life with the prospect of its being supported by both parties in government.

In 1992 there was a second round of the Brooke–Mayhew talks, with an Ulster Unionist delegation led by James Molyneaux coming for the first time to Dublin Castle, and with the Irish Government debating across the table in Belfast and London with the DUP as well. While important progress was made, especially in relation to clarifying Strand 1 or internal structures, discussions on relationships within the island of Ireland, which John Hume saw as the most crucial element, were more difficult and polemical. No party or government were really willing to show their hand. The Ulster Unionist Party were subsequently to claim that none of the often promised generosity was on display from the South. While they put forward at the last minute a sketchy inter-Irish Relations Committee, the Government stated their conditional willingness to alter Articles 2 and 3 of the Constitution, but expected as a *quid pro quo* repeal or amendment of Section 75 of the Government of Ireland Act, 1920, which Albert Reynolds cleverly juxtaposed from his first press conference.

Despite the change in government and a stronger declared willingness to alter Articles 2 and 3 as part of a balanced constitutional accommodation within the context of an overall settlement, Unionists were not interested over the next three years in resumed participation in direct talks.

In June 1993, after further efforts to improve the text of the draft declaration had failed, Albert Reynolds decided to go with the text, more or less as it had been since the previous June, which had the qualified support of the Republican Movement and the full support of John Hume. It represented the outer limit of what was possible, consistent with Ireland's international obligations. While the British Prime Minister found it interesting, and was willing to have it examined further, it was far from clear whether the British Government would be willing to negotiate on the Declaration. In the course of the autumn of 1993, the British Government in fact moved heaven and earth to wean Albert Reynolds off his peace initiative, but without success. They found him (and John Hume) fixated and unwavering on the opportunity for peace. Each time, he was told it was impossible to proceed, he replied that if necessary he would pursue the initiative without them, and would not shield them from international criticism. He accepted that peace terms could not simply be dictated by what was presented in public as a Hume–Adams initiative (although the Irish Government had always been centrally involved), and that the two Governments had to take a broader view. But it is a complete myth that strong feeling at the Fianna Fáil Árd Fheis in favour of Hume–Adams in any way affected or was required to strengthen Albert Reynolds' unalterable determination to pursue the peace initiative with the utmost vigour. At that Árd Fheis on 6 November 1993 he spoke of the 'walls of wilted flowers', and threw down the gauntlet, 'Who is afraid of peace?' He expressed his conviction that 'we can make the beginning of peace a reality, before this year is out', adding with his own characteristic and prophetic homespun wisdom, 'opportunity comes to pass but not to pause'.

Eventually, in early December 1993, the British Government sat down seriously to negotiate on the Joint Declaration. The resulting Downing Street Declaration on 15 December 1993 between the two Prime Ministers incorporated and enlarged the spirit of the original Irish initiative. The British repeated that they had no selfish strategic or economic interest. It was even-handed, but the core of it was the recognition of the Irish right to self-determination balanced by the principle of concurrent consent, and the declared willingness of the British Government to work hard for a new agreement between all the people of Ireland. It was made explicit that all parties renouncing violence could participate in talks on the way ahead. This simple equation was driven home by the British Prime Minister again and again over the following months, that Sinn Féin should renounce violence to take part in talks.

Between December 1993 and August 1994, Albert Reynolds embarked on a huge task of persuasion in public and in private. He never tired of giving interview after interview on the peace process to the Irish, British and American media. He made a number of major speeches – to the Irish Association on 10 January 1994 making clear his commitment to the equality agenda, and to the UCD Law Society on how the right to self-determination applied in international law and in practice to partitioned countries. He was willing to clarify every point that was raised. He was also willing to engage in confidence-building measures. The first, indeed, had been the previous summer, when despite enormous internal and external political and official pressure he had refused to stop President Robinson from travelling to West Belfast, where she would meet Gerry Adams, among many others. In January 1994, in creative alliance with the libertarian Minister for Arts, Culture and the Gaeltacht, Michael D. Higgins he lifted the ban on interviews with Sinn Féin under Section 31 of the Broadcasting Act. He backed the short-term visa for Gerry Adams to visit the United States in the face of intense British anger. All through this period, he had the full and active support of the most positively influential US Ambassador ever, Jean Kennedy-Smith.

If he was firm with the British, he was equally firm with Republicans. He strongly criticised the folly of the Heathrow bombing while he was in the United States in March. He rejected the 48-hour ceasefire after Easter. He made it plain that he would not accept a time-limited ceasefire, and that he would have to form a judgement on whether there was any realistic possibility of peace by the end of the summer. He was not willing to move away from the careful balance of the Downing Street Declaration.

Much to the surprise of the British Government and nearly everyone else, a complete and unqualified ceasefire was declared on 31 August 1994 and a definitive commitment was given by the IRA to the success of the democratic peace process. Seven days later, Albert Reynolds met with John Hume and Gerry Adams on the steps of Government Buildings. In a Joint Statement afterwards they recognised that Unionist agreement was needed for any peace settlement to be viable. A month later, the Loyalists responded with their ceasefire on 13 October 1994.

In the first few weeks, events moved rapidly, as Albert Reynolds moved to build and consolidate the peace and to draw a line under the physical force tradition in Irish politics. The Forum for Peace and Reconciliation with all Southern parties, and many Northern parties, except the Unionist ones, assembled in Dublin Castle under the chairmanship of Judge Catherine McGuinness, heard a wide range of evidence and drew up a report. Increased international aid was made available from the EU, the US and Australia.

An announcement was made that all Border roads would be reopened. Arrangements were made to start the release of Republican prisoners from Portlaoise. Constant pressure was maintained by Albert Reynolds on the British Government to move ahead, though they were anxious to maintain the confidence of the Unionists that no secret deal had been done. Everywhere Albert Reynolds now went, he was treated with enormous respect, in Australia and New Zealand and in the United States, where he had already established a cordial relationship with President Clinton. John Major could not ignore him, as he had delivered what had seemed impossible. He had kept faith with Republicans and Loyalists in the North, and had not misled them. Lives were being spared in Northern Ireland at the rate of about 80–90 for each year the ceasefire would last. Everyone, both Unionists and Nationalists, appreciated the benefits.

Substantial progress was being made towards completing the historic Framework Document in the summer and autumn of 1994. When published in February 1995, this was to contain a powerful statement of equality, the outline of a balanced constitutional accommodation, in which the principle of self-determination balanced by consent took centre place, superseding territorial claims of jurisdiction, and, most importantly from Albert Reynolds' point of view, an outline of North–South bodies with executive, harmonising and consultative powers and functions, which would be vital to an agreement, though there was no question of imposing these without the consent of the people of Northern Ireland.

Then political disaster struck. While the Fianna Fáil–Labour Partnership Government was an effective one, and more harmonious for most of its duration than the FF-PD Coalition, Labour had suffered a significant drop in its popularity, partly perhaps because of resentment in some quarters of its original decision to go into government with Fianna Fáil to get more of its programme implemented, but also because of the elaborate back-up it seemed to require. Labour were also uneasy about the increasing politicial dominance being established by Albert Reynolds, mainly as a result of the peace process, in which Dick Spring played an important and honourable part. While the Taoiseach and the Tánaiste initially had good working relations, a series of minor controversies affecting Fianna Fáil members of Government, where the Opposition were shrill in attack and alleging conflicts of interest, coupled with the impending Beef Tribunal report, began to create strain. When the bulky report came out, the Taoiseach, greatly to the annoyance of the Labour leadership, immediately claimed vindication. More accurately, it vindicated his integrity, but it did not express any particular approval of his ministerial decisions on export insurance cover. The affair blew over, and the Dáil debate was overshadowed by the declaration of the IRA ceasefire. The Beef Tribunal, which cost the State, directly through lawyers' fees and indirectly through EU fines, a vast amount of money, failed to find, despite a massive trawl, any evidence of political corruption which was its main *raison d'être,* and it proved a hugely expensive way of trying to stand up loose allegations or insinuations by Opposition parties in 1989.

The Labour leader, who was a barrister by training, dug his heels in over the appointment of the Attorney General Harold Whelehan to the plum judicial position of President of the High Court. The dissension became public in the latter half of September 1994, and there was an ominous stand-off. Nobody believed the issue was worth going to the brink over, and therefore expected the other party to back down. After Labour backbenchers began to express public misgivings, an accommodation was apparently reached at Baldonnell, which would have reformed the system of judicial appointments, while allowing the Whelehan appointment to go ahead after a period of grace. But a fortnight later, it emerged that a warrant for the extradition of a paedophile priest Fr Brendan Smyth had been unaccountably delayed in the Attorney General's Office for several months. This effectively reopened discussion of the suitability of the appointment, but Albert Reynolds remained determined that his understanding at Baldonnell be implemented. On Friday 11 November, Labour withdrew from Cabinet, when Albert Reynolds persisted in forcing through the appointment, regardless of its effect in undermining the spirit of partnership government. That same day, the Government lost two by-elections in Cork, having lost another two the previous summer. It was assumed that Labour would not want an election. But unnoticed by most, the arithmetic of the Dáil had been altered, and now made viable Labour's original preference for a Rainbow Coalition consisting of Fine Gael, Labour and Democratic Left, to which Fine Gael had now dropped its objections.

In a mood of rising public hysteria about alleged protection of a child-abusing priest, the resolution of the crisis ostensibly depended on the Taoiseach's statement to the Dáil on the handling of the Brendan Smyth case. A new Attorney General, Eoghan Fitzsimons, claimed to have discovered another case, which undermined the reason given by his predecessor for the delay. But neither that reason nor its invalidity were referred to by the Taoiseach in the Dáil, partly because he did not want to endorse excuses for the delay, partly because he was awaiting final clarification of the legal position, after Mr Whelehan's views had been sought, and perhaps also through an oversight. While Fianna Fáil and most Labour Ministers sought desperately to find a formula to patch up their differences, the Labour leader was stony and implacable. Even when the Taoiseach was prepared to make abject amends, Dick Spring's agreement to go back into government lasted less than an hour on Wednesday morning and was not worth the paper it was written on. Ostensibly, the Government broke down over an alleged lack of transparency over an arcane legal point. In reality, trust and partnership between the two leaders had broken down. There was a clash between two strong personalities, neither accustomed to giving way once challenged, and between differing priorities. As in November 1992, Albert Reynolds tended to rely heavily on his colleagues when it came to deciding how to handle the crisis.

With Labour pulling out of government, Albert Reynolds did not seek a dissolution, which the president had the power to refuse, but instead on the following day resigned as Taoiseach and as party leader. Warm tributes on account of his role in the peace process were paid to him in the Dáil. There was incredulity abroad. Labour, having done the rounds of the other parties, and failed once more to lever Dick Spring in as rotating Taoiseach, reverted to negotiating a full agreement with Fianna Fáil under their new leader Bertie Ahern, then pulled out at the last minute, because of an alleged new revelation about Fianna Fáil ministers' 'knowledge' of a precedent to the Smyth case. Even by the time of the Sub-Committee, this pretext was an embarrassment to the Labour Party, but in the meantime they had successfully strengthened their position in the Rainbow Coalition, holding both the key posts of Finance and Foreign Affairs. The honour and integrity of Fianna Fáil ex-ministers was effectively vindicated in the subsequent Dáil Sub-Committee set up to investigate the affair, when it was too late to make much difference.

While the affair represented a tragic miscalculation, a trial of strengths that went drastically wrong, and that brought to a premature end one of Fianna Fáil's most successful runs in office, it was grossly irresponsible to bring down the Government two and a half months into a still vulnerable peace process over issues of such little intrinsic national importance. The peace process lost a driving force, and no one in the Rainbow Coalition was able to fill Albert Reynolds' shoes.

The peace process stalled in March 1995, after Unionist rejection of the Framework Document, when the British sought to introduce upfront partial decommissioning as a new precondition and to disqualify Sinn Féin from participation in all-party talks. Sinn Féin were not admitted to talks as they had been promised, and Albert Reynolds was no longer in a position as Taoiseach to insist forcefully, if necessary, that public promises be honoured. An atmosphere of crisis developed by the following autumn. The IRA ceasefire broke down in February 1996. While Albert Reynolds' opinion continued to be sought by the media on these untoward developments, he no longer held the levers of power or had the responsibility of office. In government, he had shown an unfailingly sure instinct on the North, which was not easy to replace. His successors came to it with quite different instincts. The confidence and euphoria over peace had gone, and it has proved increasingly difficult to pick up the pieces, even when the right moves are made, often twelve months too late. Nevertheless, the hope and inspiration of a 17-month peace will not be readily abandoned by people who now know that there is a better future than the violence of 25 years, and the zero-sum game, in which in fact there are only losers and no winners. But the momentum for peace, which Albert Reynolds, working with John Hume and Gerry Adams, as well as John Major, and many others did so much to establish, is so strong that it is bound sooner or later to prevail decisively. The legacy of the peace process, as far as Fianna Fáil is concerned, is in the hands of its leader Bertie Ahern, who has tried very hard even from Opposition, to rescue it in a spirit of critical bipartisanship. Using his background as a conciliator, his role particularly in government will be to help restore and rebuild confidence in it.

13

The de Valera Papers – A Signpost

by Breandán Mac Giolla Choille

'All history is a record of man's efforts to realise ideals... We in Ireland are suffering bitterly from the false ideals that have been imposed on us... We retain, however, great reserves of spiritual strength and true idealism'.[1]

Eamon de Valera
5 February 1929

The very least that can be said of the papers of Eamon de Valera (1882–1975) is that they must be of considerable interest to all who are interested in Irish history and in the genesis of Fianna Fáil. As *prima facie* evidence to support that statement, the reader is invited at this point to read the four sample documents selected by the archivist and reproduced in these pages. They show him writing as a schoolboy, as a political leader and as a statesman.

The aspects of the papers of Eamon de Valera discussed briefly within the tight exigencies of space here will be: character of the papers; their extent and years covered; the content of the documents and their arrangement; work completed by the archivist; access to the papers and their significance; and finally the question: how the work on them can be brought to completion.

These papers are sometimes referred to as the private papers of Eamon de Valera. This is both correct and incorrect. They do contain many papers which are personal to de Valera. Examples would be papers relating to his birthdays,[2] to Christmas cards received,[3] to his eye operation,[4] to the 'X ray taken from Eamon de Valera's leg showing splinters of bullets still there from time of shooting and arrest at Ennis 15 August 1923',[5] and to the death of his son Brian in February 1936.[6] The papers of a strictly private or personal character, however, do not constitute more than a small percentage of the vast number of documents in the collection. In general the de Valera papers are mainly to be regarded as the papers of a political leader who was, in turn, President of Sinn Féin (1917–26), President of Dáil Éireann, leader of the opposition to the

Treaty of 1921 and of Cumann na Poblachta, head of a republican government from October/November 1922, President of the Fianna Fáil party (1926–59), Head of Government and Taoiseach (1932–59 with gaps[7]) and President of Ireland (1959–73). Most of the papers deal with his life as a political leader and are especially numerous and important for the period ending in the formation of Fianna Fáil.[8]

Covering the entire span of the life of Eamon de Valera, the collection numbers approximately 60,000 items.[9] They may be broadly classified as: (1) documents, written, printed and published; (2) published books and pamphlets;[10] (3) other information media. The documents comprise: letters and correspondence,[11] memoranda and reports, notes formal and informal, scripts for speeches and broadcasts,[12] election material and results, minute books,[13] press statements and interviews, diaries[14] and newspapers (bound and loose copies). Information is also preserved to a relatively minor extent in other media. The main items in this classification are: tape-recordings,[15] dictabelts,[16] films and microfilms, a record album, and photographs.[17]

The subjects covered in the papers are intimately bound up with the career of de Valera as outlined above; nevertheless some further indication of their content can be shown by mentioning some other subjects dealt with in files containing numerous items. Among these are the following: League of Nations;[18] 1937 Constitution;[19] visits and tours abroad by de Valera;[20] Anglo-Irish relations;[21] and the Emergency period (including neutrality).[22] In the collection as a whole individual files range in content from a single document to hundreds. Some examples of the large files in the 1922–23 period may usefully be cited here: Fine Ghaedheal 1922;[23] 'Misc. Letters to de Valera 1922;[24] Local Government 1923;[25] Home Affairs 1922–23;[26] and '1924 Letters to Editor, SF.'[27]

One other important feature of the de Valera papers is that they contain letters and other documents written by a large number of his contemporaries. For example, they contain letters of Michael Collins which have not been seen in print. Another example concerning his political friends and opponents are the Stack papers. Accessioned with the de Valera papers and showing the breadth of their scope were letters written by his many friends to Austin Stack while he was in prison in Belfast and Manchester, 1918–19.[28]

It is clear that at least four persons were engaged at different times to arrange the papers before they reached archival hands. None appears to have been aware of or influenced by the arrangement work of their predecessors with the end-result that there is no uniformity in the arrangement as a whole. The original plan seems to have been chronological from 1916 to the founding of Fianna Fáil. Later helpers arranged the papers by broad subject-categories and still later by devoting files to individuals. Finally the arrangement appears to have returned to the broadly chronological treatment during the presidential years. While in the immediate possession of de Valera the papers were kept in file-covers crammed into four large filing cabinets comprising 16 drawers and also in a number of boxes full of single topics such as the 1937 Constitution.[29] There is a considerable degree of overlapping in the titling of files[30] and many are vague[31] and repetitive. The over-riding consideration in the primary non-archival arrangement was probably ease of reference and secretarial day-to-day requirements to provide the relevant papers on request by Eamon de Valera. For a variety of reasons dictated by archival practices and principles it was determined to respect the original order and place reliance on the retrieval methods which the archivist would in time employ to enable historical research to proceed with maximum facility.

The archival work on the de Valera papers extended over 10 years.[32] The initial task was to survey the entire collection. As this was being done, physical first-aid was rendered to the papers and files were numbered 1 to 2634. A comprehensive list was drawn up using existing titles.[33] The cumulative effect of these steps enabled the archivist to formulate the best method of producing the necessary finding aids.[34] The final decision was that nothing less than a document by document listing or calendar would be adequate. The calendar so produced gives for each single file examined the following items of information: existing title; years covered; number of items; summary of the contents of the file; entry document by document in chronological order giving details of writer and addressee as well as excerpts quoting the authentic words used in order to indicate the main topics discussed; and details of number of pages, signatures, initials, whether manuscript/holograph, typescript or printed. The calendar thus compiled ran to approximately 2 million words (7,000 A4 pages) at the time the work was terminated.[35] The calendar was written with a view to publication and the archivist is grateful to those who helped him by devoting their skills and energy to the huge task of caring adequately for the unique papers under discussion.[36]

Access to the calendared papers of Eamon de Valera at present (1996) housed in the Franciscan Library Killiney can be gained by written application to Father Librarian in Dún Mhuire, Seafield Road, Killiney.[37] He will inform intending readers about the current position in regard to access to files. Four official openings of sections of the papers took place between June 1987 and April 1994 and they were so widely reported in the media on each occasion that intending research scholars should enrich themselves by reading the contemporary newspapers.[38]

The de Valera papers as source material are with three possible exceptions largely unexploited. They were extensively used in the still outstanding work of Dorothy Macardle[39] and in the biographies of de Valera by the Earl of Longford and the late Thomas P. O'Neill and also by him and Pádraig Ó Fiannachta.[40]

Until this goldmine of documentation is systematically and thoroughly exploited for primary source-material, the full authoritative life of Eamon de Valera will remain unwritten. Not only that but these same papers provide essential information for many scores of biographies of contemporaries of de Valera that remain unwritten and call for well-deserved attention. Worthy of mention in this regard are, as examples, Harry Boland, William T. Cosgrave, George Gavan Duffy, Frank Aiken, Kathleen O'Connell, Molly Childers, Katherine Hughes and civil servants John Joseph Walshe and John Hearne. From these papers much could be added to published biographies of persons such as Sinéad de Valera, Bob Brennan, Máire Nic Shuibhne/Mary Mac Swiney, and Austin Stack. These papers would be essential for the study of many political and other subjects such as the peace efforts in Civil War times, 1922–23; Cumann na Poblachta; the early history of foreign affairs under Dáil Éireann 1919–22; Cumann na mBan; de Valera's early advocacy of the need to establish a daily republican newspaper. In a word there is research work for many years to come in this resource of inestimable national value.

This national resource should not be left with incomplete archival attention and listing. A comparatively small sum[41] would be required to complete the outstanding percentage (approximately 25%) in the same manner as employed hitherto. The contents richly deserve to be made available to a wide and interested public through publication of an adequate guide with illustrations and also of the calendar already available as edited typescript computer print-outs. In the archivist's opinion the necessary resources should be provided, if no benefactors come forward, out of public funds. Eamon de

Valera, who served Ireland's needs for so many years of his long public life and gave his papers generously for the use of all, surely deserves generosity from this generation no less than the amount needed to complete the work on his gift of incomparable archival value.

Achoimhre:

1. D'fhág Eamon de Valera saibhreas aircíveanna thar áireamh mar oidhreacht ag an náisiún nuair a bhronn sé orainn breis agus 60,000 cáipéis ag baint lena shaol féin agus le saol na hÉireann lena linn. Tá anseo 4 samplaí díobh a thaispeánann de Valera mar dhalta scoile, mar cheannaire polaitíochta lasmuigh de na Ceithre Cúirteanna, 1922, agus mar státaire ag scríobh chuig Príomh-Aire na Breataine, 1939.

2. Sa bhronntanas seo tá cáipéisí ceannaire polaitíochta a bhí i mbéal an phobail ó 1917 go dtí 1975.

3. Tá 2634 comhad de pháipéir sa bhailiúchán. Comhaid mhóra a lán acu agus tuilleadh agus 200 cáipéis iontu. Ina measc tá raidhse ábhair i nGaeilge.

4. Ar na cáipéisí is luachmhaire iontu tá litreacha, nótaí, meamraim, agus ailt ina láimh féin ag Eamon de Valera faoi na hábhair is mó trácht lena linn – an Conradh le Sasana, 1921; bunú Fhianna Fáil, 1926; Bunreacht na hÉireann, 1937, mar shamplaí.

5. Tá caileandar (liostaí de na cáipéisí, item ar item) ina bhfuil 2 mhilliún focal agus 7,000 leathanach A4 réitithe ag an aircíveoir seo agus fáil air san ionad taisce.

6. Faoi láthair (1996) tá na cáipéisí ar oscailt don phobal ach scríobh roimh ré chuig an Leabharlannaí Oirmh., Leabharlann na bProinsiasach, Cill Iníon Léinín, Contae Átha Cliath. Go dtí seo is beag úsáid a baineadh as an saibhreas seo ag staraithe agus ag beathaisnéiseoirí.

7. Is trua nach bhfuil an liostáil críochnaithe, de cheal airgid. Is é is lú atá ag dul do chuimhne Eamoin de Valera an obair a chríochnú ar na cáipéisí a bhronn sé go fial ar an náisiún.

8. Guíonn an t-aircíveoir seo a chaith deich mbliana ag obair ar na cáipéisí rí-luachmhara seo go gcuirfear ar fáil an t-airgead (beag – timpeall £75,000 – i gcomórtas lena bhfíorluach) chun an liostáil a chríochnú agus chun na páipéir seo le hEamon de Valera a bhuanchoimeád do na glúnta romhainn.

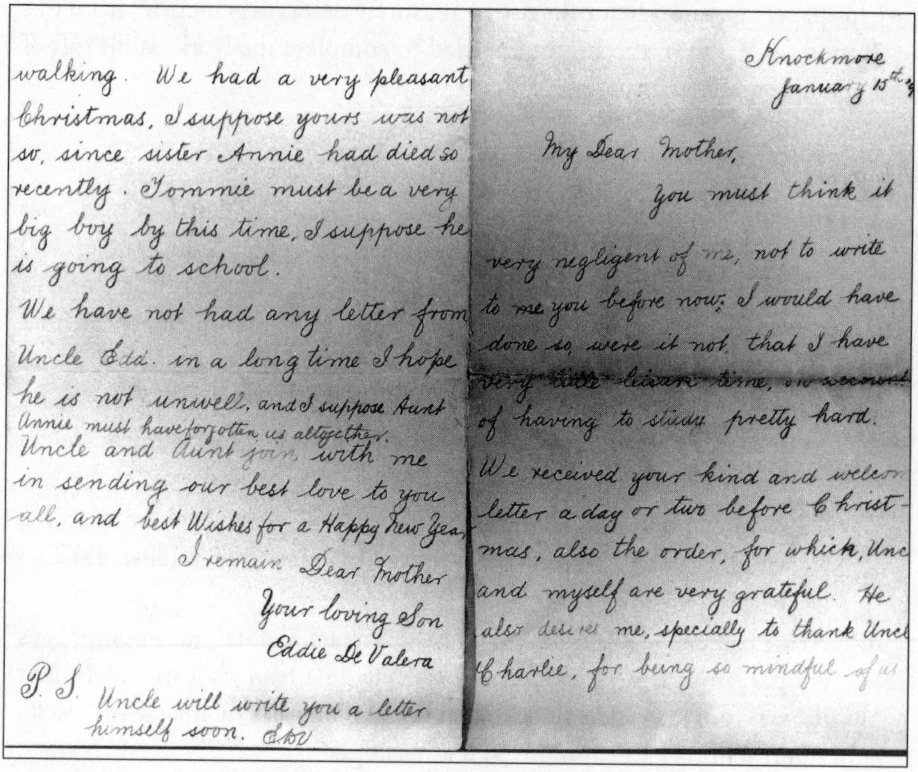

Knockmore
January 15th

My Dear Mother,

You must think it very negligent of me, not to write to me you before now; I would have done so, were it not that I have very little leisure time, on account of having to study pretty hard.

We received your kind and welcome letter a day or two before Christmas, also the order, for which, Unc and myself are very grateful. He also desired me, specially to thank Uncle Charlie, for being so mindful of us

walking. We had a very pleasant Christmas, I suppose yours was not so, since sister Annie had died so recently. Tommie must be a very big boy by this time, I suppose he is going to school.

We have not had any letter from Uncle Ed. in a long time I hope he is not unwell, and I suppose Aunt Annie must have forgotten us altogether. Uncle and Aunt join with me in sending our best love to you all, and best Wishes for a Happy New Year.

I remain Dear Mother
Your loving Son
Eddie De Valera

P.S. Uncle will write you a letter himself soon. EdV

This four-page letter from Knockmore in Bruree parish was written at the age of 15 years by Eddie de Valera eight months before going on scholarship to Blackrock College. He thanks his mother for her present at Christmas which 'came in very appropriately, as it helped to get me a portion of the books which I required at the re-opening of school.' (Quoted from p. 3, not shown here.) He refers to his uncle Pat Coll and to 'Uncle Charlie' [Wheelwright] whom his mother married after the death of Vivion de Valera. Tommy, the big boy, was his stepbrother, Rev. Thomas Wheelwright CSSR. Uncle and Aunt were Pat and Kate Coll in Knockmore. His stepsister Annie had died in 1897. At school (p. 3) there was 'very keen competition between us boys, though the most of them are better circumstanced than I am, as they stay in town [Charleville/ Rathluirc]'. He used the form Eamon from 1908 when he joined the Gaelic League (*Eamon de Valera Centenary*, Prof. J.L. Synge FRS, p. 15, 1982).

This is a draft in his own hand of a two-page statement by Eamon de Valera four days after the bombardment of the Four Courts by the forces of the

Statement from Eamon de Valera

The Republic of Ireland has not been disestablished

The so called "Provisional Government" is not the government. The legitimate Government of Ireland is Dáil Éireann which is the Government of the Republic. The Republic has not been disestablished.

Since January last the President and ministry of Dáil Éireann relying on alien powers have in their election acts ignored the regular legal and constitutional procedure and acted in an arbitrary manner — assuming dictatorial powers for which they should be held answerable in the Supreme Courts of the Republic. These irregularities have led directly to the present situation.

The men who are fighting to uphold the Republic are soldiers who took an oath of allegiance to the Republic and are acting literally in accordance with its explicit terms and the intention with which they took it.

Eamon de Valera
July 2. 1922.

Provisional Government established following the signing of the Articles of Agreement between Great Britain and Ireland on 6 December 1921. The Four Courts buildings (including the wrecked Public Record Office of Ireland and its contents) were abandoned by the republican garrison of 200 on 30 June 1922.

This one-page memorandum of 16 June 1923 was sent to Leopold H. Kerney

No. 1

June 16th, 1923.

Memo to L.H.K.
From the President.

I understand a League of Nations Congress is to
be held in Vienna on June 23rd, at which delegates from all
branches of the "League of Nations Union" will speak.

I wonder could you go yourself to Vienna for that
week, taking with you Miss K. O'Brennan for publicity work,
or, if you thought better of it, send Miss O'Brennan to do
propaganda unofficially. We would be responsible for all
reasonable expenses.

Please let me know if you can manage this and
let me have a rough estimate of the expenses.

The general idea underlying the propaganda would
be something like this:

A League of Nations to be in a position to effect
anything must be founded on justice. This clearly involves

(a) Free self-determination of nations.

(b) Equality of right amongst the constituent members
    of the League.

England, by denying the right of free self-determination to
Ireland, and by imposing on Ireland by threats a "Treaty"
which is so distasteful to the Irish people that a large
section of the population almost without arms rose up
against the armed might of those who would accept it in
league with the forces of Britain itself has struck a deadly
blow at the possibility of a League of Nations. In view of
this action of Britain the plain people of the world can only
see in the present League of Nations an organism for the
preservation of Imperial tyrannies.

P.

who was acting in Paris as representative of the Republican Government
established by P. (President Eamon de Valera), October–November 1922.
While in the USA (June 1919–December 1920) he had expressed his views
critically of the League of Nations founded in 1920 under a Covenant forming
part of the Versailles Treaty, 28 June 1919, concluded after the First World
War. The first appearance of de Valera at the 13th Assembly of the League was
in September 1932 when he became President of its Council. He was elected
President of the Assembly of the League in September 1938.

This is the first page of a three-page personal and confidential letter written in
his own hand by Eamon de Valera to the Prime Minister of Britain, Neville

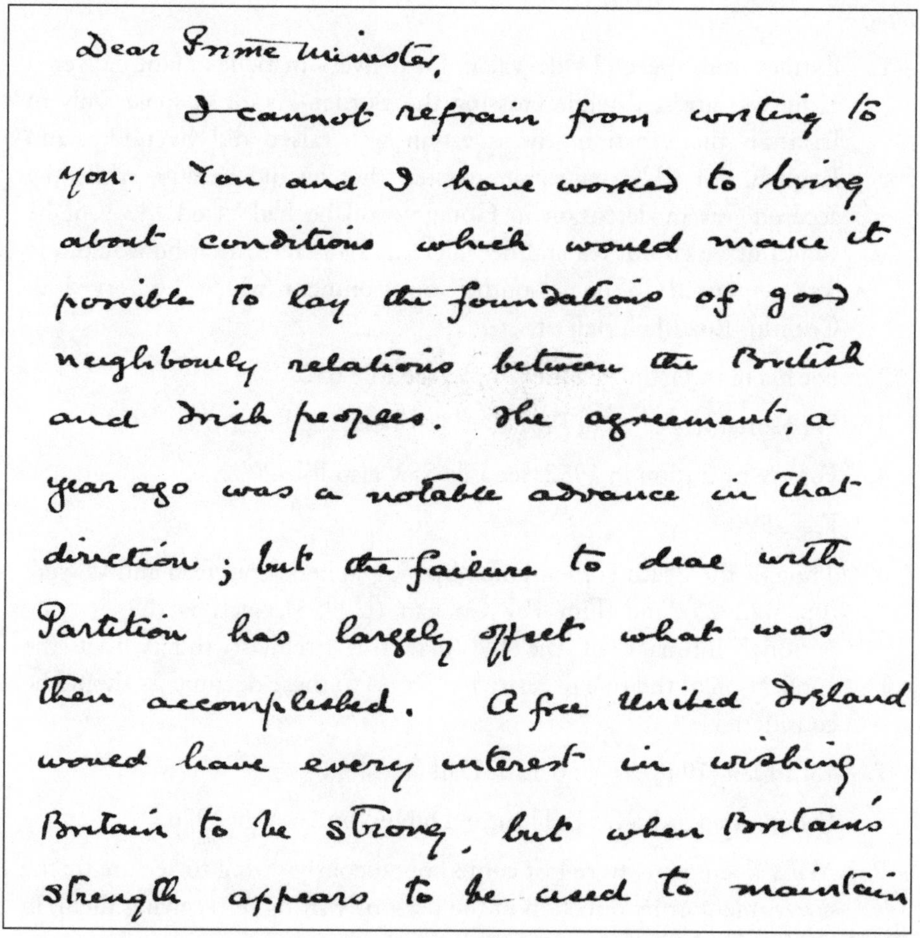

> Dear Prime Minister,
>
>   I cannot refrain from writing to you. You and I have worked to bring about conditions which would make it possible to lay the foundations of good neighbourly relations between the British and Irish peoples. The agreement, a year ago was a notable advance in that direction; but the failure to deal with Partition has largely offset what was then accomplished. A free United Ireland would have every interest in wishing Britain to be strong, but when Britain's strength appears to be used to maintain

Chamberlain (1869–1940). The agreement mentioned was the series of Anglo-Irish Agreements ending the Economic War (including the handing over of the so-called 'Treaty Ports') signed by de Valera and Chamberlain on 25 April 1938. The last sentence shown here continues: 'the division of our island no such consideration can have any force: a large section of our people, particularly the young, are led to see hope only in Britain's weakness. Can something not be done and without delay? The consequences of failure in the past to act in time are clear to see and should be a warning ... the intensification of feeling here and amongst our people in the United States makes it imperative to act quickly lest it be too late to save the situation ... Once this war [September 1939–May 1945] is begun no man can see the end.'

Notes:

1. Extract from speech by de Valera for delivery in Belfast. Not delivered as he was arrested while crossing the Border. As de V. spoke only in Irish on the occasion, the question was raised did he understand English. An RUC constable attested that he did because while the accused was in detention in Goraghwood he had asked de V. if he would like a cup of tea and de Valera had answered that he would. He was sentenced to one month's imprisonment which he served in Crumlin Road Jail, Belfast.

2. For his 80th birthday, for example, see File 652.

3. For Christmas cards of President de Valera, see File 2622.

4. For eye operation in 1952, see File 553; also File 2070.

5. File 2590.

6. Though the death is mentioned by biographers Longford and O'Neill (pp. 422–23) and Tim Pat Coogan (p. 485), such is the extreme personal intimacy of the file that this archivist thinks that the application of the rule of restricted access to these documents should be considered.

7. 13th Dáil (1948–51) and 15th Dáil (1954–57).

8. Inaugurated at La Scala Theatre, Dublin, on 16 May 1926.

9. Many documents were lost contemporaneously owing to seizure by the government or by direction of the persons writing or receiving them, in the interests of safety.

10. De Valera deposited in Killiney 367 of his books, many inscribed and/or autographed by him, and 217 pamphlets, in addition to his papers.

11. By far the largest class of documents.

12. Including the famous St Patrick's Day message 1943 in which E. de V. referred to comely maidens dancing at the crossroads. The text in its entirety (including an exhortation to promote the use of the Irish language) is seldom, if ever, cited.

13. Sinn Féin, 1923–28, six volumes; Fianna Fáil (National Executive), 1927–36, eight volumes.

14. For years 1914–61. Many of the entries are by de Valera's private secretaries, Kathleen O'Connell and Máire Ní Cheallaigh.

15. Total 86 in number. Included are conversations between de Valera and biographer T.P. O'Neill while the biography was in preparation which contain matter not published. See also next note.

16. The 83 dictabelts deserve a separate communication. Work on them was successfully undertaken over many months by Liam and Clár Ó Lonargáin and Marion Molloy. As the equipment used by E. de V. in the 1950s was long obsolete, the pioneering work done to re-record them on modern cassettes and transcribe their content merits the highest praise as being a unique action in Irish archives history. Liam Ó Lonargáin and his team also re-recorded for security reasons a large percentage of the original tape-recordings.

17. They are to be found in Files 2557–90 and 2605–17; also singly in many other files throughout the collection.

18. Years 1929 and 1932–38 in Files 2444–67 and scattered references in other files.

19. A separate guide, 196 pages of computer print-out, was prepared by the archivist and is available *in situ* with the papers themselves.

20. Years 1933–62 in Files 2491–2506. There are separate files for his American visit of 1964 and earlier years.

21. These include the 1938 negotiations ending the Economic War and the agreement about the 'Treaty Ports'. For 1932–39 see Files 950–1028.

22. See Files 1173–1205.

23. File 200 contains 422 documents relating to the Irish World Congress in Paris, January 1922.

24. File 234 contains 307 letters. This total does not include letters to and from de Valera in files with different (original) titles in the collection such as President and Chief of Staff, File 287 (333 items).

25. File 310 contains 344 items.

26. File 308 contains 327 items.

27. S.F. stands for the newspaper Sinn Féin (270 items).

28. There are 744 items covering his prison days, 1918–19.

29. Now in Files 1029-95 and 1969–99. See also the Guide already cited in Note 19.

30. One example is in relation to files of E. de V. incorporating the style President. File 278 is entitled 'President's letters written in 1923'; file 302 has the title 'President's Department 1923'.

31. Contrast 'E. de Valera's letters 1923' and 'Miscellaneous letters to de Valera 1923', Files 300 and 301. Misleading original titles occur and have been corrected by the archivist. One example is in File 333 entitled '1924 letters to Editor, S.F.' whose real contents are: L.H. Kerney Correspondence, 226 documents, letters from him to Sinn Féin, 26 documents, and Bulletins issued by him in Paris in 1924, 18 documents.

32. During this time the archivist spent 18 months on the papers of Seán Mac Eoin of Ballinalee fame and these were opened to the public on 11 February 1991. As media coverage was extensive, interested research students should consult the public prints. There are also finding aids to these papers prepared by the archivist.

33. This work which runs to 159 A4 pages was done by Eilís Mhic Giolla Choille who voluntarily devoted seven years to the de Valera papers.

34. The word archivists generally use for their lists; they are also referred to as catalogues.

35. April 1995. The reason for the termination is given in *Dún Mhuire Killiney* 1945–95 *Léann agus Seanchas*, page x, edited by Benignus Millett OFM and Anthony Lynch, Dublin 1995: 'The cataloguing of the de Valera papers was discontinued for one reason only, lack of funds. The Order spent a very large sum of money on this project. Without a grant from some source it could not afford to finance this deserving work any longer.'

36. Pride of place goes to Dr Fiachra Ó Ceallaigh OFM who invited the archivist to accept the position of Consultant Archivist to the de Valera papers in 1985 and supported him tenaciously until his elevation as Auxiliary Bishop of Dublin, 17 Sept. 1994. As well as the archivist's wife (see Note 33 above), the archivist was helped by Mark Farrell (now a director of the archives services Arcline) and Philip Hannon (now in the head office of Fianna Fáil). From start to finish the computer work on the calendar was done by Una, Bean (Niall) Mhic Giolla Choille. See also Note 16.

37. The present Franciscan Killiney (and Provincial) Librarian is Fr Ignatius Fennessy OFM who has kindly, patiently and effectively helped the writer in this present work. Thanks are also due to Fr Benignus Millett OFM who welcomed the writer warmly to Dún Mhuire in 1985 and facilitated his work there. Permission to reproduce

the documents in this article is gratefully acknowledged to the Franciscan Library Killiney.

38. For the convenience of researchers, the opening dates were: 30 June 1987 (1937 Constitution, jubilee commemoration by OFM); 20 November 1991 (1916 Rising to the Anglo-Irish Agreement 1921); and 13 April 1994 (258 files on individuals e.g. Joseph Walshe, Secretary to Department of External/Foreign Affairs). An opening planned for September 1994 to cover the Civil War and following years was not held.

39. *The Irish Republic* first published in March 1937 which is of course limited to the period ending November 1925.

40. *Eamon de Valera*, published 1970, and *De Valera*, a d'fhoilsigh Cló Morainn 1968 (iml. 1) agus 1970 (iml. 2). Tim Pat Coogan in his 1993 *De Valera, Long Fellow, Long Shadow* made minimal use of the papers but generously acknowledged that 'When the work [of cataloguing the papers by the archivist] is completed it will be a monumental contribution to our understanding of a man and an era.' T. Ryle Dwyer in his 1991–92 *De Valera: The Man and The Myths* does not mention them in his sources. Likewise, Professor Arthur Mitchell in his 1995 *Revolutionary Government in Ireland, Dáil Éireann 1919–22*.

41. Given the historical value of the de Valera Papers, the outlay necessary to complete them would be modest, probably in the region of £75,000.

14

Treasured Sundays at the Áras

by Síle de Valera

The public perception of Eamon de Valera was of a tall, austere, unsmiling and aloof man with little or no sense of humour. Here was a man whose name was synonymous with Irish politics at home and abroad, who had joined the Gaelic League, took a leadership role in 1916, was sentenced to death, spent time on the run, had to endure the tragedy of civil war, formed a political party, served in opposition, was Taoiseach for 21 years and President of Ireland for 14 years. It is no wonder that the general public only got to see the serious side of his personality and perhaps viewed him as a one dimensional character.

Given the vagrancy of his early political career, Dev had little opportunity to get to know his own children. In Lord Longford and Tom O'Neill's biography a poignant example of this was recounted by his daughter, Máirín. She remembered her younger brothers Brian and Ruairí having a conversation. One asked the other 'Who is Dev?' while the other answered, 'I think he is Mummy's father.' This was in 1920. As time passed and things became somewhat more routine in the 1930s the opportunities for father and children to get to know each other were more frequent. However, I believe it was not until later in life that Dev really had the chance to partake in family life with the advent of his grandchildren.

I was four years old when de Valera became president and I have treasured memories of Sundays in Áras an Uachtaráin where all the family would gather. We all grew up there together, from dressing up in old clothes, putting on plays, learning to drive and going to our first dance! Christmasses were particularly special.

Both Eamon and Sinéad showed a great interest in their grandchildren's education, always there to prompt, encourage and praise. No doubt this stemmed from the fact that both were teachers. That was in fact how they both met. My grandfather happened to be in an Irish class held by the Gaelic

League, which was being taught by my grandmother. Both Eamon and Sinéad believed that girls and boys had an equal right to education. While this is an accepted principle now, it was not the prevailing outlook of the time.

Sinéad's love of literature and the stage always shone through and this proved to be a healthy contrast to Dev's love of mathematics. Dev's mathematical ability led to an analytical mind. He always strove to be accurate and dispassionate in debate, to be fair and would always ensure that he would not be distracted from the core of an argument. De Valera never personalised the debate and had little time for those politicians who did, believing that it showed great weakness in the substance of their argument. He wished to pass this principle onto his children and the following story told by his son Ruairí demonstrates this very well. One evening after Dev came out of jail he was having his tea and Ruairí was playing with toy soldiers on the floor. Dev took up an empty egg shell and threw it at some of the soldiers, saying 'there's a shell'. Ruairí cried out: 'Daddy, you hit the wrong soldiers, these are the Irish.' Dev then asked 'who are the others?' and Ruairí answered 'the English'. Dev replied gently, 'no just call them the enemy'. The British politician Malcolm McDonald on hearing this story was struck by Dev's lack of bitterness towards the British in spite of his years in prison.

Whereas Dev was always known as a very strong and committed nationalist, both in cultural and political terms, this was in no small way due to Sinéad. Sinéad's father was a fervent Fenian. She, like her father, held her convictions with pride and never compromised the truth. Sinéad is often remembered as the retiring, self-effacing, gentle, quiet and petite lady at Dev's side, but it would have been a great mistake to consider her as a submissive or subordinate character. In fact, she was known by some members of the family as 'ruthless Aunty Jenny'. After all, she was a red-head. Sinéad's influence on her children was very deep and enduring. She instilled in them love and appreciation of the arts, particularly literature, music and the stage. She was considered to be a talented amateur actor in her day. Her love of nature and animals was always to the fore. Although she was very practical in her day-to-day approach to life and indeed had to deal with the economic hardships that arose particularly when Dev was in jail or on the run, she always possessed a very special childlike quality. This was immediately understood and recognised by children and young people who would seek her company. Perhaps it was this quality which made her a successful writer of children's stories. Sinéad would have preferred to have lived in a quiet and reserved way and even as a Taoiseach's and President's wife managed to preserve the time and privacy she believed was necessary for family life.

Neither of my grandparents would entertain bitterness and enjoyed the company of others who would challenge their views on life either in the political or religious sphere. Although the sad events of the Civil War were to set Michael Collins and Eamon de Valera on different paths, both Eamon and Sinéad maintained an abiding respect and fondness for Collins. It might surprise some to know that Collins sent messages to my grandmother to see if she and the children were alright during the Civil War and a poignant letter from Sinéad is recorded in Leon O'Broin's book, *In Great Haste*. Within ten years of the Civil War, Collins' nephews were playing with the de Valera children. I was very proud some years ago to accept an invitation from Michael Collins' nephew, Liam Collins to be his personal guest at the celebrations to commemorate Collins' birth. Although I would not have agreed with the 'Big Fellow's' stance on the Treaty, he was a man of great courage and conviction and someone for whom I have had long-term admiration.

I have fond memories of my grandfather listening patiently as I nervously attempted to sing along with my feeble efforts on the guitar. From his facial expression you would have been convinced he was listening to a genius! One of my favourite pursuits, like so many teenagers, was a love of horses and horseriding. For many years, I went horseriding in Blackrock and every Sunday afternoon when we would visit the Áras, Dev would tell me of his fears of an accident. He was always fearful of horseriding since the tragic death of his son Brian who was killed when his horse bolted in the Phoenix Park. Even with this sad memory, he always attended the Dublin Horse Show and he used to bring me along with him on occasion.

My love of history goes back to when I was ten or eleven years of age and so I suppose it was not so surprising that this interest would lead me to a fascination with politics from my teens. Dev was very aware of my political interests and when I was asked by Fianna Fáil for the first time to read the Proclamation at the 1916 ceremonies in Arbour Hill, he sent me good wishes the night before to help dispel my nerves. Dev always encouraged my political pursuits and never viewed the fact that I was female as a disadvantage in the world of politics. Growing up, I remember a map of Clare in brass hanging on the wall of the State Dining Room in Áras an Uachtaráin: this had been presented to him by the people of Clare. Little did I think that some years later, I would have the honour of representing that constituency myself.

On Sunday evenings, all the family would be seated around a large table in the dining room in the Áras having high tea. It was there that the discussions would begin. Everyone at the table would seem to have a different view on every subject, some I suspect holding the opposing view just for the sake of a good debate. Everyone could join in no matter how young. The proceedings were, of course, chaired by Dev. Your view was entertained as long as it was somewhat logical. This taught me never to enter an argument without having thought it through and being able to cite evidence for stating any claim.

Dev had a very good sense of humour and once he had started laughing he could find it difficult to control his mirth. He would often tell us a story with great glee of my father, Terry, as a young child refusing to take a certain disagreeable medicine which Sinéad was attempting to administer without success. When Terry protested, Dev would decide to administer the medicine himself. Soon Terry was aware of a slimy, foul-smelling substance sliding down his throat. Dev had won the struggle! Later, as Terry climbed the stairs, he remembered calling out 'dirty fellow, filthy fellow, I wish he would go back to jail again!' Dev always told the story with great gusto.

The loyalty that was shown to Eamon de Valera by his supporters throughout his long political career was phenomenal. It was very often a very quiet and unassuming presence but when the need arose that loyalty would be fiercely demonstrated. That support went very deep and meant a lifetime of service for many. When Dev died on 29 August 1975, he was mourned as an international statesman, as a friend, a colleague, as a comrade-in-arms and as the indulgent grandfather that he was.

15

Fianna Fáil agus an Ghaeilge

le Nollaig Ó Gadhra

Tá sé chomh maith agam, is dócha, tosú le píosa soiscéalaíochta a ghealfaidh croíthe na seanlaoch sa pháirtí, mar beidh tuilleadh le rá ar ball. An méid seo a leanas mar sin: 'Ón gcéad lá riamh d'aithin Fianna Fáil tábhacht na Gaeilge i saol an náisiúin. Níorbh rosc gan bhrí acu 'Éire shaor, Éire Ghaelach'. Thuig siad an dualgas atá ar an eagraíocht agus ar gach Rialtas a gcion díchill a dhéanamh leis an nGaeilge a shábháil agus a chur faoi réim arís ar fud na tíre. I ngnóthaí poiblí agus riaracháin, i gcúrsaí oideachais agus cultúir bhain siad leas as gach deis chun ionad na teanga a neartú sa nGalltacht.

'D'aithin Fianna Fáil go háirithe páirt na Gaeltachta in obair seo na hathbheochana agus is iomaí scéim a cheap siad chun an Ghaeltacht a chaomhnú agus a neartú mar chuisle Gaelach an náisiúin. Níor mhiste gearrchúntas a thabhairt ar chuid den obair atá ar bun ar mhaithe leis an nGaeltacht.'

Bhain mé an sliocht sin as 'Chapter Thirteen – Gaeltacht' sa leabhar *The Story of Fianna Fáil -First Phase* a d'fhoilsigh an páirtí sa bhliain 1960 – bliain tar éis do de Valera éirí as an gceannasaíocht agus Seán Lemass teacht i réim mar Uachtarán an pháirtí agus Taoiseach ar an Rialtas. B'fhéidir go raibh 'Ré Lemass' tosaithe, ach má bhí, is léir go raibh blas láidir an tseansaoil le brath ar an gcaibidil seo faoi chúrsaí Gaeilge agus Gaeltachta – an t-aon chaibidil sa leabhar, dála an scéil, a bhí i nGaeilge.

I measc na gceannteideal a bhí sa chaibidil tar éis an Réamhrá sin thuas, nuair a tosaíodh ag ríomh obair Fhianna Fáil don teanga, bhí na cinn seo a leanas: Oideachas, Meánscolaíocht, Scoláireachta (sic), Postaí Ceannasacha, Seallaí agus Brúanna, Coláistí Gaeilge, Scéimeanna Cultúrtha (ina measc luaitear reachtáil Feiseanna agus deontais chun úirlisí ceoil a sholáthar agus a fhoghlaim), Spórt agus Aclaíocht, Geilleagar agus Sóisealacht lena n-áirítear Talmhaíocht, Tithe Gloine, Iascach agus Foraoiseacht agus Tionscail mar a deirtear 'Tá gach iarracht is féidir á dhéanamh leis na tionscail déantóireachta atá sa nGaeltacht cheana e.g. cniotáil, fíodóireacht, bróidnéaracht, fúáil srl. a chaomhnú, a neartú agus a leathnú. Ar an gcaoi chéanna táthar ag iarraidh, i gcónaí, na portaigh d'fhorbairt le haghaidh soirn agus leictreachais. Níl faillí déanta ach oiread i dtionscal na feamainne – agus tá cuid mhaith déanta cheana féin.' Leanann píosa eile faoi 'Thithe, Bóithre, Uisce srl.' agus 'comhoibriú le Eagraíochtaí atá ag obair ar son na Gaeltachta ina ndeirtear an méid seo a leanas : 'Tá Aire na Gaeltachta ag comhoibriú go tréan le gach eagraíocht atá ag gníomhú ar son na Gaeilge agus ar son na Gaeltachta e.g. Conradh na Gaeilge, Comhaltas Uladh, Cumann Lúth-Chleas Gael, Gael-Linn agus Cumainn éagsúla eile.

Moladh ar bith ráthúil ar mhaithe leis an nGaeltacht scrúdóidh Aire na Gaeltachta go cúramach báúil é. Leanfaidh Fianna Fáil go dílis dúthrachtach, díograiseach, den obair ar mhaithe leis an nGaeltacht'.[1]

Tá cuma na haislinge agus an idéalachais ar chuid den chaint seo ach tá cuma na sean-aimsire uirthi freisin. Fiú má bhí an dream a scríobh lán-dáiríre – agus seans go raibh más duine uasal cosúil le Donncha Ó Briain ba mhó a bhí i mbun pinn ag an am – is léir freisin go raibh easpa smaointe dearfacha agus easpa cláir raidiciúil ar Aire na Gaeltachta féin.

Is fiú cuimhneamh ar an am a cuireadh an leabhar seo faoi 'Chéad Tréimhse Fhianna Fáil' i gcló. Ní raibh na seascadaí lena réabhlóid theilifíse agus chultúir idirnáisiúnta buailte linn fós i gceart. Ach bhí Fianna Fáil 34 bliana ar an saol agus 22 bhliain den tréimhse sin caite acu i mbun an rialtais sna 26 chontae. Go praiticiúil ní raibh ach duine amháin, Eamon de Valera, tar éis a bheith i gceannas ar an bpáirtí le linn na mblianta fada sin. Ní raibh an Comhphobal Eorpach ach ina naíonán 3 bliana ag an am agus muintir na hÉireann dall go maith ar an saol ar fud na hEorpa, seachas sa Bhreatain béal dorais. B'shin 36 bliana ó shin – rud a fhágann go bhfuilimid tar éis a bheith ag trácht go dtí seo ar léargas agus ar thuiscint Fhianna Fáil ar scéal na Gaeilge leathshlí trí shaolré an pháirtí go dtí seo sa 'Chapter Thirteen' úd a bhí luaite i mBéarla amháin!

Ach chun an scéal ar fad a thuiscint níos soiléire agus chun iarracht a dhéanamh a bheith cothrom do gach éinne – mar a gheall mé a bheinn nuair a ghlac mé leis an gcuireadh flaithiúil oscailte seo – ní mór dul siar píosa eile agus plé níos doimhne a dhéanamh faoin scéal ar fad a bhaineann le tábhacht na Gaeilge i saol an náisiúin agus faoin bpáirt a bhí ag iarracht na hathbheochana Gaeilge in athbheochan bheatha an náisiúin sa chéad seo.

Ní dóigh liom go n-easaontódh duine ar bith le bunbhrí na cainte ag Pádraig Mac Piarais nuair a mhaígh sé 'that the Irish Revolution began when the Gaelic League was founded in 1893'.[2] Cé gur minic conspóid faoin pholaitíocht a bhain leis an athbheochan chéanna, ní shéanfadh éinne, dar liom, gurb é slánú mhuintir na hÉireann mar aonad neamhspleách ar leith, ag a mbeadh a gcultúr agus a dteanga féin, an bhun-aidhm choitianta a bhí ag formhór na réabhlóidithe in Éirinn ó aimsir De hÍde agus Mhic Néill i leith. Tá a leagan féin den scéal ag de Valera sa Réamhrá don Bhunreacht a chuir sé faoi bhráid an phobail in 1937 agus go háirithe in Airteagal 1 den Bhunreacht – an ceann nach luann daoine ariamh nuair a bhíonn leasuithe ar Airteagail 2 agus 3 á moladh acu! Deirtear sa Chéad Airteagal sin 'Deimhníonn náisiún na hÉireann leis seo a gceart doshannta dochloíte ceannasach chun cibé cineál Rialtais is rogha leo féin a bhunú, chun a gcaidreamh le náisiúin eile a chinneadh agus chun a saol polaitíochta is geilleagair is saíochta a chur ar aghaidh de réir dhúchais is gnás a sinsear.'[3] Sílim féin go bhfuil blas níos fearr ar an leagan Béarla sa chás seo ag deireadh an Airteagail, mar a bhfuil trácht ar fhorbairt a dhéanamh ar chúrsaí an náisiúin 'in accordance with its own genius and traditions'.[4] Tar éis nach bhfuil an focal 'traidisiún' luaite sa leagan Gaeilge den ráiteas! Glacadh leis coitianta, le fada an lá, go raibh dlúthcheangal idir traidisiún liteartha agus intleachtúil na Gaeilge agus forbairt, saibhriú agus cur chun cinn an náisiúin trí chéile. Bhí an meon seo ag teacht leis an méid a bhí le fáil sa litríocht ó thosaigh an choimhlint idir Gaeil agus Gaill sa tír – scéal a chuaigh i ngéire nuair a bhí cúrsaí talún agus easaontas creidimh le cur san áireamh chomh maith. Bhain tábhacht leis an nGaeilge mar dhlúthchuid den réabhlóid náisiúnta ó aimsir Davis i leith – ag an am céanna go raibh cluas an mhóraimh a raibh Gaeilge acu ag an gcainteoir dúchais as Uíbh Ráthach, Dónall Ó Conaill, fear nár mheas aon tábhacht mórán a bheith leis an saibhreas chultúir, agus a d'admhaigh gur chuma leis má bhí an teanga ag dul ar chúl go tréan lena linn féin. Ní mór áfach gach imeacht staire a shuíomh i gcomhthéacs, agus bheadh sé chomh deacair d'fhear as Uíbh Ráthach a cheapadh go raibh an Ghaeilge i mbaol báis sa chéad dhá scór bliain den 19ú céad, agus a bheadh sé a cheapadh, fiú i 1960, go mbeadh na ceantair Ghaeltachta mar atá siad faoi láthair ag deireadh an chéid seo.[5]

Is fíor gur chuir Conradh na Gaeilge oideachas ar ghlúin óg iomlán idir 1893 agus 1916 a ghlac ceannas ar an réabhlóid náisiúnta as sin amach. B'í an teanga croí na hoibre ach bhain sé le níos mó ná sin, gach rud ó thírghrá, go féinmhuinín, go aithne ar an saol lasmuigh de dhomhan an Bhéarla. Ach nuair a thug muintir na Chéad Dála (ar oidhrí Chonradh na Gaeilge gach uile dhuine acu nach mór dár le De hÍde féin, nuair a scríobh sé an Réamhrá le *Mise agus an Conradh*[6] in 1931) faoi athbheochan na Gaeilge caithfear a rá go macánta nach raibh aon fhianaise neodrach ann a chruthódh do lucht teangeolaíochta, abair, go bhféadfaí an aisling a chur i gcríoch. Aisling gan bhonn, gan chiall, gan bhunús a bhí ann mar sin? B'fhéidir é. Ach dúradh an rud céanna faoi aisling na saoirse agus an neamhspleáchais ag an am. Ní dóigh liom gur chreid mórán de lucht na haislinge in 1916 agus sna blianta ina dhiaidh sin go n-éireodh chomh maith sin leo.[7] Ba bheag duine acu a mheas, dar liom, go bhfeicfí an lá nach mbeadh fágtha d'Impireacht na Breataine ach cúpla oileán fánach anseo is ansiúd. Go mbeidís ag glanadh as Hong Kong féin, agus gurb é an t-imní is mó a bheadh ar chúlbhinseoir an 1922 Club ná cad a tharlódh dá ngéillfí orlach maidir le Sé Chontae na hÉireann, in Albain agus sa Bhreatain Bheag!

Fíric staire í gurb iad muintir na hÉireann is túisce a chuir tús le cealú an chórais impireachta ba mhó a tharla sa stair go dtí sin.[8] Sin fáth eile nach maith leis na Sasanaigh go meabhrófaí an taifead staire sin dóibh. Ní mhaithfidh siad go deo dúinn an scian sa droim a thug lucht Éirí Amach 1916 dóibh – agus iad i lár an Chogaidh Mhóir ba mhó sa stair go dtí sin. Sin é an fáth freisin a ndéantar ceap magaidh d'aislingí cultúir agus teanga de Valera go háirithe i Sasana (agus ar RTE gan amhras mar a bhfuil an lá ag staraithe de dhath áirithe i gcónaí!) – mar go raibh an dá cheist ceangailte chomh dlúth sin le chéile ag an Sinn Féin nua eagraithe faoi cheannas de Valera ó 1917 ar aghaidh. Bhuaigh siad Olltoghchán na bliana 1918 agus, ní hionann agus polaiteoirí eile a raibh cleachtadh ag muintir na hÉireann orthu, chuaigh siad ar aghaidh le Dáil Uile-Éireann (32 chontae) mar a raibh an Ghaeilge in uachtar ar an gcéad lá.[9]

Tá scéal na Gaeilge sa chéad agus sa dara Dáil fíor-spéisiúil. Sa leabhar a scríobh mé ar an Chéad Dáil Éireann, feictear an deacracht phraiticiúil a tharla láithreach nuair a féachadh leis an teanga náisiúnta a chur san áit a bheadh aici in aon 'ghnáth'-Pharlaimint Náisiúnta (sa Danmhairg, san Íoslainn, san Ioruaidh abair) agus an fhírinne shearbh nach raibh eolas ar an teanga ná tuiscint ar a hoidhreacht ag go leor den dream ba dhíograisí a bhí ag iarraidh í a chosaint, agus a bhí sásta bás a fháil chun ár gceart mar riarthóirí ar ár ngnóthaí féin, a chosaint. An iontas ar bith é, ar bhealach, go raibh na Sasanaigh féin, an Príomh-Aire Lloyd George (a labhraíodh Breatnais san oifig lena rúnaí Tom Jones), an *Irish Times*, maithe Choláiste na Tríonóide agus go deimhin cuid mhaith de na heaspaig freisin ag trácht ar mhíphraiticiúlacht na haislinge ag na 'impractical idealists'? Mar go borb macánta, fuarchúiseach, níor éirigh le haon náisiún a bhí chomh buailte sin maidir lena teanga dúchais, a hoidhreacht chultúrtha, gan trácht ar bheocht na bpobal ina raibh an dúchas fós beo sa phobal, an taoide a chasadh roimhe sin. Bhí muintir na hÉireann chun tosaigh i réabhlóid chultúir agus athbheochana teanga na dtíortha iar-choilíneacha sa bhfichiú aois chomh maith, cé nár thuig siad féin é sin ag an am b'fhéidir.[10] Ansin in 1947 bunaíodh stát Iosrael. Réitíodh ceist na teanga in imeacht 30 bliain ...

D'éirigh leis na hIosraelaigh rud a dhéanamh le linn don chuid eile againn a bheith ag caint faoi! Tá a fhios agam nach raibh an scéal mar an gcéanna. Tá a fhios againn, mar shampla, gur ceann de na nithe ba mhó a chabhraigh le h-athbheochan na hEabhraise ná gur baineadh leas iomlán as an nua-theicneolaíocht chun an teanga a mhúineadh, agus leas as na mórmheáin raidió agus teilifíse chun í a bhunú i ngnáthshaol an stáit nua. Gan trácht ar an tréimhse a bhí ar gach saoránach óg a chaitheamh san Arm, chun snas a chur ar an teanga a bhí foghlamtha acu! Agus gur bhain an chéad sé mhí den tréimhse sin le dul i dtaithí ar *úsáid na teanga*, mar gnáth-theanga oibre i gcibé scil nó gairm a bhí i gceist ag an saighdiúir óg a leanúint nuair a bheadh an tseirbhís náisiúnta déanta aige/aici.

Córas sách docht, sách mídhaonlathach a bhí ann, le fírinne, ar feadh glúine. Ach tá tábhacht amháin ach go háirithe le sampla Iosrael dar liom. Chruthaigh siad gur féidir é a dhéanamh taobh istigh den ghlúin nó dhó. Go deimhin, tá daoine áirithe ann a mheasann nach féidir athbheochan teanga mar seo a chur i gcríoch ar chor ar bith mura dtugtar faoi in imeacht glúine nó dhó.

An chéad rud eile nach foláir a mheabhrú dúinn féin b'fhéidir gurbh í aidhm athbheochan na Gaeilge an t-aon chuid den aisling a tháinig slán ar fad ó dhrochfhuil an Chogaidh Chathartha. Bhí Gaeilgeoirí díograiseacha ar an dá thaobh sa scoilt uafásach sin a tharla in 1922. Go deimhin deirtí gur chaith Conraitheoirí bliain iomlán beagnach ag marú a chéile go neamhthrócaireach agus gan de chomhthuiscint idir na seanchairde sa chúis ach a gcomhspéis i leas na Gaeilge. Nílim chun ainmneacha a lua cheal spáis.[11]

Glacaimis leis freisin gurb é Rialtas Chumann na nGaedheal, idir 1922 agus 1932, a leag síos an chuid is mó ar fad den bhunpholasaí stáit a bhain le h-athbheochan na Gaeilge. Go polaitiúil, ba mhaith an rud é sin, mar chiallaigh sé go raibh comhaontas náisiúnta ann faoi dhubhriachtanas na Gaeilge tar éis an Chogaidh Chathartha agus go ceann glúine nó dhó eile. Bhí difríochtaí béime ann áfach. Go ginearálta thuill de Valera agus muintir Fhianna Fáil cáil níos mó mar lucht taca na teanga le himeacht aimsire. Is cinnte go ndeachaigh go leor Gaeilgeoirí a ghlac leis an Saorstát in 1922, mar gur mheas siad go slánódh an stát céanna an teanga tríd an gcóras oideachais, le

Fianna Fáil ar ball. Agus chuir cuid d'iompar Chumann na nGaedheal i mbun polasaí Gaeilge dóibh olc ar a lucht leanúna féin fiú amháin. Cé gur ceanglaíodh cáil 'Compulsory Irish' ar Fhianna Fáil sna caogadaí agus sna seascadaí, ba é Rialtas Chumann na nGaedheal a chuir tús leis mar pholasaí. Agus cé gur mhaígh Fine Gael ar ball gur theip air ('present methods have failed'), a mhalairt glan atá fíor. Ní shéanfadh éinne an dul chun cinn a rinne an teanga ag gach leibhéal beagnach sa chéad 50 bhliain tar éis bhunú an stáit. Ach theip go dona ar an stát i réimsí áirithe, ní toisc na Gaeilge éigeantaí ach toisc *nár cuireadh* i bhfeidhm i gceart í.[12] Má thógtar an réimse oibre is mó a bhíodh i gceist, soláthar seirbhísí dátheangacha ón stát, theip ar an stát an comhcheart sin a chinntiú do mhuintir na Gaeltachta féin. D'éirigh leis an iarracht i gcásanna áirithe. Mar shampla, rinneadh socrú sonrach ar leith maidir leis na Gardaí agus na cúirteanna dúiche i gCorca Dhuibhne, i nGaillimh agus i gConamara – agus tá toradh sásúil ann go fóill.[13] Ní dhearnadh an socrú céanna i nGaeltacht Mhaigh Eo ná i nDún na nGall – agus tá an toradh míshásúil le feiceáil ansin freisin le fada an lá!

I mbeagán focal, níor iarradh i dtromlach na gcásanna ach scrúdú Gaeilge d'oifigigh stáit agus iad ag dul i mbun oibre. Ní dhearnadh socruithe a chinnteodh go bhféadfaidís a gcuid oibre *a dhéanamh trí Ghaeilge* nuair ba ghá sin. Go deimhin ba mhó béim a bhí ar sheanfhocail agus mionphointí gramadaí sna scrúduithe iontrála ná tástáil ar chumas an iarrthóra chun obair shainiúil éigin a bhain leis an ghairm a dhéanamh *trí mheán na Gaeilge*.[14] Arís, easpa tuisceana ó thaobh na teangeolaíochta agus na sochtheangeolaíochta de. Bhí polaitíocht i gceist freisin gan amhras.

Ní féidir, cheal spáis, plé mion a dhéanamh anseo ar na beartais bhreise éagsúla a rinne Fianna Fáil ar son na teanga nuair a tháinig siad i gcumhacht in 1932. Is cinnte go raibh díograis agus dóchas breise i measc Gaeilgeoirí agus lucht Gaeltachta nuair a tháinig de Valera i gcumhacht. Tá trácht déanta againn cheana féin ar chuid de na scéimeanna éagsúla faoi cheannteidil éagsúla a mhaígh Fianna Fáil féin in 1960 a bheith ag cabhrú leis an bpolasaí athbheochana a bhí mar an dara haidhm ag an bpáirtí ón tús. Ceann de na rudaí ar baineadh triail as sna 1930aí ar ndóigh, agus a bhí faoi mar a bheadh macalla Gaelach den fheachtas in aghaidh dleachtanna talún ag an am, ná bunú cúpla coilíneacht Ghaeltachta ar thalamh méith na Mí. Dhá iarracht ba mhó a luadh – Baile Ghib mar a meascadh daoine ó thrí Ghaeltacht éagsúla agus Ráth Cairn inar lonnaíodh pobal as Conamara. Tá stair spéisiúil dá chuid féin ag iarrachtaí seo Ghaeltacht na Mí freisin ach, ó thaobh na haiste seo, ba cheart a lua gur díoladh an polasaí ag an am mar bheart taibhseach a chuirfeadh mallacht Chromail ar ceal. Chealófaí an phlandáil ollmhór a tharla san 17ú aois trí dhá scór ghabháltas beag a lonnú i lár na Mí. Agus féach gur fhan muintir na Mí go dtí 1967, sar ar áitigh siad ar Rúnaí Parlaiminte na Gaeltachta ag an am, Pádraic Ó Fachtna ó Cho. Lú, aitheantas Gaeltachta a thabhairt don áit.[15]

Ach le filleadh ar an saol tar éis an chogaidh agus an imirce mhór a bhánaigh an Ghaeltacht sna blianta sin nuair a bhí an Bhreatain le atógáil tar éis an Chogaidh. Ná ceap nach raibh daoine buartha ón tús faoi staid na Gaeltachta agus faoi staid na Gaeilge sa Ghaeltacht nuair a bhí daoine ag imeacht leo agus an saol ag dul i bhfeabhas don dream sa bhaile. Duine de na saineolaithe ba mhacánta agus ba oscailte faoin scéal seo ab ea an tOllamh Brian Ó Cuív a bhí pósta ar iníon le de Valera – tuismitheoirí an TD Eamon Ó Cuív atá ina chónaí i gCorr na Móna i dtuaisceart Chonamara anois. Seasann a shaothar *Irish Dialects and Irish Speaking Districts,* a foilsíodh i 1947, teist na haimsire i gcónaí.[16] Mar a sheasann moltaí na Comhdhála 'A Board for the Gaeltacht'[17] a foilsíodh i 1953 agus go leor meamram eile a bhain le bunú Roinn na Gaeltachta mar Roinn ar leith i 1956 agus bunú Ghaeltarra Éireann mar chomhlacht stát-urraithe le bord neamhspleách i 1957. Seán Ó Loinsigh a roghnaigh de Valera mar Rúnaí Parlaiminte i Roinn na Gaeltachta ar theacht ar ais dó i mbun oifige don uair dheiridh i mí Mhárta 1957. Cuireadh tús le nós ón uair sin ar aghaidh go dtosaíodh polaiteoirí óga sa pháirtí i Roinn na Gaeltachta – rud a thabharfadh deis dóibh a gcuid Gaeilge a chleachtadh i mbun cúramaí praiticiúla san oifig. Níor bhain Gearóid Mac Pharthaláin ná Mícheál Ó Móráin leis an nglúin sin. Ach féach mar a thosaigh Pádraig Ó Fachtna, Gearóid Ó Coileáin, Máire Geoghegan-Quinn agus Pat the Cóp Ó Gallchóir sa Roinn sin ó shin. Ar ndóigh bhí polaiteoirí níos críonna a ghlac cúram na Gaeltachta orthu féin i bhFianna Fáil ag amanna éagsúla, de bharr cúraim ar leith nó sainspéise. Ina measc bhí Seoirse Ó Colla, nach maireann, a bhí ina Aire Tionscail agus Tráchtála agus ina Aire Airgeadais le linn dó a bheith ina Aire Gaeltachta, Cathal Ó hEochaidh a choinnigh Aireacht na Gaeltachta dó féin le linn dó a bheith ina Thaoiseach, tar éis 1987, agus Seán Mac Uilliam a bhí ina Aire Cosanta chomh maith le bheith ina Thánaiste sa chéad Rialtas a cheap Ailbhe Mac Raghnaill, in 1992.

Ceann de na beartais dheireanacha a rinne de Valera sar ar éirigh sé as an bpolaitíocht ghníomhach ná gur bhunaigh sé Coimisiún um Athbheochan na Gaeilge in 1958. Tomás Ó Fiaich (Cairdinéal ina dhiaidh sin) a bhí mar Chathaoirleach air don chuid is mó den am cé nárbh é a bhí ann i dtosach.[18]

Rinne an Coimisiún obair mhór le linn ré nuair a bhí an saol ag athrú go tréan – ré Lemass, tionscail iasachta á mealladh go hÉirinn agus chun na Gaeltachta ar ball, bunú RTE, ré JFK agus na seascadaí, Vatacáin II ....

Mar a tharla, mhair an Coimisiún i mbun oibre go dtí 1964 agus tharla 'díospóireacht mhór náisiúnta' ar scéal na Gaeilge ansin ag am nuair a bhí an LFM ag feidhmiú mar thaca le lucht cáinte na Gaeilge éigeantaí i bhFine Gael. Spéisiúil go leor, labhraíodh Ceannaire nua an Lucht Oibre, Breandán Mac Fheorais agus Leas-Chathaoirleach an pháirtí san am, Proinsias Mac Aonghusa, go tréan ar thaobh na hathbheochana[19] – cé gurbh iad an Lucht Oibre, faoi cheannas Mhic Fheorais, a dhíbhunaigh an Ghaeilge sa státchóras agus sa chóras oideachais sa Chomhrialtas a rinne siad le Fine Gael faoi cheannas Liam Mhic Chosgair, tar éis Olltoghchán 1973.

Ní féidir an scéal ar fad a phlé go mion anseo ach amháin le rá gur dearnadh an chéad chúlú ón aidhm náisiúnta teanga mar a bhíodh ón tús, ag Fianna Fáil, in 1964 nuair a fuarthas amach go raibh ardstátseirbhíseach sa Roinn Airgeadais ag smaoineamh ar aidhm na hathbheochana a shainmhíniú mar 'to restore Irish as *a* general means of communication'. Mheas lucht na cúise gur cheart trácht ar 'the national aim is to restore Irish as *the* general means of communication'! Lean raiceanna, caint san aer faoin difríocht idir an dá ráiteas, daoine eile fós ag rá nár cheart aon aidhm dhocht mar sin a bheith ann, ach an teanga a shábháil agus a úsáid agus fág faoi ghlúin eile, ar ball, an staid dheiridh a leagan amach dóibh féin![20] I mBéarla ar fad, nach mór, a tharla na conspóidí!

Ach is í fírinne an scéil nár cuireadh aon chóras ceart pleanála nua don teanga i bhfeidhm tar éis 1977, agus cé gur maith ann cuid de na hiarrachtaí deonacha agus leathdheonacha a rinneadh ó shin, níl aon aidhm chinnte, plean, struchtúr, córas tástála ná cód imeachtais ag an stát don Ghaeilge, breis is 100 bliain tar éis do Chonradh na Gaeilge teacht ar an saol, agus 70 bliain tar éis d'Fhianna Fáil a bheith bunaithe.

Tá an saol ag athrú, agus cé go dtuigeann gach éinne an brú uafásach ón saol Angla-Mheiriceánach atá ar na pobail Ghaeltachta ach go háirithe, níl an scéal ar fad go dona. Ná éadóchasach ach an oiread. Fuair muid Údarás don Ghaeltacht sa deireadh. Donncha Ó Gallchóir a thug ar an saol é agus Máire Geoghegan-Quinn a thug an chéad chruinniú le chéile ag tús 1980. Níl sé sásúil ar fad agus is cinnte nach bhfuil aon athrú ar scéal an rialtais áitiúil atá go hainnis i gcónaí, ach mar sin féin, tá obair mhaith déanta ag an Údarás taobh amuigh den phríomhchúram atá orthu maidir le soláthar fostaíochta. Tá Bord na Gaeilge ann ó lár na seachtóidí, ach tá sé thar am go leagfaí amach clár oibre soiléir don dream sin freisin – agus go ndéanfaí comhordú idir iad agus na heagrais dheonacha. Tá fás agus forbairt faoi na Naíonraí agus faoi Ghaelscoileanna. Ach ní mór a bheith an-chúramach faoi cé acu an bua é seo – nó comhartha nach bhfuil Gaeilge á labhairt sa bhaile in an-chuid tithe Gaeltachta féin, gan trácht ar ghnáthbhunscoileanna na tíre. Bíonn an teanga faoi chaibidil go rialta ag Comhchoiste Gaeilge an Oireachtais – agus tá tacaíocht láidir tugtha ag feisirí éagsúla de chuid Fhianna Fáil d'obair an Bhiúró do Theangacha Neamhfhorleathana i bParlaimint na hEorpa. Ach níl aon úsáid rialta á baint as Gaeilge sa Dáil – rud a bhí, sa chéad Dáil! Labhair an Taoiseach Ailbhe Mac Raghnaill faoi seo nuair a rinne sé comóradh oifigiúil ar 75 bliana na Dála, i dTeach an Ard-Mhéara ar an 26 Aibreán, 1994. Ag labhairt i nGaeilge dó, mheabhraigh sé dá raibh i láthair nach mbeadh bealach níos fearr ann chun ómós a thabhairt don ghlúin réabhlóideach dhaonlathach úd ná go n-aontódh na páirtithe eatarthu féin chun cuid d'obair na Dála cibé scéal é, a dhéanamh trí mheán na Gaeilge *ar bhonn rialta*. Dúirt sé níos déanaí, ag labhairt i mBéarla dó faoin Chéad Dáil:

'The Irish language was used exclusively in its proceedings, as has been recounted in the Oireachtas Award-winning book on *An Chéad Dáil Éireann agus an Ghaeilge* published in 1989 to mark the 70th anniversary of the foundation of the Dáil ...

'Consideration might be given, as I said, on the basis of all-party consultation, to the idea of conducting some part of our proceedings *on specific occasions* in Irish. There could be no more fitting way to honour the founding fathers of Dáil Éireann, 75 years ago, than to rededicate ourselves, like them to the open and public expression of Ireland as a nation with a rich cultural heritage of its own, derived in substantial part from our own distinctive national language.'[21]

Cad a tharla ó shin?

An féidir go mbeidh rud éigin substaintiúil déanta ag Fianna Fáil maidir leis an scéal seo faoin am a bheas an páirtí féin ag comóradh 75 bliana a bhunaithe – i gceann cúig bliana eile?

Arís, féach an méid a bhí le rá ag Mac Raghnaill, i nGaeilge an uair seo, ar an ócáid chéanna: 'Ar an gcéad lá sin rinneadh gach rud trí Ghaeilge, is sin mar a bhí i bhfad ina dhiaidh sin. Mar sin, mar chuimhne ar na daoine a bhí páirteach, ba cheart dúinn iarracht a dheanamh cuid dár ngnó a dhéanamh trí Ghaeilge. Ní bheidh sé éasca ach níl bealach níos fearr chun iad a chómoradh. Ar ndóigh beidh orainn é seo a phlé leis na páirtithe go léir'.[22]

Tá tábhacht leis an óráid sin, dar liomsa,mar go gceanglaíonn sí oidhreacht Fhianna Fáil go dlúth le traidisiún na Chéad Dála, ainneoin na ndeacrachtaí móra a chothaíonn sin do na páirtithe go léir. Tá tábhacht leis freisin, mar gur thuig Mac Raghnaill, fear nach raibh aon cháil mhór Ghaeilge air féin, an bhunfhíric teangeolaíochta nach leor an 'cúpla focal', nach mairfidh an chorr-chosaint fhánach ag an díograiseoir mór, an óráid shiombalach thart faoi Lá le Pádraig. Caithfear gnó na Gaeilge a cheangal isteach mar chuid den ghnáthshaol mar rud praiticiúil nádúrtha dóibh siúd a bhfuil sí acu cheana féin, fiú más mar shruth mionlach i saol na tíre a bheas an ghnáth-úsáid sin. Ach tabharfaidh an deis úsáide phraiticiúla sin misneach do go leor, agus deis do go leor daoine dul sa tseans agus clárú leis an gclub de réir a chéile. Chuala mé an t-iar Uachtarán ar Fhianna Fáil a rá uair amháin nár éirigh leis greim a choinneáil ar an nGaeilge a d'fhoghlaim sé ar scoil, mar nach raibh béim ar bith ar an scrúdú cainte, nó an cur chuige cumarsáide san am sin. Tá feabhas ar an scéal ó shin, dóibh siúd atá dáiríre faoi Ghaeilge mar ábhar, ach tá an easpa gnáthdheiseanna chun an Ghaeilge a chleachtadh *sa ghnáthshaol* ann i gcónaí. Sin é an fáth gur chinn Mac Raghnaill agus a bhean a gcuid páistí a chur chuig Coláistí Gaeilge a leag béim ar leith ar bheo-úsáid na teanga - Coláistí na bhFiann, céard eile? Agus rinneadh beart phraiticiúil maidir le díol agus cóiriú Thearmann Lir i gCo. na hIarmhí, i bhfad sar ar ceapadh TD de chuid an Dáilcheantair sin ina Thaoiseach!

I mbeagán focal, agus is léir go bhfuil ábhar leabhair iomláin sa tréimhse staire atá i gceist, ba é an laige ba mhó a bhí ar pholasaí Fhianna Fáil i dtaobh na teanga ná an laige chéanna a bhain le muintir na hÉireann trí chéile.

An t-aon mholadh deimhnitheach a chuala mé ag éirí as óráid an Taoisigh Mhic Raghnaill ag comóradh 75 bliana na Chéad Dála, ná moladh a rinne Máire Geoghegan-Quinn nuair a labhair sí ar an gCeathrú Rua chun a 21 bhliain sa Dáil a chomóradh i mí Mhárta, 1996. Dar léi, gur cheart smaoineamh ar Chomhairle um Stádas na Gaeilge a bhunú, rud a bheadh cosúil, ar bhealach, leis an gComhairle um Stádas na mBan. Bheadh an Chomhairle seo ag faire, agus ag faire go géar, le ceart na Gaeilge agus lucht úsáide na Gaeilge a chosaint ar gach ócáid is féidir agus i ngach gné den saol.

Mar rud amháin, dhéanfadh an Chomhairle monatóireacht ar gach Bille nua ar bhealach a chinnteodh nach rithfí reachtaíocht ar bith gan a rá go soiléir cén tionchar a bheadh ag an Acht nua ar leas nó aimhleas na Gaeilge sa phobal.[23] Lobby don Ghaeilge? Cinnte! An difríocht a bheadh idir é agus an tOmbudsman, mar shampla, ná go mbeifí ag iarraidh cur le stádas na Gaeilge i ngach gné den saol trína shocrú go cinnte go mbeadh soláthar ann i ngach beartas nua chun Gaeilge chomh maith le Béarla a láimhsiú, agus ar an dóigh sin, go mbunófaí 'Cód Cleachtais' de réir a chéile, mar atá sa Bhreatain Bheag, i gCeanada, sa Bheilg srl.

Tá impleachtaí aige seo d'Fhianna Fáil féin chomh maith gan amhras. Chiallódh sé go gcaithfí Gaeilge agus Béarla a chur ar chomhchéim tríd an eagraíocht go léir – mar ní haon mhaith a bheith ag soiscéalaíocht chuig gach éinne eile, mura bhfuil rud éigin ar siúl agat féin. Ba thús maith é dá ndéanfaí an Ardoifig a dhátheangú nó, níos fearr fós, obair Áras de Valera a dhéanamh as Gaeilge ar fad go hinmheánach. Is fearr unsa dea-shampla ná na hóráidí Ard-Fheise go léir. Fiú na cinn inar dúirt de Valera féin dá mbeadh rogha le déanamh aige idir athbheochan na Gaeilge agus aontacht na tíre go roghnódh sé athbheochan na Gaeilge!

Níl aon ghá rogha mar sin a dhéanamh ar ndóigh. Go deimhin mura mbímid cúramach is fearr an dearcadh a bheas ag an státchóras ó thuaidh i leith na Gaeilge ná go leor den dearcadh aineolach a fhaightear ó dheas. Ach bhí an pointe á dhéanamh ag Dev ar ndóigh, go bhféadfaí filleadh ar fhadhb na Sé Chontae arís is arís eile.

Easpa tuisceana ar mhéad na faidhbe, easpa spéise i gcur chuige teangeolaíochta agus easpa pleanála deimhnithí, mar sin, na comharthaí sóirt is mó a bhain le polasaí Fhianna Fáil ón tús maidir le Gaeilge. Ní rabhadar pioc níos measa ná dream ar bith eile, idir Státairí agus muintir Shinn Féin agus an IRA a lean orthu tar éis 1926. Tá a fhios agam ó bheith ag freastal ar Ardfheiseanna éagsúla le scór go leith bliain gur mó líon na nGaeilgeoirí agus gur mó an fonn chun Gaeilge a labhairt a bhíonn le feiceáil ag Ardfheis Fhianna Fáil, de ghnáth, ná aon pháirtí eile b'fhéidir. Ach ansin is mó freisin líon an lucht leanúna atá ag Fianna Fáil ná aon dream eile. Ábhar mór buartha dom, áfach, gur in aois atá go leor den lucht Gaeilge ag dul – an ghlúin a chuaigh trí chóras na Gaeilge éigeantaí! Tá aineolas dochreidte maidir le Gaeilge agus go deimhin maidir le stair na tíre agus an pháirtí féin ag roinnt le go leor den óige.

Scéal é seo ar cheart don cheannasaíocht a bheith buartha faoi – agus rud éigin a dhéanamh faoi – trí chomhdháil Ógra Fhianna Fáil a reachtáil trí Ghaeilge mar shampla? Ansin arís, is dócha go bhfuil óige Fhianna Fáil níos fearr faoin Ghaeilge ná go leor óg-eagraíochtaí polaitíochta eile. Ní bheadh sin deacair! Fiú i gcás an dreama a choinnigh le Sinn Féin i gcónaí, is spéis liom go bhfuil an leagan Gaeilge dá ainm in úsáid i gcónaí ag Proinsias De Rossa agus gur chuir sé snas ar a chumas Gaeilge, mar a rinne Tomás Mac Giolla roimhe sin, le linn dó a bheith imtheorannaithe. Ar éirigh le Gerry Adams an rud céanna a dhéanamh? Is Gerry Adams a thugtar air sna mórmheáin éagsúla i gcónaí.

Ba mhinic an tOllamh Tomás De Bhaldraithe, beannacht Dé leis, ag trácht ar fhonn a bheith ar de Valera níos mó Gaeilge a chur in úsáid *laistigh* dá eagraíocht pholaitiúil féin. Ach ní go ró-mhaith a d'éirigh leis, fiú ag leibhéal na gCumann sa Ghaeltacht féin. Is cuimhneach linn ar fad raiceanna a tharla faoi roghnú iarrthóirí nach raibh focal Gaeilge acu fiú i dtoghcháin rialtais áitiúil i nGaeltachtaí chomh láidir le Conamara. Níor glacadh riamh le riail a déarfadh go gcaithfeadh Gaeilge a bheith ag iarrthóirí nó go mbeadh air/uirthi í a fhoghlaim laistigh de thréimhse áirithe. Ní thuigim ó thalamh an domhain cén fáth nach bhfuil dhá theanga riachtanach do bhaill tofa Fhianna Fáil – tá siad chomh riachtanach céanna le cúrsaí cumarsáide teilifíse a chosnaíonn an oiread sin ar an bpáirtí!

Nótaí:

1. *Fianna Fáil – An Chéad Tréimhse.* Baile Átha Cliath, 1960. Leathanaigh 85–87.

2. In óráid ag comóradh Robert Emmet san Academy of Music, Brooklyn, New York, ar an 2 Márta, 1914 dúirt Mac Piarais: 'A new junction has been made with the past: into the movement that has never wholly died since '67 have come the young men of the Gaelic League. I have said again and again that when the Gaelic League was founded in 1893, the Irish Revolution began.' Féach freisin an bhéim a leagann Daniel Corkery ar thábhacht na hóráide Fíníní seo, agus an fo-nóta atá aige faoi Lionel Johnston 'one whose grandfather was a Captain of Yeomanry at New Ross in 1798' in *Imeachtaí na Teanga Gaeilge/The Fortunes of the Irish Language,* Cló Mercier, Corcaigh, 1956. Leathanach 127.

3. Bunreacht na hÉireann/Constitution of Ireland. 1937. Airteagal 1 *(An Náisiún).*

4. *Ibid.* Leagan Béarla. Article 1. *(The Nation).*

5. Féach *The Death of the Irish Language – A Qualified Obituary* le Reg Hindley, Routledge, Londain agus New York, 1990 leis an bport is éadóchasaí a fháil. Féach freisin *An Ghaeltacht (Oifigiúil) – agus 1992?* le Nollaig Ó Gadhra, Coiscéim, Baile Átha Cliath, 1989, mar a bhfuil

leas bainte as taighde an Dr Hindley in Aguisín 1. Tá port beagáinín níos dóchasaí le fáil anseo. Tuigtear dom go bhfuil Hindley tar éis maolú áirithe a dhéanamh ar an phort éadóchais ó shin i leith de bharr imeachtaí éagsúla. Féach freisin a raibh le rá ag an Ollamh Gearóid Mac Eoin ag an gcéad Chomhdháil Mheiriceánach don Léann Ceilteach i 1986 nuair a thrácht sé in Ollscoil Ottawa ar 'The Future of the Celtic Languages' agus dúirt: 'There seems to be no reason to doubt that the present surviving Celtic languages, Breton, Irish Gaelic, Scottish Gaelic and Welsh, will all, one by one, cease to be spoken as traditional community languages within a very few generations.'

6. De hÍde, Dubhghlas, ina Réamhrá le *Mise agus an Conradh* (go dtí 1905). Oifig Dhíolta Foilseachán Rialtais, Baile Átha Cliath, 1931.

7. Tá léargas an-mhaith ar atmisféar na linne sin le fáil sa chuntas *Dóchas agus Duainéis* le Aindrias Ó Muimhneacháin. Duaisleabhar Oireachtais i 1974 a d'fhoilsigh Cló Mercier, Corcaigh agus Baile Átha Cliath.

8. Féach, mar shampla, an dá leabhar leis an Ollamh Nicholas Mansergh, *The Irish Question 1840–1921*, Allen and Unwin, London, Third Edition 1975 agus *The Unsolved Question – The Anglo Irish Settlement and its Undoing. 1912–1972*. Yale University Press, New Haven and London, 1991.

9. *An Chéad Dáil (1919–1921) agus an Ghaeilge,* Duaisleabhar Oireachtais le Nollaig Ó Gadhra, Coiscéim, Baile Átha Cliath, 1989.

10. Féach, mar shampla, *The Will of a Nation,* paimfléad a scríobh an Dr Eoin McKiernan, don Patrick Butler Family Foundation, St Paul, Minnesota, 1963.

11. Ó Muimhneacháin, Aindrias, *Dóchas agus Duainéis*. Féach 7 thuas.

12. McKiernan, Eoin, *The Will of a Nation*. Op. Cit.

13. Féach *The Use of Irish in District Courts in Gaeltacht Areas – Report to Bord na Gaeilge* a réitigh Thomas O'Malley agus Eamonn Ward, Roinn an Dlí, Coláiste na hOllscoile i nGaillimh, 1991. Féach freisin Feidhmiú Polasaí an Stáit ar thairiscintí Seirbhísí tré Ghaeilge ón *Earnáil Phoiblí do Phobal na Gaeltachta* – Tuairisc d'Aire na Gaeltachta ar an staid faoi láthair. Réitithe ag Údarás na Gaeltachta agus Bord na Gaeilge, faoina gComh-Chathaoirligh Donncha Ó Gallchóir agus Proinsias Mac Aonghusa, 1991.

14. Féach an plé a rinneadh air seo i dTuarascáil Dheiridh an Choimisiúin um Athbheochan na Gaeilge, Baile Átha Cliath, 1964. Féach go háirithe Roinn III, An Ghaeilge i gCúrsaí Riaracháin Phoiblí.

15. Tá cuntais mhaithe ar ghnéithe éagsúla den scéal le fáil in *Gaeltacht Ráth Cairn*, sraith léachtaí comórtha a chraol Raidió na Gaeltachta, i 1985 agus a chuir Mícheál Ó Conghaile in eagar do Chló Iar-Chonnachta, Béal an Daingin, Conamara, 1986.

16. *Irish Dialects and Irish Speaking Districts* le Brian Ó Cuív, Institiúid an Ardléinn, Baile Átha Cliath. Athchló 1971.

17. *A Board for the Gaeltacht,* meamram a sheol Comhdháil Náisiúnta na Gaeilge chuig an Taoiseach ar an 22 Deireadh Fómhair, 1953. D'fhoilsigh an Chomhdháil an Meamram i bhfoirm leabhráin don phobal freisin.

18. D'éirigh an Monsignor Ró-oirmh. Máirtín Ó Braonáin, M.A., B.D., B.C.L., Ph.D., P.P., V.F., as cathaoirleacht agus as comhaltas an Choimisiúin ar an 11 Meitheamh 1959. Ceapadh an tAthair Tomás Ó Fiaich, Ollamh le Stair i gColáiste Phádraig, Maigh Nuad, agus Uachtarán Chumann na Sagart, mar chathaoirleach, ar an 11 Meitheamh, 1959 céanna.

19. Ag labhairt ag Feis na Bóinne i nDroichead Átha i 1963, dúirt Mac Fheorais go raibh Gaeltacht bheag i gCo. Lú nuair a bunaíodh an stát 40 bliain roimhe sin. Cháin sé na daoine a dúirt go bhféadfaí scéal na Gaeilge a fhágáil faoi iarrachtaí deonacha amháin agus dúirt: 'If the Gaeltacht is to be saved the State must have a strong effective and radical plan to save it and this plan must immediately be put into effect ...'

    'The voluntary organisations such as The Gaelic League, Gael-Linn, An Réalt, Cumann Gaelach na hEaglaise, Cumann na Sagart and particularly in the northern part of the country, Comhaltas Uladh do great work, and they deserve the gratitude of all who would like to see a Gaelic Ireland. But it is sheer hypocrisy and pretence to say that a major question like the saving of the language or the preservation of the Gaeltacht can be solved by leaving it to voluntary organisations.' Leathanach 28 de *Corish Speaks – Speeches on National Affairs by the Leader of the Labour Party* in eagar ag Proinsias Mac Aonghusa, agus foilsithe ag New Century Publications, Dublin, 1966.

20. Féach, mar shampla, an cás maith atá déanta ag Martin Brennan S.J. in *The Restoration of Irish* a foilsíodh mar aiste in *Studies* in Eagrán an Fhómhair 1964, le caoinchead an eagarthóra, Roland Burke Savage, S. J. Bhí aistí ag cáineadh gnéithe d'iarracht na hathbheochana tar éis a bheith in *Studies* in eagráin an earraigh agus an tsamhraidh den irisleabhar an bhliain sin. Agus deir an tEagarthóir go raibh air iarraidh ar an Athair Máirtín Ó Braonáin an cás eile a chur 'as no one submitted an article presenting an alternative viewpoint'.

21. Óráid an Taoisigh, Albert Reynolds, TD 'at a State Reception for the 75th anniversary of Dáil Éireann'. Teach an Ardmhéara, Baile Átha Cliath, Dé Máirt, 26 Aibreán, 1994.

22. *Ibid.*

23. *Lá* Béal Feirste, 4.4 1996. Féach freisin *Anois*, 31.3.1996.

16

The Evolution of Ógra Fianna Fáil

by Mary O'Shea

It was visionary, idealistic and committed young people who founded Fianna Fáil, under the leadership of Eamon de Valera in 1926. They believed that it was through the formation of a new national political movement that their ideals of a united Ireland, social and economic advancement and equality of opportunity for all could best be achieved. Therefore in the context of any analysis of the contribution of young people to the development of Fianna Fáil it is important to remember that in every decade since the foundation of the party, young people participated at all levels of the organisation, in cumainn (branches), Comhairlí Ceanntair (district councils) and Comhairlí Dáilcheantair (constituency councils). At various stages of the party's history younger generations came to the fore to lead the party into different eras. Of particular note in this respect were personalities such as Jack Lynch, Donogh O'Malley, Brian Lenihan, Neil Blaney and Charles J. Haughey and many others who in the late 1950s and early 1960s revamped and rejuvenated the party under the leadership of Seán Lemass.

In acknowledging that background however it is nonetheless true to say that politics in Ireland particularly up to the 1960s was very much dominated by the great political figures of the War of Independence and the Civil War era. The founding fathers of Fianna Fáil continued to play a dominant role in the party right up to the late 1950s. It was not until 1974–75 that a specific youth section of the party was established to cater for the needs of young people in the party and to provide the vehicle for attracting the support of a fast-growing young electorate reflecting significant demographic change in a modern and young Ireland.

Fianna Fáil at its various stages in government introduced legislative measures and decisions that had a significant impact on the population as a whole but particularly on young people. There are numerous examples of this. Two however will suffice to illustrate this point. The radical house building programme in urban and rural Ireland in the first decade of Fianna Fáil's period in power was truly remarkable. An average of 12,000 local authority houses were built each year from 1932–42. This was achieved despite the fact that during the war years raw materials were in short supply with a consequent decline in construction activity. In the mid-1930s up to 17,000 houses were built in one year. This compares with 4,000 local authority houses being built in 1996.

The second example was the introduction in 1966 by the Minister for Education, Donogh O'Malley, of free post-primary education in tandem with a free school transport system. It was without question one of the most important milestones in the history of modern Ireland. For the generation of people born from the mid-1950s onwards the provision of free second-level education created genuine opportunities for so many of them in terms of intellectual, social and economic advancement denied to previous generations of Irish people. It is interesting to note that many of the leading personalities of Young Fianna Fáil from 1977 onwards were products of the O'Malley revolution in education.

As a general principle, political parties in government have less time to devote energy and attention to party organisational matters. The demands of being in government absorb almost all their energies. Periods in opposition are generally used to revamp and rejuvenate the organisation. Fianna Fáil are no different in this respect. It was in this context with the Fine Gael/Labour Government taking office after the 1973 General Election that Fianna Fáil decided to establish a specific youth organisation. The 1974 Árd Fheis passed motions calling for youth to be given a chance and calling for action by the party in the field of youth activity. Fianna Fáil was the first political party in Ireland to recognise the need to establish a youth section. This was undertaken for the young members already in Fianna Fáil but more importantly to encourage the recruitment of more young people into Fianna Fáil. In the words of Seamus Brennan, the then General Secretary: 'for a party with such a record it has not succeeded in bringing in its quota of idealistic and motivated young people.' In establishing a youth section the organisation at large was acknowledging the changing demographic structure in Ireland starting to become so evident in the 1970s with an ever-growing proportion of young people in the population. Increasing the participation of young people in politics and attracting a young electorate was very important for the development of Fianna Fáil throughout the 1970s and beyond.

In the winter of 1974 the first edition of a new party journal – *Iris* – appeared and contained notes on decisions taken at National Executive meetings. It was announced that in early 1975 a national youth conference was to be held. The purpose of the conference was to: (a) ascertain the views of the young members of Fianna Fáil; (b) demonstrate to the public that Fianna Fáil was genuinely concerned about youth affairs; and (c) to examine future youth involvement in the party.

The first National Youth Conference was held in the Burlington Hotel in January 1975 and had four delegates from each Dáil constituency selected by the senior Comhairle Dáilcheantair. By the time of the second national youth conference a national youth scheme had been formulated and the essence of this involved the establishment of a youth sub-committee in each CDC (Comhairle Dáilcheantair). The functions of these sub-committees were to: (a) convene at least once annually a constituency youth conference composed of all cumainn members in the constituency under the age of 25 years; and (b) to promote youth involvement in the constituency.

The functions of the constituency conference were: (a) to elect three persons from the conference to act as observers to the Comhairle Dáilcheantair; (b) to elect four delegates to represent the constituency at the National Youth Conference (the CDC would then add a further four); (c) to undertake projects of interest to the youth of Fianna Fáil in the constituency and to promote the party among young people generally; (d) to make recommendations on youth affairs to the CDC; and (e) to carry out such specific instructions transmitted to it from bodies with authority to do so. In contrast to the position of Ógra Fianna Fáil today within the structure of the overall party these beginnings now seem humble and the subservient status of Ógra at that time is clearly evident.

However a structure was established and from that point onwards greater development of the role of young people within the party was possible. Some of the young people involved in 1975 were not happy and were impatient with the progress being made. They wanted direct representation on the National Executive – the governing body of the party. One unnamed Kerry delegate speaking at the first conference wanted elections to the National Executive held at the annual national youth conference to 'give the business a bit of bite'. Delegates wanted the young delegates to have more say in organising future youth conferences. In particular they wanted greater influence over and control of the conference agenda. Very many thought that a disproportionate amount of time was given to senior front-bench speakers from the platform (a regular complaint over the years about Árd Fheiseanna).

The 1977 General Election had a very visible and high profile youth campaign and a special advertising programme geared to winning the young vote was adopted. The election results brought in a range of new young talented members to the Fianna Fáil ranks in Dáil Éireann, among them the present leader of Fianna Fáil Bertie Ahern TD, who in his day proved to be a most effective and inspiring Chairman of Ógra Fianna Fáil (1980–1983). The increased status of young people within the party was reflected in the Taoiseach Jack Lynch's eleven nominees to the Senate. Among them was Mary Harney, whose impressive and outspoken contribution to the emerging young Fianna Fáil, particularly in Trinity College Dublin, brought her to the attention of the party leadership.

In reviewing the minutes and journals of the early years of Ógra Fianna Fáil, it is obvious that the annual National Youth Conference was the cornerstone around which all youth activity within the party revolved. A further significant development took place in 1979 when Áine Kitt and Seán Ó Riain became the first elected representatives of young people within Fianna Fáil to join the National Executive. At the 1980 youth conference, one member from each Euro constituency was elected by the delegates to the National Executive. The successful candidates were Aidan Eames (Connacht/Ulster), Sean O'Connor (Dublin), Mary Hanafin (Leinster) and Paul Long (Munster).

By 1979 the national youth scheme was developing and the integration of Ógra Fianna Fáil with the senior organisation, not just as observers but with voting rights at all levels of the organisation was beginning. In the structure of party headquarters, the position of Ógra Fianna Fáil was also recognised. In the late 1970s Mary Kavanagh was given administrative responsibility for the youth section. The appointment in 1980 of Áine Kitt as National Youth Officer showed that the party was committing substantial human resources to this growing section of the party. In 1980, Bertie Ahern TD was appointed as the first National Chairman of Ógra Fianna Fáil. He was responsible for giving a greater national public profile to Ógra. He toured the country to assist in the establishment of new units and to encourage existing members. He also presided over the establishment of a national youth committee which was a sub committee of the National Executive. This was a very significant development. It gave greater autonomy and a greater say to young people in the direction of Ógra Fianna Fáil.

The appointment of Aidan Eames as National Youth Organiser in 1981 represented a further development within the administrative structure of Ógra Fianna Fáil. The role of the youth organiser was to service existing units of

Ógra, establish new units, visit constituencies and third level institutions and generally to ensure the ongoing growth and development of a nationwide youth organisation. The National Youth Organiser was also responsible for the organisation of the National Youth Conference which to the present day has proved to be the major political and social event of the Ógra calendar. The appointment of current Senator and former TD Frank Fahey as Chairman of Ógra Fianna Fáil (1983–85) represented the beginning of a new chapter in the emerging Ógra Fianna Fáil. He was the main motivator behind the formulation of a National Youth Action Plan which resulted in, among other things, the very successful Ógra Fianna Fáil 'Buy Irish Campaigns' in the early 1980s. His appointment coincided with a Fianna Fáil period in opposition from December 1982. During this time the party under the leadership of Charles J. Haughey devoted considerable energies to developing the party particularly Ógra Fianna Fáil. Ógra during this time acquired more power and developed a greater presence within the overall party structure. I remember joining Fianna Fáil as a university student in UCC at this time. I did not come from a traditional Fianna Fáil family but the lack of pedigree was irrelevant. Fianna Fáil was putting out its hand to interested people to join, to hold officer positions, be active in policy formulation and to start preparing candidates for the next local elections.

In 1983 it was decided to give Ógra delegates the right to vote at candidate selection conventions in local, Dáil and European elections. At a Dáil selection convention, for example the Ógra Fianna Fáil organisation in a constituency are entitled to two voting delegates. This was very important recognition of the role of young people within the party and resulted in more attention than ever from senior members of the party towards Ógra Fianna Fáil. In some constituencies however, such attention became excessive particularly where the internal candidate rivalry was intense. Two votes from Ógra could decide who was to represent Fianna Fáil in a Dáil election in a given constituency. Consequently attempts were made in the early years in some constituencies to manipulate Ógra and overt interference by certain groups within a constituency was not uncommon. However, direct representation on the National Executive ensured that such interference was kept to a minimum.

The decision to put an age limit on membership of Ógra Fianna Fáil was to have important implications for the organisation. It has proved to be an ongoing dynamic in ensuring recruitment of younger members to Fianna Fáil. The reality is that generations move on once they reach the age of 25 and younger members come to the fore. This creates an ongoing challenge for Ógra and some difficulties as well. Very often four or five talented members in a given constituency unit can reach the age of 25 together and their collective departure can lead to the creation of a void in that unit and it can take some time for it to be built up again. Throughout the evolution of Ógra Fianna Fáil from the late 1970s onwards, this proved to be an ongoing problem and continues to represent a challenge in the latter half of the 1990s.

In perusing party journals such as *Iris, Vision* and others one noticeable fact emerges: women have always played a very strong role in the development of Ógra Fianna Fáil. Many young women began their political careers within the organisation and were elected to the National Executive for the first time through it. They found it easier to progress through Ógra than through the main organisational structure.

It is also worth noting that many of the young people photographed in editions of *Iris* and *Vision* in the 1970s and 1980s have maintained their involvement in Fianna Fáil to the present day. Many current members of the present Fianna Fáil National Executive began as Ógra delegates. When they left Ógra they succeeded in being re-elected to the National Executive either as constituency delegates elected by their Dáilcheantair or as 'Committee of 15' members elected by the delegates at the Árd Fheis. Indeed quite a number of the present parliamentary party began their careers with Ógra Fianna Fáil, as did many local councillors throughout the country.

Policy formulation since the 1980s has been a very important feature of Ógra's contribution to Fianna Fáil. Whether in government or opposition, preparing policy documents and presenting them to the relevant minister or front-bench spokesperson is very important to Ógra.

It was obviously more difficult for Ógra Fianna Fáil to take on and challenge policy decisions when the Party was in government. There were times when Ógra members, particularly at annual youth conferences, would openly clash with Fianna Fáil government ministers. Ógra members however were also facilitated in having an input to party policy and access to government ministers to present their points of view.

Ógra, whether at constituency or national conferences, has always invited speakers from other organisations and with other perspectives. This facilitated a constructive exchange of views with 'experts' in particular areas of responsibility and ensured access to a broad spectrum of views on particular issues.

While acquiring the right to vote at Fianna Fáil selection conventions was important to Ógra Fianna Fáil, of more importance to the party overall was the need to have younger candidates selected to contest local and general elections. Just as the 1979 local elections were an important launching pad for many in Fine Gael, so the 1985 local elections proved to be a watershed for Fianna Fáil and Ógra Fianna Fáil. Over 70 young candidates contested the 1985 local elections and 39 were successful – a more than 55% success rate. The most difficult part of this achievement was the candidate selection process within the party. There was considerable internal opposition in some constituencies towards younger candidates. Indeed many were imposed on the local electoral ticket by the Dáilcheantair with encouragement from national headquarters. Of crucial importance was the resolution passed by the 1984 Árd Fheis that 'every local electoral ticket was to have one candidate under the age of 25'. While this was not universally applied it did prove to be an effective backup to those who were promoting young people in certain constituencies and in ensuring that where good quality young candidates were available they were given their opportunity. The then Chairman of Ógra Fianna Fáil, John Browne TD, provided strong leadership in ensuring that the spirit of the Árd Fheis motion was adhered to throughout the country.

Quite a number of those elected in the 1985 local elections were subsequently elected to Dáil Éireann. Two such councillors were Mícheál Martin and Seán Haughey who became chairmen of Ógra Fianna Fáil. Mícheál Martin TD was Chairman from 1989–94 and with Noel Whelan, National Youth Organiser (1989–93) developed a very strong emphasis on policy formulation. Seán Haughey TD was appointed Chairman by Bertie Ahern TD and with Joan Keating, Membership Officer, providing skilful leadership at this stage of Ógra's evolution. They have been particularly successful in establishing Fianna Fáil in most of the Regional Technical Colleges around the country. Furthermore the 1991 local elections witnessed the vast majority of those young candidates elected in 1985 retaining their seats, in most cases with an increase in votes despite a difficult climate with Fianna Fáil in government. Consequently the 1991 local elections resulted in only four new young councillors being elected. The present Fianna Fáil parliamentary party has the youngest age profile of all the parties. Ógra Fianna Fáil can claim some success in contributing to this reality. The ongoing need for younger candidates to emerge was reflected by the then Taoiseach Albert Reynolds' decision to nominate Billy Kelleher and Brian Crowley (elected to European Parliament in 1994) to Seanad Éireann in 1993. Albert Reynolds, both as a Minister and Taoiseach, was typical of many senior members of Fianna Fáil in giving considerable time and energy to the deliberations of Ógra Fianna Fáil, a factor which has ensured its importance in the overall scheme of things.

Clearly, therefore, the establishment of a specific youth section in Fianna Fáil was of major importance in the development of the party from the late 1970s onwards. It proved to be a very effective vehicle for attracting young people to Fianna Fáil. Furthermore young people in Fianna Fáil through the Ógra structure were given an opportunity to grow and develop politically to a far greater extent than they would have through the existing cumainn structure. Ógra helped to give the party a younger profile at all levels but particularly at county council and parliamentary party levels. This contribution cannot be underestimated. The unique structure of Ógra and the degree to which it was integrated with the mainstream organisation has been very successful. The presence of Ógra delegates at Comhairle Ceantair, Dáilcheantair and National Executive meetings has brought a new fresh dimension to internal debate within the party which benefits all.

It can also be argued that Ógra raised policy considerations of social and environmental issues to an even greater plane within Fianna Fáil policy formulation. Ógra members have consistently through its various conferences fought for greater social justice both in Ireland and the Third World. Ógra members also developed a strong environmental emphasis particularly under the chairmanship of Tom Kitt TD (1987–89) and gave Ógra exceptional leadership in campaigning for the closure of Sellafield and other related environmental issues.

Finally, Ógra members developed over the years a greater insight into the problems of Northern Ireland through exchange visits and meetings with political groups from Northern Ireland at various seminars and conferences.

Democracy is the cornerstone of our society. Fianna Fáil through the formation of a specific youth section has made a noble contribution to the ongoing development of Irish democracy. At the first National Youth Conference where Ógra Fianna Fáil had its beginnings, Jack Lynch the leader of Fianna Fáil expressed these sentiments:

> Whether it be to join and support or indeed to strongly oppose us, we in Fianna Fáil exhort each and every young person in this State to become involved in political organisations, pledged to maintain our parliamentary democracy and pledged to use the democratic machinery to defend the fundamental rights and freedoms of our people.

One such person who embodied all that was best in Ógra Fianna Fáil – commitment to social justice, to the re-unification of the people of Ireland and to democracy itself – was a former Chairperson of Ógra Fianna Fáil, Dublin North Central, the late Veronica Guerin who as a journalist challenged the single greatest threat to our modern democracy – drugs. Many Ógra members of Veronica's era will remember an active, campaigning and committed political activist who personified the spirit of an emerging younger generation of Fianna Fáil members.

17

Building Blocks for the Future

by Eamon Ó Cuív

My father-in-law, who was in his seventies when I got to know him, was a quiet man of deep conviction who lived more by example rather than by any loud proclamation of his views. He lived all his life in Connemara, farming a small farm, and experienced the hard times and also saw the vast changes that occurred in Ireland between the turn of the century and the late 1980s.

I remember one day making a jocose remark about Fianna Fáil and questioning its achievements. I knew he was a strong Fianna Fáil voter but I was not expecting the vehement and reasoned lecture I got on Fianna Fáil and its achievements for the next half an hour. During that time he traced for me the work done by Fianna Fáil from its foundation and the way it had transformed the lives and status of ordinary people during the previous 50 years. He outlined for me the poverty and helpless position that they were in when Fianna Fáil was founded. He explained to me the way they had in very practical ways tackled the problems faced by the people of his generation. He mentioned the opening of the bog roads, the provision of work in the winter time that was both practical and useful in the area and also gave them an income, the provision of social welfare and many other of the Fianna Fáil achievements. There was also the whole question of the lifting of a people who had been so long used to being subjugated and giving them a say in the running of their own country. It was the heady mix of practical changes allied to giving status to ordinary people that created this loyalty to Fianna Fáil. Time and again over my years in Connemara the same message has been given to me by the older people. When you ask about Fianna Fáil they explain how Fianna Fáil made them independent by giving them an income of their own, how it put meat on the table and shoes on people's feet at a time when these were scarce commodities. There is always also, the same sense of the pride that it gave the people in themselves and their hope for the future.

I have never gone along with the popular myth that people nowadays are very different from the way they were thirty, forty or even seventy years ago.

Of course, during the last seventy years huge changes have taken place both in a material sense and also particularly in relation to communications and formal education. However, it would be foolish and arrogant of us to think that our generation is any more intelligent or discerning than previous generations.

As a practising politician and accepting the above facts I was very interested to explore what was the secret that attracted so many people to give so much to Fianna Fáil over the last seventy years in terms of commitment, dedication and voter loyalty.

Strange as it might seem it was only when I went to live in Connemara that I really began to understand and think deeply about the Fianna Fáil organisation. Growing up in Dublin I had a lot of contact with the founder of Fianna Fáil, Eamon de Valera, as a grandfather and I understood and had a good knowledge of him as a statesman. However, during my school years I had very little experience of Fianna Fáil on the ground. Living in Connemara, since 1974 I got to understand its vitality and motivation and began to realise that the great strength of Fianna Fáil is the loyalty and commitment that so many ordinary people give to the party. The test of leadership is not the isolated actions of the great but their ability to communicate ideas and aims and to get large numbers of people to subscribe to them.

In my view political success for Fianna Fáil in the future will largely depend on whether we can, in the modern context, attract the same level of commitment and dedication as in the past. It would therefore seem appropriate after seventy years to try to examine what made our party so different and great, not as a nostalgic look at the past, but more as building blocks for the future.

The sceptics will say that times change and this cannot be done. However my political experience tells me that this is not true and that our biggest problem lies with our own self-confidence and belief.

There is no doubt about the commitment of the ordinary voter of former years to Fianna Fáil.

There is a lovely true story told in the Maam Valley about the last time Eamon de Valera stood for election. A party car called to collect a woman who always voted for Fianna Fáil to bring her to the polling booth. When the car called she was washing her feet in a tub outside the house. The driver of the car said that he would call back after a while and bring her to vote.

However, she replied:

'I am not going with you to vote this time.' Taken aback the driver asked, 'Why?' She said 'This is the last time I will ever be able to vote for Eamon de Valera and I am going to do it the hard way.'

The woman walked the six miles that day to the polling booth and the six miles home as a demonstration of her commitment and appreciation of Fianna Fáil and Eamon deValera.

However, it would be a foolish person who would believe that the same commitment and dedication to Fianna Fáil and its people cannot exist in the 1990s. One small example will illustrate how the technology might change but the commitment can stay the same.

During the local election of 1991, a neighbour of mine travelled at his own expense all the way from Cork to Cor na Móna in Co. Galway and back to cast a vote for Fianna Fáil. Our biggest problem is, however, that the number of people nowadays with that dedication is less than in former times.

What was the magic mix that made Fianna Fáil? I believe that there were a number of important elements to it and I will try to indicate what I think the main ingredients were and what direction we should take for the future.

The basics of the Fianna Fáil success story was based on three elements: definite ideological aims, practical policies and good organisation.

On the organisational front a conscious effort was made right from the beginning to give an important say in the party to the ordinary people at cumann level. Long before the academics were extolling the merits of participatory democracy and the 'bottom up approach' Fianna Fáil had put in place probably the most intensive and extensive network of branches of any political party in the world. All levels of the party including the National Executive, the Comhairlí Dáil Cheantair, the Comhairlí Ceantair sprung from the local cumann which was the real power base of the party. The extensive nature of the party which is still largely with us in rural Ireland is seen by the number of cumainn in rural constituencies. I have calculated that in the rural part of my own constituency we have a cumann for approximately every 300 persons on the voters' register. This would represent a cumann of 10 or 20 people for approximately every 200 Fianna Fáil voters or in other words a cumann member for every 10 to 15 households. What this means is that the Fianna Fáil organisation in such areas is fully representative of and in touch with the local Fianna Fáil voters. Another big factor in the organisation was its egalitarian nature. It made no difference what profession or background you came from in the election of officers. The role of delegates to the various levels of the organisation was to convey the message from the ground to the top of the organisation as well as conveying the messages from the various organisation levels back to the ground. Another very important part of the organisation was the fact that the local TD attended cumann meetings and thereby heard at first hand what the local organisation was thinking on both local and national matters. One must never forget that the status given by participation at all levels in Fianna Fáil to very ordinary people was a highly motivating factor. The fact that they had direct access to politicians including government ministers gave them importance in their own communities.

In the modern context, it is very interesting to compare the vote being achieved by Fianna Fáil in rural areas at present to that in the cities. I do not think that it is any coincidence that the Fianna Fáil vote in rural areas, where there is a very intensive and extensive organisation as outlined above is still very strong, while in the urban areas where there are much fewer cumainn, our vote also tends to be much lower and their influence and penetration into the community consciousness is also weak.

A matter of great concern to a lot of Fianna Fáil members in recent times has been the drift away from basing policy on what public representatives hear on the ground. More and more the organisation feels that representative bodies, interest groups and experts of all types have a bigger say in policy than the ordinary cumann member. This trend is evident over a long number of years and it is common to a lot of political organisations, but it must not be accepted if we wish to maintain the primacy of the ordinary member of our party in determining policy.

In terms of effective policies, the early years of Fianna Fáil were particularly marked by a 'can do' attitude. In the 1930s in very difficult economic circumstances major social issues were tackled in a direct simple and effective way. Aggressive policies were followed in agriculture with land division, in industry with the setting up of an indigenous industry base, in housing and social welfare, to mention but a few. All polices were directed towards the clear needs of the ordinary people, Irish solutions were found for Irish problems and despite the economic war and world depression, the lives of the ordinary people improved. There is no doubt that a large part of the prosperity enjoyed in this part of the country now is based on the work and foundations of that period. As a result the people of the country have never had it as good as they have had it in the last ten years. It is also true to say that particularly since the return to power of Fianna Fáil in 1987, the country has done exceptionally well on a macro-economic level. Therefore, we must ask why is there not greater support for Fianna Fáil now than during its early formative period. It would appear that one of the big problems in relation to policy is that we have so many consultative bodies and so many vested interests that must be consulted before we can take direct action where the people see a need for something to be done. A simple example of this is our inability to go and do something over a long period in relation to rural roads, although every rural TD, will tell you that this is the issue that takes most time at cumann meetings in rural Ireland. The experts of course, will tell us that from an economic point of view these roads don't have any great significance and, unfortunately, for too long their view was heeded. However, what the ordinary people would tell you is that these are the roads that they have to travel everyday coming and going from their houses, and that the economy should be run for the people and not the people for the economy; that it is no good having a high GDP if a person cannot get with ease to and from their home. Similar situations arise in relation to school transport, general rural infrastructure, schools, medical services etc.

In urban areas we refuse to listen to people living in high-rise flats who are anxious to live in conventional houses. They see money spent all around them and they cannot understand how the money cannot be funnelled to solve the greatest problem they face. In both rural and urban areas people see plenty of work to be done and are getting impatient with the excuses and difficulties put up when suggestions are made that this work could quite usefully be done by people who are unemployed. They feel that there must be a way of organising society to ensure that those who want to work can work. They see the huge social and crime problems caused by unemployment and its huge cost and cannot understand why this money cannot be diverted to more productive purposes. They are not impressed by arguments by experts who say it cannot be done or only certain types of work are allowable. They think back to the opening of the bog roads, the draining of the land carried on under schemes in previous times where there was direct benefit to the local community, and they ask themselves why, if it was possible then, it is not possible now?

Economists tend to forecast the future by basing it on the past and this can often lead to total failure. We must once again build the future by tackling with vigour and determination the problems we see around us and we must not let spurious difficulties stand in our way. We must end social segregation, unemployment, provide an adequate rural infrastructure and tackle the other social problems in society with simple effective policies.

The last, but probably the most important element of Fianna Fáil since its foundation has been the ideals or common bond on which the party was formed. This amongst all else was the real strength of the party in the past and must again become its real strength in the future. The cynics will tell you of course that Fianna Fáil failed in its main aims of unifying the country, restoring the Irish language, maintaining people on the land, promoting the ruralisation of industry and making the country as economically self-contained and self-sufficient as possible.

Obviously, none of these aims have been achieved in full, but like all ideals, they are ideals because they are nearly impossible to achieve, but are goals that we must work towards. In recent years there has been great emphasis based on the pragmatic in Fianna Fáil. It is my belief, however, if we do not renew our commitment to the high ideals of the party in a very real sense, we will cause the decline of the party from a national movement to a very ordinary political party with very modest support. It was the ideals and vision of the party that bonded people from different economic and geographical circumstances into one large family. It was these ideals that gave common purpose to people from both rural and urban backgrounds and to the people from areas in Dublin's inner city and prosperous suburbs such as Foxrock. Of course, it was also the idealism that was the main engine of the phenomenal drive forward made by this country in the last seventy years largely under Fianna Fáil Government. If we examine how the party has performed in relation to its stated aims we will find that major progress has been made towards each and every one of its goals.

It is true to say that a United Ireland has not been brought about. However, when Fianna Fáil came to power in 1932, even the 26 counties had only a very limited form of independence. In the intervening years, the full position of Ireland as an independent State has been recognised in all international fora. The economy of this part of country has now grown to the point that the words spoken by Eamon de Valera at the foundation of the party, that the best way we could bring about the unity of this country would be to make it economically attractive, is now coming true.

At the foundation of Fianna Fáil the Irish language was in rapid decline and Irish culture was at a low ebb. Compare this to the modern Ireland where the Irish language is thriving in the most unexpected places and where Irish music, games, dancing and culture are now recognised worldwide. There is still much to be done on the cultural front, but there is no doubt that there has been tremendous successes in this regard taking into account the mammoth task set.

181

It must have appeared over the years that the building of a vibrant rural Ireland would prove impossible and was but a pipe dream. There is also no doubt that there are huge problems to be faced in rural Ireland due to population decline etc., however, anybody who lives in rural Ireland will recognise that the policies of maintaining people on the land and ruralisation of industry played a very important part in creating the modern vibrant rural Ireland of today. All we need now is a new commitment to avoid the mistakes made by other developed and developing nations by not accepting the destruction of the rural communities and their replacement by large socially segregated urban conurbations. Anybody who looks at the towns and cities of this country would see that such policies are not only necessary for rural Ireland, but vital to preserve these towns and cities from the worst type of development. In this regard, a lot of the policies being espoused by groups such as Rural Re-Settlement and even political parties such as the Green Party, stem from the basic Fianna Fáil philosophy. It is important that we reclaim our heritage in relation to these matters.

In an interdependent world it would appear that the ideal of this country being self-contained and self-sufficient is rather quaint. Obviously, international trade is now vital to Ireland's interest. However, if the 1980s taught us nothing else, it should have taught us the danger of becoming an economy unable to stand on its own two feet. We must ensure that economically the future of this country will be determined primarily by the people of this country and not by foreign hand-outs. For as long as it lasts, money coming from Europe should be spent wisely in ensuring long-term self-development and not wasted as some super-dole or hand-out from a bottomless pit.

We must be self-sufficient and not indulge in foreign borrowing for non-productive reasons. Above all else we must realise that the root of our future social and economic development must lie with ourselves in the first place, starting with each community and each county, then with the country, and finally with Brussels.

The greatest and most enduring legacy of Fianna Fáil since its foundation has been the giving of a self-belief and pride to a people that had suffered subjugation and defeat for eight hundred years. The self-confident new Ireland we have is largely a result of the work of our party.

I have no doubt that if we re-dedicate ourselves with the same vigour and enthusiasm as that shown by the people in 1926, then Fianna Fáil will have as important a part to play in the next seventy years as it had in the last seventy.

Name Index